Fergus P. Hughes
University of Wisconsin-Green Bay

Children, Play,
and Development

Allyn and Bacon
Boston London Toronto Sydney Tokyo Singapore

Series Editor: *Sean W. Wakely*
Series Editorial Assistant: *Carol L. Chernaik*
Production Administrator: *Annette Joseph*
Production Coordinator: *Susan Freese*
Editorial-Production Service: *Cyndy Lyle Rymer*
Cover Administrator: *Linda K. Dickinson*
Cover Designer: *Suzanne Harbison*
Manufacturing Buyer: *Megan Cochran*

Copyright © 1991 by Allyn and Bacon
A Division of Simon & Schuster, Inc.
160 Gould Street
Needham Heights, Massachusetts 02194

Library of Congress Cataloging-in-Publication Data

Hughes, Fergus P.
   Children, play, and development / Fergus P. Hughes.
      p.   cm.
   Includes bibliographical references (p. 225) and indexes.
   ISBN 0-205-12644-8   KING ALFRED'S COLLEGE
   1. Play.   2. Child development. WINCHESTER I. Title.
HQ782.H84   1991
155.4′ 18—dc20

Printed in the United States of America

10 9 8 7 6 5 4   95 94 93 92

Photo Credits

pp. 1, 25, 97, 100, 104, 136, 141, 161 © Frank Siteman; pp. 20, 42, 55, 72, 76, 144, 165, 181 by
Ron Wood; p. 33 by Robert Harbison; p. 45 by Neil Goldstein; p. 69 by Ken Karp; p. 119 by
David Kelley; pp. 131, 195, 207, 217 by Talbot D. Lovering; p. 186 by Shirley Zeiberg; p. 201
by Larry Fleming.

Text credits appear on page 256

THE UNIVERSITY OF WINCHESTER

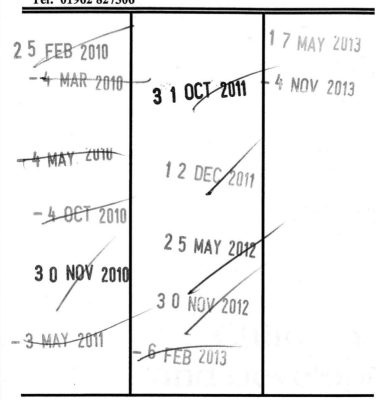
Play,

nent

*To my wife, Bonnie, for her love and support,
and to my sons, Peter and Jonathan,
for reminding me every day of the value of play
in the lives of children*

Contents

CHAPTER THREE
The First Two Years of Life   45

CHAPTER FOUR
The Preschool Years: From Two to Five   69

CHAPTER SIX
Gender Differences in Play   119

Preface

Sixteen years ago, Dr. Ruth E. Hartley, the chairperson of the department in which I worked, announced her retirement and asked me to assume the responsibility of teaching her course on children's play. It was an intimidating request. Ruth had developed the course, and she was one of the country's leading experts on play. I was an assistant professor who had defended my doctoral dissertation less than two years earlier. I told Ruth of my apprehension about being able to take her place in the course, because of the vast difference in our experience. She was amused. "I know you can teach my course," she said. "If you truly understand children's development, then you understand the essence of children's play."

It was only gradually that I began to understand what Ruth meant. Play is both a reflection of and an influence on *all* areas of children's development: intellectual, social, emotional, and physical. As Ruth herself described it, play is "the essential ingredient," the vehicle by which children communicate, socialize, learn about the world around them, understand themselves and others, deal with their problems, and practice some of the skills they will use in the future. And for those who study child development, the observation of children at play can provide a wealth of information.

That play is a central, all-encompassing characteristic of children's development is the major point throughout this book. In the first two chapters, providing historical, theoretical, and cultural overviews of play, the reader will discover that play is found in most human cultures, past and present, and occurs among the young of every advanced animal species as well. Chapters Three, Four, and Five focus on the development of play from infancy through adolescence; my goal in these chapters was to demonstrate that the development of play mirrors the physical, social, intellectual, and emotional development of the child. Chapters Six and Seven describe the individual differences in play attributable to gender, physical and emotional challenges, and particular stress situations. Such differences tell us much about differences in our cultural expectations for children and about the dynamics of the socialization process. Finally, Chapters Eight, Nine, and Ten specifically highlight the ways in which play facilitates, respectively, the intellectual, social, and emotional development of the child.

The book is written primarily from the perspective of developmental psychology, and the goal was to blend the major theoretical perspectives on play with up-to-date reviews of the research literature. While the intended audience includes anyone interested in children's play, this is not a how-to book. Every effort was made to enhance the book's appeal by making it as readable as possible. However, it is hoped that the book will also challenge the reader. I emphatically reject the view that books must be simplified, in writing style and the ideas they present, if they are to reach a wide audience.

It is expected that this book will be used in college classrooms, either as the main text in courses on children's play or as a supplement in child development courses or in those dealing with early childhood education. While an attempt was made to incorporate practical examples wherever possible, it is fair to say that this book is not characterized by an applied focus. I leave it to practitioners in the fields of education and psychology and to their students to devise appropriate applications. It is my hope, however, that I will have given them the solid grounding in theory and research that will enable them to do so.

Acknowledgments

I would like to acknowledge the contributions of a number of people who have helped me make this book a reality. Ruth Hartley's influence has already been mentioned. Thank you, Ruth, for being the first to stimulate what has become for me a long-standing interest in children's play. Sean Wakely, my education editor at Allyn and Bacon, was the first to help me see the promise in a writing project of this type. He shared and helped to shape my vision of what it was that I wanted to do. His encouragement, his solid practical suggestions, his willingness to listen, and his general good humor combined to make this project a pleasure to work on.

I would also like thank the reviewers who offered their suggestions for improvement of the manuscript: Ruth Barnhart, Iowa State University; April Beavers, Concord College; Marcia L. Oreskovich, University of Northern Colorado; Anne Rusher, Texas Christian University; Barbara Heim Scott, University of Florida; and Amy Toole, Suffolk B.O.C.E.S. I was fortunate to have constructive reviews. When they liked what I had written, they told me so, and when they disapproved, they made helpful suggestions for improving, sometimes even including reference materials. One can ask no more from reviewers than I received from those who worked on this project.

Finally, I would like to thank my student assistants, Bernie Dirkman and Susan Jacquet, for the extensive amount of library research they cheerfully accepted, engaging in what was often the most tedious sort of detective work. Their contributions made the task of writing this book considerably easier for me.

Children, Play, and Development

CHAPTER ONE

Historical
and Theoretical
Viewpoints

Scott, a first-grader with little interest in competitive sports, agreed to join a school soccer team only because his parents insisted on it. However, playing soccer frightens Scott, and on the evening of each game he is so overcome by anxiety that he can scarcely eat his dinner. Six-month-old Michelle can spend extensive amounts of time exploring the contents of her mother's purse; she seriously and methodically inspects every item she discovers before moving on to the next one. Elaine loves her job as a copyeditor for the local newspaper; she often comments to friends that she feels almost guilty to be drawing a salary for doing something that she enjoys so much.

When Scott is on the soccer field, is it accurate to describe him as a child at play? Is Michelle playing when she examines the contents of her mother's purse? And what about Elaine? When she is at the office, is she working, or is there a sense in which her work is really a playful activity?

A Definition of Play

What exactly is *play*? What is the dividing line between *play* and *work*? Can an activity be both play and work at the same time? Can an activity begin as one and gradually evolve into the other? Actually, there is no simple definition of play, and the borderlines between play and other activities, such as work, exploration, and learning, are not always clear. Nevertheless, psychologists have identified a number of elements that are typical of play, and so we will now try to arrive at a definition of play by examining some of these generally agreed upon essential characteristics.

Essential Characteristics of Play

Before an activity can be described as play, it must contain five essential characteristics (Rubin, Fein, & Vandenberg, 1983). First, play is *intrinsically motivated*. It is an end in itself, done only for the sheer satisfaction of doing it. A second, related characteristic of play is that it must be *freely chosen* by the participants. If children are forced—or even gently pressured—into play, they may not regard the assigned activity as play at all. In one study (King, 1979), for example, it was found that if a kindergarten teacher assigned a play activity to her pupils, they tended to regard it as work, even though they described the identical activity as play if they were allowed to choose it themselves.

A third essential characteristic of play is that it must be *pleasurable*. Children must enjoy the experience or it cannot be regarded as play. If we think of Scott, the first-grader who reluctantly agreed to play soccer only because his parents wanted him to, it becomes apparent that his activity on the soccer field fails to satisfy any of the characteristics of play that have been mentioned thus far. Soccer is certainly not intrinsically motivating for Scott; his motivation for doing it is to please his parents. It is not a freely chosen activity because it was chosen for him by his parents. Finally, an activity that engenders so much stress in the participant can hardly be described as pleasurable!

A fourth characteristic of play is that it is *nonliteral*. That is, it involves a certain element of make-believe, a distortion of reality to accommodate the interests of the player. This is particularly true of the symbolic play that is so characteristic of the preschool years, when children spend much of their time experimenting with new

2

roles and playing out imaginary scenes. Finally, play is *actively engaged* in by the player. The child must be involved, physically, psychologically, or both, rather than passive or indifferent to what is going on.

The image of play presented here is certainly a positive one. It conjures up idyllic visions of happy, carefree children who are totally at ease. Some psychologists wonder, in fact, if play has been overly romanticized. For example, Sutton-Smith and Kelly-Byrne (1984) suggest that it is unfair to ignore the fact that children at play often engage in behaviors that are cruel, brutal, vulgar, or obscene. Children sometimes terrorize and humiliate one another as they search for ways of establishing positions of dominance, with the result that smaller, weaker children are often forced to do things against their will and are teased and even physically assaulted if they refuse.

None of play's five essential characteristics precludes behaviors that are cruel, brutal, and terribly exploitative. However, since they are neither pleasurable nor freely chosen, the activities of the child who is victimized by the cruel games of others cannot be described as play, even though they occur in a playful atmosphere. Such is the difficulty of attempting to apply neat and simple definitions to so broad a category of behaviors as those involved in children's play.

Play and Work

Whatever play is or is not, there seems to be general agreement that play differs in some ways from what is regarded as work. The major difference between the two is that, even when work is enjoyable, it is still extrinsically motivated, whether the goal is to earn money, to enhance one's status, to feel useful, or to attain success in one's chosen field. Work is sometimes freely chosen, like play, but the option to avoid work of any sort is rarely available in our society. A person is fortunate who regards work as pleasurable, as did Elaine in the opening section of this chapter; for many workers it is not. The nonliteral element that typifies play is not usually found in work activities, except perhaps in the case of actors. And finally, work does resemble play in the last characteristic: Both are actively engaged in, to some extent at least, by the participants.

The History of Play in the Western World

In order to understand the various theoretical perspectives on the significance of children's play to a child's development, and to appreciate current American attitudes toward play, it is important to know something about the history of conceptions of childhood, not only in this country, but in the entire Western world. Let us now look briefly at childhood in its historical context, with particular reference to the attitudes of adults toward children's play.

From Ancient Times to the Middle Age

For a thousand years before the birth of Christ, the recorded history of all the major cultures in the eastern Mediterranean world indicates a fairly similar view of childhood. Children were never romanticized, as they often are today; they were not seen as naturally innocent and pure. However, they were thought of as helpless, incapable of directing their own affairs, and having special needs, including the desire and the need to play. Play was an understandable and an acceptable part of children's lives. In ancient Egyptian wall paintings, for example, children can be seen playing with balls and dolls, as well as jumping rope (French, 1977).

Children in ancient Greece were seen as naturally playful, and play was allowed and even encouraged. Children were also seen as naturally more unformed, unruly, helpless, fearful, cheerful, and affectionate than adults. Even though childhood and children's activities were appreciated, the role of the adult was to guide the child gently into becoming a useful and responsible citizen (French, 1977). The gentle and respectful nature of this guidance is illustrated by the writings of the philosopher Plato. Although he described the young boy as "the craftiest, most mischievous, and unruliest of brutes" (*Laws,* Book 7, p. 808), Plato was also concerned that excessive adult supervision could be harmful. Spoiling children can make them "fretful, peevish, and easily upset by mere trifles," he wrote, but harsh childrearing approaches can make them "sullen, spiritless, servile, and unfit for the intercourse of domestic and civic life" (*Laws,* Book 7, p. 91). Although perhaps less gentle in their approaches to child guidance, the ancient Romans shared the Greek view of children as affectionate, cheerful, and playful, but they saw children as being in need of discipline tempered with affection (French, 1977).

The special nature of childhood continued to be recognized in the Western world throughout the early Christian era and up until the Middle Ages, approximately 12 centuries after the birth of Christ. The early Christian view was that a child is important to God, has a soul, and therefore is not to be abused by adults. Indeed, the Church had a special role in promoting the welfare of children. Although children in the Middle Ages were not sheltered from the hardships and realities of life (as is often the case today), neither were they seen as miniature versions of adults, and special childhood activities, including play, continued to be thought of as both acceptable and appropriate (Borstelmann, 1983).

The Renaissance Perspective

Negative attitudes about children, and about the need for them to have special activities, began to surface in Europe during the period known as the Renaissance (1300–1600 A.D.). While the Renaissance is generally recognized as one of the most creative periods in European history, a time of openness to new ideas in all areas of the arts and sciences, children apparently did not benefit from this open-mindedness. For example, it was common practice to place children in the custody of a nurse or a succession of nurses, who usually saw their caretaking roles in purely monetary terms. Children were believed to be of little importance compared to adults and were said to lack strength, wit, and cunning. Often they were the subject of jokes and were placed in the category of fools and senile old people (Tucker, 1974). A more commonly heard phrase was "Who sees a child sees nothing" (Whiting & Whiting, 1968).

All distinctions between the world of childhood and that of adulthood vanished, it seems, during the Renaissance. Children were put to work as soon as was reasonable, because idleness was considered both sinful and unprofitable (Tucker, 1974). It was only in elite families that children were sent to school, and that was not a pleasant prospect for them; there, they would spend long hours in the care of stern, unfeeling teachers. Nevertheless, there seems to have been time enough for play as well, and many of what we would call children's play activities can be observed in paintings depicting scenes from everyday life in Renaissance Europe.

However, it is not only children who can be seen playing. Since there was no distinction between the world of children and that of adults, people of all ages played the same games and chanted the same nursery rhymes. In fact, the only real nursery rhymes were those composed specifically for the nursery, and the only chants that truly belonged to the world of childhood were lullabies (Tucker, 1974). Riddles were typically made up by adults and for adults, and many popular chants that have come down to us from that period were originally sung by adults and often contained interesting political or social messages. For example, the children's rhyme "Sing-a-Song-of-Sixpence" was an adult song telling of King Henry VIII's love for Anne Boleyn and other events at the beginning of the Protestant Reformation (Opie & Opie, 1957; Borstelmann, 1983).

Interestingly, it was during the Renaissance that, in southern Germany, the toy-manufacturing industry was born. Along with homemade toys, such as kites and tops, that had been seen during the Middle Ages, now there were also lead soldiers, elaborate wooden dolls, and glass animals. We should not presume, however, that these toys were made for children. The lack of a distinction between the child's world and that of adults is nicely illustrated by the fact the Renaissance toys were intended not only for children but for adults too. In fact, many toys of this era, and of the seventeenth and eighteenth centuries, as well, were so elaborate and so delicate (e.g., teasets, dolls, dollhouses) that it is likely that children were not allowed even to touch them (Somerville, 1982).

In the seventeenth century, as the Renaissance era was coming to an end, European attitudes about children and about play were beginning to change. There arose what has been described as a "new consciousness of childhood" (Pinchbeck & Hewitt, 1969); children began to be seen as worthy of attention and having developmental needs and problems that were different from those of adults. The seventeenth century was also a period of enthusiastic colonization of the New World, and because of colonization patterns, the major European influences on American attitudes toward work and play came from the countries of France and England.

French Influences

As Europe emerged from the Renaissance at the dawn of the seventeenth century, the French attitude toward play could be characterized as one of acceptance, and this acceptance has continued to one degree or another until the present day. Even though the Catholic clergy took a dim view of play without the redeeming social value of work, they were apparently powerless to prevent its occurrence (Aries, 1962).

Perhaps the most complete record of children's play in seventeenth-century France can be found in a diary kept by Jean Heroard, the physician who attended young King Louis XIII. Louis was hardly a typical French child of the time. What is more, the diary seems to contain a number of exaggerations and distortions intended to put the child in the best possible light (Marvick, 1974). Heroard claimed, for example, that Louis understood human speech when he was only five weeks old; on being told that God placed him in the world for a purpose and therefore he must be good and just, the infant responded with a knowing smile!

If we disregard Heroard's self-serving suggestions about Louis's remarkable precocity, the diary tells us much about the seventeenth-century attitude toward children in general and toward play in particular. Louis had windmills to play with, hobby horses, and whipping toys resembling modern tops. By the age of seventeen months, the future king was able to play the violin and sing at the same time. (Perhaps this is another bit of exaggeration.) As a toddler, he played ball exactly as did the adults of his time, and by the age of two, he had a little drum to bang on and was already becoming a skillful dancer. At four, he liked to play cards and to shoot with a bow and arrow, and by the age of six, he was beginning to play chess and to enjoy parlor games (Aries, 1962).

The most revealing feature of Louis's play is its similarity to that of the adults of his time. As a matter of fact, many of Louis's playmates were adult servants and courtiers. Play that involved music, athletic skills, board games, and parlor games was engaged in by noblemen and noblewomen of all ages, because beyond the age of infancy there was no separation between the games of children and those of adults. Indeed, as was true during the Renaissance, virtually no distinction existed in the early seventeenth century between the world of children and the world of adults; there was as yet no concept of childhood innocence, and there was little separation between work and play.

As the century progressed, however, a separation gradually appeared between the worlds of childhood and adulthood and between the games of children and those of adults. The games of children (and fools) were physical in nature, whereas adults, at least those of the nobility who aspired to some degree of sophistication, played only games of intellect and wit. Work and play were increasingly thought of as separate activities. Work became the center of adult life, while play came to be seen as an activity reserved for children and for those with childish minds. Nevertheless, play continued to be at least tolerated in France, as it was not to be in England, and the French retained a definite appreciation for the period of childhood.

The French appreciation for childhood, and for children's natural activities, was later embodied in the writings of France's most influential philosopher of the eighteenth century, Jean-Jacques Rousseau (1712–1784). Rousseau (1911/1762) expressed the philosophy of **naturalism.** "God makes all things good," he wrote. "Man meddles with them and they become evil." Children come into the world not as empty organisms waiting for experience to shape them but as original human beings equipped by nature with an innate plan for their development. The child is more than an incomplete version of an adult, and adults must appreciate children for who they are. "Childhood has its own way of seeing, thinking, and feeling, and nothing is more foolish than to try to substitute ours for them," wrote Rousseau in *Emile,* his classic work on education, which appeared in 1762.

Rousseau believed that little harm would come to children if they were allowed to grow without excessive adult supervision. The first 12 years of life should be a time of leisure, during which the only education should be negative. That is, adults should try not to teach virtues to children but only prevent them from acquiring vices. "Give him no orders at all, absolutely none," wrote Rousseau. "Do not even let him think that you claim authority over him."

The widespread acceptance of Rousseau's ideas tells us as much about the age in which he lived as about the character of the French people. Eighteenth-century Europe witnessed the emergence of the spirit of Romanticism, in which childhood was glorified and childhood innocence celebrated. It is unlikely, of course, that all French people of the time agreed with Rousseau's views on child development or that the average citizen read his books (or anything else for that matter). However, it reveals much about the French view of life that Rousseau should gain so large an audience in that country. His ideas were not as well received in England, even in the Romantic era, nor was he as widely read in the American colonies as was John Locke, whose ideas will be discussed in the following section. As we shall see, England offered a scarcity of the fertile soil in which the radical democratic ideas of naturalism could grow.

British Influences

As in other European countries, there was in seventeenth-century England a growing awareness of the child as an individual with special needs and a world view different from that of adults. Nevertheless, this enlightened perspective did not lead to a greater acceptance of children's play. In fact, while the French maintained an appreciation for play, even as they relegated it to the realm of childhood, the emphasis in England in the seventeenth and eighteenth centuries was almost completely on the value of work for both children and adults. What was responsible for the overwhelming emphasis on work and the corresponding deemphasis on play in England? Actually both religious and philosophical reasons contributed to the devaluation of play in English life.

The religious influence most responsible for the devaluation of play in England was the rise of Protestantism. While Catholicism stressed the necessity of faith in achieving salvation, the Protestant view was that faith alone would not suffice. Hard work was also necessary, and self-discipline; material success was thought to be indicative of good moral character. Play was viewed as the opposite of work and so was both sinful and irresponsible. In the words of the theologian John Wesley, "He who plays as a boy will also play as a man." (One can assume that this statement was meant to apply to girls and women as well.)

As Rousseau was later to become the preeminent philosopher of France, the philosopher whose views on the nature of children would be the most widely accepted in England was John Locke (1632–1704). Locke was representative of seventeenth-century thinking in his belief that each child is a unique and valuable human being whose developmental needs must be recognized by adults. Not surprisingly, he also represented the religious tradition in which he was raised. The son of Puritan parents, Locke held ideas on childrearing that were quite consistent with the Puritan world view, which will be discussed in the following section. They were also consistent with those of virtually every other Protestant sect in England at the time.

Locke apparently loved children felt a special empathy with them, and yet he neither romanticized them nor recommended that they be indulged. Instead, he argued that the child needs firm adult direction. A central assumption of Locke's theory was that the human organism is empty at birth—that the mind of the newborn is a **tabula rasa**, or blank slate—and that all knowledge of the world comes through the senses. It follows that the environment is all important in shaping a person's direction, and so, beginning in infancy, the foundations of good character must be laid down by parents.

Indulgence must be avoided because children have no natural awareness of what is best for them. Their natural tendency is to seek freedom to do what they want and to exert control over the world around them; but other than satisfying their basic physiological needs, parents must never give children what they cry for. "Children must leave it to the choice and ordering of their parents, what they think properest for them, and how much: and must not be permitted to chuse for themselves," Locke wrote in *Some Thoughts Concerning Education* (1964/1693, p. 41). Parental direction is necessary for the mind to be "made obedient to discipline and pliant to reason when it [is] most tender, most easy to be bowed" (p. 54).

Although he emphasized the value of firm direction for children and even went so far as to suggest that their feet be immersed in cold water every day to harden them against the chilly English climate, Locke's views on childrearing and education were actually quite humane. He advocated gentle and respectful approaches to parenting. For example, he condemned both physical punishment and excessive nagging and argued in favor of methods that would help children develop their own internal controls. Furthermore, it was his hope that as children matured, parents would need to exert their authority less and less, so that the parent-child relationship would eventually come to be based on equality. Parental authority, wrote Locke in *Thoughts*, "should be relaxed as fast as their age, discretion, and good behavior could allow it. . . . The sooner you treat him as a man, the sooner he will begin to be one."

Locke's ideas were widely circulated during the late seventeenth and the eighteenth centuries, not only in England but throughout Europe and in the colonies of the New World. His ideas about the importance of firmness, rationality, discipline, and moral education were enthusiastically received. Although his philosophy was certainly more respectful of children as individuals than was the Renaissance perspective, Locke was no advocate of naturalistic childrearing approaches. Indeed, the "natural" elements of childhood were those that needed correction, and while he did not actually condemn play, Locke made it clear that work, rationality, and discipline were the central ingredients in a child's optimal development.

In summary, the ideas of Protestant reformers had a dramatic impact on British attitudes toward childrearing in general and toward work and play in particular. Locke, influenced by his Protestant upbringing and by a revolutionary seventeenth-century view of the child as a distinct and original creation of God, came to have a significant influence on British, and later on American, beliefs about children. Work and self-discipline were seen as paths to eternal salvation, to material success, and to mature rationality; play was at best a distraction, at worst a sin against God. The result was that play was virtually suppressed by the middle and end of the eighteenth century. Many English towns even went so far as to enact laws forbidding certain forms of play, such as playing with tops or running races in the public streets.

Childhood in the United States

The Puritan Legacy

The earliest permanent settlers in what would become the American colonies were the Puritans, a religious reform group who left England in 1630 to seek freedom of expression in a new world. The Puritan influence was widely felt in the colonies of New England. This group was to have a significant impact on later U.S. attitudes toward work and play, although they themselves, and their influence on U.S. thought, are often misunderstood.

The Puritans are often stereotyped as a harsh, unfeeling people who treated their children with a sternness bordering on cruelty, and had little use for play of any sort. In fact, this was not the case at all. Puritan views on childhood, as exemplified in the writings of John Locke, were considerably more humane and enlightened than were the views of most of their contemporaries (Somerville, 1982).

The Puritans were reformers, after all, who envisioned a world that was new and better than their own. Reformers tend to be future-oriented people, and the children of Puritan society were highly valued as representing the hope of the future. They were seen as individuals in their own right instead of mere family replacements, a status that was indicated by the names they were typically given (Somerville, 1982). The European pattern of naming had always been to bestow on a child the name of a parent or other relative. In fact, siblings in the Middle Ages often were given identical names, and were referred to not by name but by labels indicating their birth order (Illick, 1974). By contrast, the Puritans gave names that symbolized their hope for a better society under God (Prudence, Thankful, Safe-on-High), and the very fact that Puritan children received original names is an indication that they were perceived as unique and original human beings.

The Puritans believed that children needed a considerable amount of discipline and instruction if they were to live orderly and responsible lives. The child was thought to be born ignorant and sinful but at least capable of being enlightened (Borstelmann, 1983). Proper discipline would make this partially rational but evil-natured creature behave reasonably and thereby reflect credit on its parents in the eyes of God.

In terms of instruction, the Puritans thought it important to provide children with the knowledge, and particularly the religious knowledge, that would enable them to serve God better and increase the chances of their own salvation. To that end, the Puritans were the first Americans to publish books especially intended for children, and until the early eighteenth century, most books written in English and addressed to a child audience were written by Puritan authors (Somerville, 1982).

Not only were Puritan adults sensitive to the special needs of children and aware of developmental differences between their children and themselves, they also did not despise all forms of playfulness, as is commonly believed. Nevertheless, it is true that play was discouraged in the life of the Puritan child. Play was not seen as evil in itself but as an activity that would distract a child from the study and vocational training that were needed to acquire appropriate self-discipline. From a practical standpoint, it is hard to imagine a Puritan child having much time for play, in any case, since school began as early as seven in the morning, six days a week, and did not end until four or five o'clock, and since children were expected to perform their household chores as well (Illick, 1974).

Ultimately, the Puritan experiment in the colonies was doomed to failure, because by the end of the seventeenth century, each new generation seemed to lose some of the religious zeal of its predecessor (Walzer, 1974). Nevertheless, the Puritans had a lasting influence on American attitudes toward children, as developmentally different from adults and as symbols of the hope of a better future. They had another type of influence as well, perhaps one that has been less positive. Despite a degree of acceptance that was almost revolutionary for its time, there were also elements of rejection in the Puritan attitude toward children. The reasonable behavior that was the purpose of discipline and instruction was thought to be against a child's basic nature; thus, the goal of childrearing was to make children into something that by nature they were not. Such a view hardly constitutes acceptance of children in their own right, and might be described as an effort to subdue the very individuality that the Puritans were among the first to recognize in the child.

In the Puritan attitude toward children, therefore, there was a degree of ambivalence that was to evolve in this country into a feeling of uncertainty about the value of childhood and the relative importance of the seemingly natural activities of children and adults, play and work. As a part of our Puritan legacy, this ambivalence would continue for several centuries. Some would argue that it continues to the present day (Walzer, 1974).

Colonial Times

In the colonial United States of the eighteenth century, the Puritan legacy of ambivalence about the value of children was evident, and perhaps as a result, there was a certain ambiguity about the relationship between work and play (Walzer, 1974). On the one hand, colonial parents were genuinely interested in their children, rejoiced at their births, played with them, gave them presents, wrote letters to them when separated, and grieved considerably when a child died. There seemed to be in the colonies a greater fondness for children and a closer relationship between parent and child than was found in England at the time.

On the other side, however, early American parents engaged in many activities that distanced them from their children. Infant abandonment, a common occurrence in Europe, was rare in the New World, but very young colonial children were often "put out." That is, they were given over to the custody of nurses, schools, tutors, or assorted relatives, a practice that modern Americans would certainly see as unusual. As an illustration of this practice, in May 1782 Pamela Sedgewick of western New England wrote of her young daughter to her cousin Betsey Mayhew in Boston: "I have a little prattler, your namesake. If you do not burden yourself with a family before [she] is old enough to leave her mama, I intend to send her to your care. So you see, my dear, you must not expect to get rid of trouble by living single" (Walzer, 1974).

The rejection of children in colonial America also took another form: the complete submission of the child to parental control. It was the parents' role, as it had been in Puritan times, to shape children according to their own strongly held religious convictions, a practice that Walzer (1974) refers to as "infanticide by smothering." In that sense, children had value only insofar as they served as extensions of and reflected well upon their parents. Again, there was that curious contradiction. How could children be appreciated in their own right and at the same time be seen as creatures in desperate need of shaping and correcting?

Compared to the seventeenth-century view, the eighteenth-century American view of childhood was considerably more diversified. There was a blending of Locke's environmentalist views with the new Romanticism typified by Rousseau's naturalistic perspective. The question of the relative influences of nurture and nature on development was now raised in earnest: Are children nothing more than reflections of the sum total of their experiences, or are there innate characteristics that play a role in determining who and what a person grows to be?

The Nineteenth Century

As the British had established colonies along the eastern seaboard, there had been extensive French colonization in the American South and Midwest. It is apparent that early American attitudes about play came to reflect the perspectives of both countries. The British emphasis on discipline, hard work, and moral rectitude was definitely reflected in nineteenth-century American thought, although to a lesser degree than in the mother country. In fact, British visitors to the United States in the early 1800s were horrified by what they considered the irreverent and disrespectful behavior of American children; they typically attributed this state of affairs to overindulgence by American parents, and they expressed surprise at the degree of intimacy and familiarity that characterized parent-child relationships in this country (Borstelmann, 1983). British observers typically described Americans as more relaxed, frivolous, and fun loving than they. Perhaps they might still do so, just as we still tend to describe the British as being somewhat serious and formal.

As has already been mentioned, the French had always maintained an attitude of greater acceptance toward play and toward the naturalness of childhood than had the British. How, then, would a French visitor have described Americans of the nineteenth century? While the British saw them as lacking in discipline, French observers characterized Americans as rather serious minded compared to themselves. Typical were the views of Alexis de Toqueville (1805–1859), who toured the new republic in the early 1800s and described our colonial ancestors as a sober and serious people, unable to enjoy play unless it was integrated in some way with work (Toqueville, 1946/1835). Early American play was, indeed, somewhat work oriented in nature. Supposed play activities, such as raising a barn or making a quilt, were obviously related to the necessary work of an agricultural society. This blend of work and play probably reflected a blend of the early British and French influences on the American colonies. The net result of these competing perspectives was an American ambivalence about play that carried through the nineteenth and into the twentieth century, compounded by the diverse and continuous immigration pattern that created a multicultural American society.

There are numerous illustrations of the nineteenth-century ambivalence toward children and play. On the one hand, the mid-nineteenth century is often regarded as a period in which parents exerted considerable psychological, rather than physical, control over their children (Davis, 1976). That is, the emphasis was on strong parental authority, with little empathy for the child, on the repression of personal feelings, and the encouragement of children's practicing self-control motivated by feelings of guilt.

Yet this also was a period in which American children were encouraged through their play to become more mobile and to achieve greater degrees of mastery over the environment. Toys became increasingly complex; for instance, there appeared a variety of miniature vehicles, such as trains, that were made up of many parts and presented a challenge to the player as well as a source of education. Board games appeared at this time, and these required skill and a flair for competition. The first cap pistol was produced in 1859, allowing a child a new means of expressing aggression and mastery over the environment (Davis, 1976). The message to children was that they must look inward to control themselves and also turn outward to attain a degree of mobility and control over their surroundings.

Twentieth-Century Attitudes

In the first 10 years of the twentieth century, there were efforts to lessen the repressive internal controls that had previously been fostered in children, with a corresponding increase in willingness to let children—and adults for that matter—express their feelings openly (Davis, 1976). There was also greater parental interest in understanding the perspectives and feelings of their children. The interest, at least temporarily, was not in molding the child into a satisfactory adult but in reaching the child, in understanding children as they were. This was the era in which the child study movement began to flourish, a movement characterized by efforts to develop a genuine science of child development and typified by the writings of the renowned American psychologist G. Stanley Hall (1844–1924).

Again, however, attitudes toward children would become distinguished by that ambivalence, attributable to our multicultural heritage, that was inherent in the American way of thinking since Puritan times. Even as the trend was beginning toward a greater appreciation of the individuality and special developmental characteristics of children, a new force was emerging in American psychology. This was the appearance, between 1910 and 1920, of the theory of **Behaviorism,** as set forth in the writings of the man who would be the most influential of all American psychologists, John B. Watson (1878–1958). Influenced by the ideas of John Locke, Watson also believed that the mind is a blank slate at birth and that people grow to be what they are made to be by the environment (Langer, 1969). "Give me a dozen healthy infants," wrote Watson, "and my own specified world to bring them up in and I'll guarantee to take any one at random and train him to become any kind of specialist I might select—doctor, lawyer, artist, merchant, chief, and yes, even beggarman and thief, regardless of his talents, penchants, tendencies, abilities, vocations, and race of his ancestors" (Watson, 1925, p. 82).

Considering the importance of the environment in setting a person's developmental direction, it follows that parents must take an active, even aggressive, stance when raising their children. They must be firm, logical, and consistent, and they must realize that sentiment has nothing to do with childrearing. Watson even advised parents not to kiss or cuddle their children, because cuddled children grow up to expect cuddling as adults; they become chronic complainers, always expecting sympathy from other people. (See the boxed item, which contains some of Watson's advice to parents.)

How did children's play fit into the behaviorist view of the world? Play was seen not as a valuable end in itself but as a means of bringing about social reform. Its value was that it could be a learning experience that allowed children to cultivate socially acceptable behaviors (Davis, 1976). A reader of *Parent's Magazine* in the early 1930s wrote to ask, "Must boys fight?" The magazine's response was that fighting can actually have value in "cultivating strength and skill. . . . As our boys grow older they can be shown how the energy that might be spent in fighting can be utilized in wholesome sports or other worthwhile activities." Perhaps she was responding to the behaviorist emphasis on reinforcement when cultural anthropologist Margaret Mead wrote in the late 1920s that Americans tend to see play as a reward for work, rather than thinking of work and play as natural separate-but-equal features of everyday life.

In the mid- and later-twentieth century, there was a growing recognition that the perspectives on childrearing that typified the years through the 1920s were unduly

---

A Behaviorist Speaks about Childrearing

Some Thoughts from John B. Watson

Even granting that the mother thinks she kisses the child for the perfectly logical reason of implanting the proper amount of affection and kindliness in it, does she succeed? The fact that . . . we rarely see a happy child is proof to the contrary. The fact that our children are always crying and always whining shows the unhappy, unwholesome state they are in. Their digestion is interfered with and probably their whole glandular system is deranged.

There is a sensible way of treating children. Treat them as though they were young adults.

Let your behavior always be objective and kindly firm. Never hug and kiss them, never let them sit on your lap. If you must, kiss them once on the forehead when they say good night. Shake hands with them in the morning. Give them a pat on the head if they have made an extraordinarily good job of a difficult task. Try it out. In a week's time you will find how easy it is to be perfectly objective with your child and at the same time kindly.

SOURCE: From *Psychological Care of Infant and Child* (pp. 80–81) by J. B. Watson, 1928. New York: Norton.

narrow. Most post–World War II parents would consider John Watson's advice on childrearing both bizarre and cruel, for example. The trend in the past 40 years has been toward a degree of autonomy and freedom of expression for children that has no precedent in either ancient or modern history (Davis, 1976). Play has at last been accorded a place of significance in a child's development. Not only are children now *allowed* to play, but it is believed that they should play, because play affords the opportunity for intellectual and social development as well as for emotional release. Here we can see the influences of both psychoanalytic and cognitive-developmental theorists.

Before we conclude, however, that we have finally come to a total acceptance of children's play, we should recognize that many psychologists continue to wonder if we are as tolerant of play as we believe. Many (e.g., Hartley, 1971; Logan, 1977; Elkind, 1982, 1987) suggest that our acceptance of play—and of children in general—is highly conditional. Ruth Hartley (1971), one of the pioneer researchers in the area, worried that play is often misunderstood by parents and even by early childhood educators, who see it as a natural part of childhood but one that has little developmental value. Cross-cultural psychologist Richard Logan (1977) suggested that even as we argue that children should be allowed to play, we unconsciously resent them for having the opportunity to do so while we adults must work to earn a living. David Elkind (1981, 1987) has expressed repeated concern that children today are being forced to grow up too fast, and childhood activities like play are replaced at earlier and earlier ages with the "meaningful" life pursuits of educational and occupational success.

Theories of Play

What is the value of play in a child's development? Is play necessary? What function does it serve?

In an effort to answer questions of this sort, psychologists have proposed a number of theories of play (see Table 1.1). As these theories are discussed, it is important to keep in mind that no one theory has ever been able to explain completely the significance of play in children's development. In fact, no one theory is adequate to explain any aspect of child development. Theories must be seen as only tentative models, helpful frameworks within which child development and behavior can be better understood.

Classic Theories

Early play theories, those that appeared in the latter part of the nineteenth century and the early years of the twentieth, emphasized the biogenetic significance of play. That is, they described play as an instinctive mechanism that either promoted optimal physical development or reflected the evolutionary history of the human species. For example, Herbert Spencer (1873), in his **surplus energy theory,** described play as necessary to allow children to discharge pent-up energy. He argued that nature equips human beings with a certain amount of energy to be used in the process of survival. If

TABLE 1.1   Theories of Play

Theories	Reasons for Play	Greatest Benefits
Surplus Energy		
H. Spencer	To discharge the natural energy of the body	Physical
Renewal of Energy		
G. T. W. Patrick	To avoid boredom while the natural motor functions of the body are restored	Physical
Recapitulation		
G. S. Hall	To relive periods in the evoutionary history of the human species	Physical
Practice for Adulthood		
K. Groos	To develop skills and knowledge necessary for functioning as an adult	Physical, intellectual
Psychoanalytic		
S. Freud, A. Freud, E. Erikson	To reduce anxiety by giving a child a sense of control over the world and an acceptable way to express forbidden impulses	Emotional, social
Cognitive-Developmental		
J. Bruner, J. Piaget, B. Sutton-Smith	To facilitate general cognitive development To consolidate learning that has already taken place while allowing for the possibility of new learning in a relaxed atmosphere	Intellectual, social
Arousal Modulation		
D. E. Berlyne, G. Fein, H. Ellis	To keep the body at an optimal state of arousal To relieve boredom To reduce uncertainty	Emotional, physical

this energy is not used for that purpose, it must be discharged somehow, and children discharge their excess energy in play. Spencer was right, or course, in the sense that play can indeed be used to release energy; parents and teachers often notice that children are more relaxed after vigorous exercise. However, adults also notice the exact opposite phenomenon: A child will often play to the point of sheer exhaustion, and appear to be even more energized afterward than before!

A view of play that was almost the opposite of Spencer's was expressed by G. T. W. Patrick (1916). The purpose of play, according to Patrick, was the **renewal of energy**. When children are tired and relaxed, play keeps them occupied and helps them avoid boredom while they wait for their natural energy supply to be restored. However, while such a theory might explain the sedentary play that children often engage in, how would it account for the rough-and-tumble play that also makes up a part of any healthy child's day?

G. Stanley Hall, one of the leading figures in the early years of American psychology, and one of the first to write extensively about childhood and adolescence, had a unique perspective on the meaning of children's play. According to his **recapitulation theory,** each person's development reflects the evolutionary progression of the entire human species. An infant crawling about at play might be reflecting some unspecified period in human evolution when humans walked on all fours; a first-grader playing "cops and robbers" might be reliving the experiences of a prehistoric ancestor whose daily activities included hunting and gathering food. Hall's was certainly an intriguing theory of play (and of human development in general), but it was based on a rather unsophisticated view of physical anthropology. It is a theory that would find little acceptance among developmental psychologists today.

A final biogenetic theory was expressed by Karl Groos (1901), who suggested that play is the body's natural way of preparing itself for the tasks of adult life. Just as a kitten chasing a ball of string is rehearsing skills that will later be used in stalking food, the child who plays "house" may be preparing for the experience of someday running a household. In fact, much of children's play does resemble adult activities, particularly when children begin to explore adult roles in dramatic play. However, many children's play activities bear little real resemblance to activities pursued in adulthood and can be seen as preparation for adult life only in the most general sense.

None of the early play theories, with their emphasis on instinctive, and often unspecified, biological mechanisms, has strong advocates among modern psychologists, yet each contains at least some element of truth. Their importance, however, is primarily historical. More typical of the modern view are theories that emphasize the psychological value of play and its significance to a child's intellectual, social, and emotional development. Let us turn now to an examination of some of these contemporary theories.

Contemporary Theories

Psychoanalytic Theory

According to psychoanalytic theorists, most notably Sigmund Freud (1856–1939) and Anna Freud (1895–1982), play's value is primarily emotional in that it allows children to reduce anxiety (Freud, 1974). But why would a child suffer from anxiety in the first place? There are two types of anxiety that characterize the years of infancy and childhood.

Objective anxiety is fear of the external world. Infants and young children realize their helplessness and know that they must rely on the good will of others to have their basic needs met. The fear of abandonment is particularly strong in early childhood, and this is not surprising since a child, unlike an adult, needs a caretaker for its very survival. Play reduces objective anxiety by giving a child the illusion of power and control. The rattle a baby plays' with becomes an extension of the body and provides the child with a greater sense of power. An older child building a tower of blocks or playing with dolls or miniature life toys is reducing the ordinarily large and overwhelming world to a size that he or she can handle. Play provides at least the temporary illusion of being in command. In much the same way, the child who plays at being a monster can, by reversing roles, allay a fear of monsters, and the child who punishes a doll can work through anxiety at being punished by a parent.

A second form of anxiety experienced by children is **instinctual anxiety**. Anna Freud (1974) observed that "the human ego by its very nature is never a promising soil for the unhampered gratification of instinct. . . . Its mistrust of their demands is always present." She added that "the effect of the anxiety experienced by the ego is . . . [that] defense mechanisms are brought into operation against the instincts, with all the familiar results in the formation of neuroses and neurotic characteristics" (pp. 58–59).

Psychoanalytic theorists believe that an infant playing with a toy derives a sense of power that helps relieve objective anxiety.

Psychoanalytic theorists noted that many of a child's feelings, including anger, unreasonable fear, sexual curiosity, and the wish to be messy or destructive, are frowned upon by adult society. Since the powerful adults in his or her world disapprove of these feelings, the child comes to fear expressing them, and soon the very feelings themselves, whether or not they are translated into behaviors, trigger a reaction of anxiety in the child.

Play allows the child to explore unwelcome feelings without the repercussions of adult disapproval. For instance, the desire to break a window, strike a playmate, or wallow in the mud may frighten a child, but in play the child is free to be both destructive and messy, within limits, of course. Many timid children become aggressive when squeezing and pounding ceramic clay, destroying a sandcastle, or punching a Bobo doll, and the cleanest, neatest children are often the first to be covered to the elbows in fingerpaint.

The psychoanalytic perspective on play is also reflected in the writings of Erik Erikson (b. 1902). Erikson rejected as unduly narrow Freud's view that the major function of play was anxiety reduction. He suggested that play can also have an ego-building function, since it brings about the development of physical and social skills that enhance a child's self-esteem. During the first year of life, play centers on the exploration of the child's own body. In the gradual recognition of their sensory and motor skills (e.g., looking, listening, talking, walking) and in the exploration of their own bodies (e.g., playing with their hands and feet), children come to have an understanding of themselves as different from other people. Erikson called play with one's own body autocosmic play.

Children in the second year of life begin to go beyond their own bodies in play and to acquire mastery over objects, including toys. This form of mastery play further enhances the ego, and Erikson referred to it as microsphere play.

Finally, during the preschool years, children at play move beyond mastery of their own bodies and mastery of objects to mastery in social interactions. Playing with peers, sharing both fantasy and reality with them, and demonstrating skills in a social setting are all elements of macrosphere play, which again strengthens children's egos, as they realize that they can be successful in the larger social world. Erikson suggested that successful macrosphere play helps children better understand their culture and the social roles that they, and everyone else, are expected to assume.

The Cognitive-Developmental Approach to Play

Rather than emphasizing its emotional value, cognitive theorists typically regard play as a tool for facilitating intellectual growth. Jerome Bruner (1972) and Brian Sutton-Smith (1967), for example, both maintained that play provides a comfortable and relaxed atmosphere in which children can learn to solve a variety of problems. Later, when children are confronted with the more complex problems of the real world, the learning that took place during play is of great benefit to them.

Perhaps the most extensive treatment of play by a cognitive theorist can be found in the writings of the Swiss biologist and philosopher Jean Piaget (1896-1980), the author of what is certainly the most influential of all theories of children's intellectual development. Piaget (1962, 1983) maintained that a primary function of

ch - adapting to diff. writ. situations

all living organisms is to adapt to the environment. Such adaptation is necessary for survival and can be physical, as when an overheated organism perspires to cool the body down, or psychological, as when people adapt their ways of thinking to incorporate new information presented to them. Physical adaptation is necessary for the survival and growth of the body; psychological adaptation ensures the continued growth of the intellectual structures of the mind.

> *Assimilation and accommodation.* Adaptation involves two processes that usually occur simultaneously: assimilation and accommodation. **Assimilation** means taking new material from the outside world and fitting it into one's already existing structures. In a physical sense, the body assimilates food by digesting it, breaking it down so that it eventually becomes a part of the body itself. In an analogous manner, we are able to assimilate new intellectual materials—ideas, concepts, points of view— into the existing structures of our minds, so that those new ideas eventually become incorporated into our own world views.

Accommodation, on the other hand, is the adjusting of the structure in reaction to the newly incorporated material. Thus, the body accommodates to food by salivating, by stomach contractions and the flow of gastric juices to break down the foreign substance, and eventually by growing and changing. So, too, does the mind accommodate new intellectual material, as when a person adjusts his or her perspective on life, even ever so slightly, after incorporating a new idea. The point is that growth, either physical or intellectual, will not occur unless *both* assimilation and accommodation take place.

Assimilation and accommodation generally occur at the same time, but there are instances in which one occurs to a considerably greater extent than the other. Play, according to Piaget, is the dominance of assimilation over accommodation. That is, it is the incorporation of new intellectual material into already existing cognitive structures without a corresponding alteration of the structures themselves. As a concrete example, six-year-old Peter finds an empty cardboard box and determines that for his purposes it is not a box at all but a rocket that will take him to the moon. Thus, Peter forces reality to conform to his perspective rather than adjusting his way of thinking to fit reality. The object he is playing with is, after all, only a cardboard box.

Piaget spoke of play as a consolidation of newly learned behaviors: A child first learns something new and then repeats what is learned over and over again until it becomes an established part of his or her repertoire (Rubin, Fein, & Vandenberg, 1983; Sutton-Smith, 1985). As an example at the level of motor activity, a child who is learning to use a skateboard must first learn how to stand on it without falling and must rehearse the basic maneuvers involved in balancing until these become firmly established routines. Only after the simpler motor patterns are consolidated can the child move on to more elaborate ones, but such consolidation obviously involves the rehearsal of old learning rather than the learning of something new.

> *Play and learning.* While play is not synonymous with learning in Piaget's theory, it can certainly facilitate learning. For example, an infant's play with a rattle, a sponge, a ball, or a spoon could improve eye-hand coordination, balance, and physical

NLS/RP

When children engage in make-believe play with objects, they often force reality to conform to their perspectives rather than accommodating to reality.

strength, and could teach about differences in size, shape, texture, and weight that characterize objects in the physical world. Symbolic, or pretend, play, which emerges during the child's second year, also has the potential to become a significant learning experience. For example, a child who builds a fortress out of sticks might try to make it as realistic as possible and in the process might learn something about logical classification, part-whole relationships, measurement, balance, and spatial relationships. In that sense, make-believe play can lead to what Piaget called **games of construction,** which he saw as representing an area of transition between symbolic play and "nonplayful activities, or serious adaptation" (Piaget & Inhelder, 1969, p. 59). Finally, the rule-oriented games of the elementary schoolchild may not be engaged in for the specific purpose of learning and typically involve the consolidation of skills rather than intentional efforts to learn new ones, but they can easily stimulate intellectual growth. In such games, children learn to share, to remember and follow rules, and to acquire new skills as they move from one level of mastery to another.

In summary, play in Jean Piaget's cognitive-developmental view is not identical to learning, since play requires no accommodation of one's intellectual structures to reality. Play involves the consolidation of physical and mental activities that have been previously learned. Nevertheless, play facilitates learning in that it exposes a child to new experiences and new possibilities for dealing with the world.

Arousal Modulation Theories

One of the distinguishing features of play is that it is intrinsically motivated. It is done for no apparent reason other than the sheer satisfaction of doing it. As we have seen, both psychoanalytic theory and that of Jean Piaget accepted the concept of internal motivation, whether it was to reduce anxiety or to consolidate previously learned activities. However, behavioral learning theorists in the United States (e.g., Hull, 1943) have always maintained that external motivation—and specifically the need to satisfy one's basic physiological needs—is at the root of even the most psychologically sophisticated behaviors. As an example, the attachment motivation that causes an infant to form a bond with its mother is a secondary drive, in that it is originally based on the recognition that mother is the one who feeds the infant. Thus, the child bonds to its mother because it associates her with the satisfaction of a physiological need (Joffe & Vaughn, 1982).

The motivation for some behaviors, however, cannot be explained in terms of basic physiological needs; these behaviors include play and exploration of the environment. Human beings, and lower animals as well, play with and explore their surroundings simply because they want to; there is no reason for these behaviors that can be understood in terms of physiological need reduction. Learning theorists attempted to explain play, therefore, by referring to the concept of internal, rather than external, motivation, and more specifically to the concept of arousal modulation.

The underlying premise of any **arousal modulation theory** of children's play is that there is some optimal level of central nervous system arousal that a human being tries to maintain (Berlyne, 1969). The ideal environment, therefore, affords neither too much nor too little stimulation but just enough to keep a person optimally aroused. What is this optimal level? It falls somewhere between uncertainty and boredom. When there are new or confusing stimuli in the environment, the person feels confused and uncertain, and the level of central nervous system arousal is elevated. To reduce this level, the person must explore the environment in order to reduce its uncertainty. In contrast, when there is a lack of stimulation in the environment, the person is bored and seeks stimulation to maintain the desired arousal level. It is here that play comes in, because children use play to generate environmental stimulation where a sufficient amount does not already exist (Berlyne, 1969).

Similar views of play as arousal modulation were offered by Ellis (1973) and Fein (1981), who suggested that children's play provides a variety of forms of stimulation to an organism in need of it. Included are kinesthetic, or physical, stimulation, perceptual stimulation, and intellectual stimulation. Children at play produce novel effects and at first are made apprehensive by the uncertainty of the new situation. Later, however, as the uncertainty of the situation is reduced, the effect of play is generally positive. It is then that children will work to create new uncertainties, which they immediately proceed to reduce, thus perpetuating a cycle of creation and reduction of uncertainty. Many a frustrated parent will comment that when their children play they often flirt with danger. Indeed, children appear to enjoy activities characterized by degrees of novelty and risk, such as playing with fire, climbing trees, playing monsters, and so forth. Perhaps children include this element of danger, of limits testing, because they are seeking stimulation unavailable in nonplayful activities.

Summary

Play has five essential characteristics. It is intrinsically motivated, freely chosen, pleasurable, nonliteral, and actively engaged in by the participants. Early theories of play emphasized its biological and genetic elements, such as its biologically determined role in releasing the body's excess energy or in preparing a child for adult living, while contemporary theories stress the emotional, intellectual, and social benefits of play. For example, the psychoanalytic perspective is that play is a defense against anxiety, cognitive theories emphasize play's intellectual value, and arousal modulation theories suggest that children play in order to provide themselves with an optimal level of stimulation.

From the time of the ancient Egyptians until the end of the Middle Ages in Europe, children were thought of as having special needs and special activities, including that of play. During the period of the Renaissance, however, children came to be thought of as having little importance compared to adults and were fully integrated into the adult world, in the sense that people of all ages worked and played together.

In the seventeenth century, a new consciousness of children developed. They were now seen as deserving attention and as having developmental needs and problems that were different from those of adults. The French were always more accepting of play than were the British. In France, play came to be seen as suitable only for children, while in England play was seen as a frivolous activity that interfered with a child's development of discipline and time for work. The Puritan legacy in the United States has been an ambivalence about children and about the value of play: Compared to the British, Americans have been closer to their children and more indulgent with them, yet, unlike the French, they have not fully accepted children's playfulness. Americans today, however, are more accepting of play and more aware of the special developmental characteristics and needs of children. There remain questions, though, about the extent of that acceptance. Some psychologists argue that we try to accept play but do not understand its functions, while others believe that we begrudge children the opportunity to play and make efforts to hurry them into adulthood.

Key Terms

Accommodation

Arousal Modulation Theory

Assimilation

Autocosmic Play

Behaviorism

Games of Construction

Instinctual Anxiety

Macrosphere Play

Microsphere Play

Naturalism

Objective Anxiety

Recapitulation Theory

Surplus Energy Theory

Tabula Rasa

CHAPTER TWO

Ethological and Cultural Perspectives

One of the pleasures of owning a young pet comes from sharing in the almost limitless exuberance of their play. A young animal, such as a puppy or a kitten, is often a very appropriate playmate for a child. When we watch a puppy frolicking in an open field, chasing a ball, or engaged in mock fighting, we realize how similar such behaviors are to those of children, and we sense that there is a certain universality to play that cuts across human cultures and even across animal species.

In the first chapter of this book, we took the long view, examining children's play from a historical standpoint. Now we turn to what might be called a wide view, not looking to the past, but comparing human and animal play in the present time, and then examining the variety of playful activities observed in diverse human cultures. The purpose of these comparisons is not so much to learn about life in other societies or about the habits of lower animal species as it is to come to a better understanding of our own culture. Understanding the characteristics of animal play may provide us with insights into the significance of children's play; the study of life in other cultures may offer us clues about the values that are reflected in the play of U.S. children.

Characteristics of Animal Play

As we begin our discussion of play in lower animals, there are three important points to remember. First, play is not found in all animal species, but only in those, such as mammals and some species of birds, that are higher up the phylogenetic ladder (Reynolds, 1981). It seems that play is characteristic of only the most sophisticated life forms.

The second point is that play is generally found only among the immature members of a particular species; it is rare among adults. Human adults have been accused of forgetting how to play, but in fact the human adult is more likely to engage in play of some sort than are the adult members of most other animal species.

The third point is that, even though there are obvious similarities between human and animal play, we must be careful not to carry the comparisons too far. Research on animal play may be used to suggest possible explanations for human play, but a link between human and lower animal behaviors of any sort is far from being clearly established. We must be particularly careful not to impose human feelings or intentions on the behavior of lower animals, since animal behavior, including play, is not governed by consciousness, rationality, or free choice.

Play as Simulation

Like human play, the play of animals is characterized by an element of pretense. In fact, the one most distinctive feature of animal play is that it involves taking skills ordinarily displayed in one context and applying them in contexts in which their true functions cannot possibly be achieved (Fagen 1984). For example, a puppy may engage in playful biting in a variety of situations, such as when it spies the evening newspaper or its favorite old slipper. The "normal" context of biting, however, is in situations that require aggressive behavior, as when the animal is threatened and must defend itself or is in competition with another dog for the same piece of food. Similarly, when a kitten plays with a piece of string, it is demonstrating many of the behaviors that would ordinarily be used in stalking a mouse. Again, however, in play these behaviors are out of context.

The "pretend" component of animal play resembles the nonliteral component of human play discussed in the previous chapter and may explain why play is found only in the more sophisticated animal species. It takes a certain amount of plasticity, or flexibility, for an animal to display behavior patterns in a variety of out-of-context settings. By way of contrast, more primitive organisms respond instinctively with programmed behaviors to specific forms of environmental stimulation.

Play can be thought of as a simulated type of activity. That is, it allows the player, animal or human, to try out behaviors without having to face any serious consequences. Real fighting could result in bodily harm or even death; play fighting is usually harmless, but it gives the animal a chance to try out skills that might some day be needed if a real fight should occur (Reynolds, 1976, 1981). An analogous situation in a human setting might occur when a college student asks a friend to quiz her on the material she is studying for an upcoming exam. The quiz is a simulation; it offers the student a chance to try out her test-taking abilities in a situation that is free of risk because it is free of consequences. While the student would probably not describe the mock quiz as play, it certainly contains an element of pretense.

Taking a simulated quiz is intended to help a student perform better on a real examination, and it may do so, but does the same principle work for lower animals as well? Do animals who engage in a good deal of play demonstrate greater skills in real-world situations than do animals of the same species who rarely play? It appears that they do. What is not clear, however, is *why* they do. The direction of cause and effect is extremely difficult to establish in research on the ultimate benefits of animal play. For example, Chalmers and Locke-Hayden (1985) discovered a relationship between amount of play and the possession of various skills (manual dexterity, agility, and the ability to compete for food) in young marmosets. Those who played the most later proved to be the most motorically skilled and the most efficient when it came to seeking food. However, there is more than one possible explanation for this finding. It might indeed be the case that the animals' experiences at play really caused an improvement in motor skills. It is also possible, however, that animals who are naturally the most skillful to begin with are the ones who play most often, either because of their greater innate ability or because they simply have more opportunities for play (Chalmers, 1984).

Play and Aggression

One of the intriguing features of animal play, particularly that of mammals, is the frequency with which it contains elements of aggressive activity: chasing, hitting, biting, butting, wrestling, and scratching. It has been found, for example, that 80 percent of the play of young rats is aggressive in nature.

While prolonged, intense, nonplayful aggression may indeed be an indicator of emotional disturbance, human parents often condemn aggressive activity of *any* sort in their children and consider even playful aggression to be a sign of immaturity. It is interesting, however, to observe that aggressive play in animals actually indicates the maturity of the organism. Such play increases in frequency as the animal grows up and becomes particularly noticeable at about the time that the animal is mature enough to establish its position within the hierarchy of the group (Reynolds, 1981). Successful acts of aggression may earn for a particular animal a higher position of dominance in relation to its peers.

Although play in lower animals often resembles aggression, it also differs from serious acts of aggression in a number of ways. First, even aggressive play still seems to be a joyful experience; chimpanzees, for example, will fight in play, but at the time they will be displaying a "play face," a facial expression indicating that their attacks on one another are all in fun. Second, unlike real aggression, aggressive play is altered so that none of the players will get hurt. Animals will put limits on their strength, particularly when playing with a younger partner (Bekoff, 1972). Third, aggressive play is characterized by role changes: A player may decide to go from being the aggressor to the victim and back again. Such role changes would not occur in real fighting. Finally, there are pauses in aggressive play, as there are not in genuine incidents of aggression. Players may stop what they are doing to engage in a bit of exploration before going back to the original activity.

Why is there such a marked similarity between play and aggression in lower animals? Play seems to be a type of fine-tuned aggression, and one that appeared later in the evolutionary development of the species. The sophistication of play is that, at least in the case of playful aggression, the animal is able to inhibit an activity before it is finalized. A playful kitten may bite its owner's hand, but it knows when to relax its jaw pressure so as to avoid inflicting serious damage.

Play and Socialization

Even when play involves a high degree of mock aggression, it still provides opportunities for intense, prolonged intimate contact with peers. In fact, a relationship between animal play and socialization has been fairly well established in the research. Play in animals is related not only to their phylogenetic position, but also to the extent to which they must adapt to their peer groups. Animals who are the most "social," who must assume specific positions within a social order established by their peers, are the most likely to engage in play (Bekoff, 1972; Vandenberg, 1978). Monkeys clearly fall into this category, and in fact, there have been more research papers written about the play of monkeys than about that of all other mammals combined (Muller-Schwarze, 1984).

Among the earliest and most influential studies of the social play of monkeys was that carried out by Harlow and Harlow in 1962 at the University of Wisconsin. The Harlows manipulated the amount of peer play that young rhesus monkeys could engage in. In one condition, a group of monkeys were raised by their natural mothers but were allowed no contact with peers at all; in a second condition, monkeys were given a cloth mother-substitute to attach themselves to their real mothers but were allowed to play extensively with peers. The Harlows found that the group raised by their natural mothers but prevented from playing with peers later appeared to be somewhat retarded in their social and sexual development. As a result, their age-mates rejected them and even displayed aggressive behaviors toward them (Harlow & Suomi, 1971; Novak & Harlow, 1975). On the other hand, those allowed to interact with peers, even though denied contact with their real mothers, later appeared to be socially and sexually normal. It seems, therefore, that peer play provides some important socialization experiences for rhesus monkeys, experiences that even the most nurturing parent is not able to provide.

Can rhesus monkeys deprived of peer play ever recover as adults? It appears that they can. Although their age-mates reject them, younger monkeys are apparently willing to play with them (Novak & Harlow, 1975). Thus it seems that the nature of monkey's social play changes with age, and that the type of play they engage in may serve one particular stage of development but not others; in other words, social play seems to serve different developmental functions at different ages (Vandenberg, 1978). Perhaps in social play the animal can try out certain behaviors in a safe setting; social blunders, if developmentally appropriate, will be forgiven by one's age-mates. Such blunders will not be forgiven, however, if, as in the case of the Harlows' play-deprived monkeys, they are seen by peers as below their appropriate level of development.

Harlow (Harlow & Harlow, 1962; Novak & Harlow, 1975) identified four different stages in the social play of his laboratory rhesus monkeys, and these stages have been validated as well on monkeys in the wild. There is the *reflex* stage, in which the infant monkeys do nothing other than cling to their playmates. Then there is the *manipulative stage,* in which they manipulate one another as they would an object in their environment. The third stage involves *true social interaction,* in which there is running, chasing, and a variety of rough-and-tumble activities. Finally, there is the stage of *aggressive play,* occurring at about the time the young monkeys are expected to negotiate their position of dominance within the group hierarchy.

To summarize the current state of knowledge about animal play, we know that the appearance of play depends on the phylogenetic level of the animal, with lower life forms responding more or less automatically to environmental stimulation, while more sophisticated organisms can vary their behaviors and, as in play, apply them in situations out of context. We know that play and aggression are closely linked in mammals. Play and aggression often physically resemble one another, and in fact, aggressive play is considered one of the most mature forms of mammalian play. The two differ in that play occurs in settings that are free of risk and consequences, while aggressive behaviors occur in real-world settings in which the animal's actions could have very serious consequences. Finally, play in mammals seems to be intimately related to the socialization process. It is not known exactly which skills are transmitted during play; it is probable that the specific skills that are transmitted depend upon the level of maturity of the organism. In any case, an animal deprived of social play opportunities during childhood may later be at a social and sexual disadvantage when compared to its age-mates.

Animal and Human Play

Now that we have discussed some of the general characteristics of animal play, we come to the ultimate question. What, if anything, can research on the play of lower animals tell us about the play of the human child? As was mentioned earlier, great care must be taken to avoid easy generalizations across animal species. However, there are some obvious similarities between the play of human beings and that of other mammals:

1. In all mammalian species, including humans, play is characteristic of the immature organism and is found in adults to a considerably lesser degree.
2. Play in all mammalian species involves an element of pretense, of the application of behaviors in out-of-context situations. In a sense, the organism at play is flexible enough to make reality conform to its own needs, rather than adapting its behaviors to the environment.
3. Play provides, for human beings and lower animals alike, an opportunity to practice, in a safe setting and without consequences, many of the skills that are needed for success in the real world. In that sense, play allows the immature animal to prepare for adulthood, although this should not be taken as evidence that such practice is the sole, or even the major, purpose of play.
4. Play allows opportunities for intimate physical contact and intense social interaction, including the chance to experiment with social roles and role reversals. Play experience is related to successful social and sexual functioning in monkeys, and it certainly can be said that some forms of play promote social development in the human child.
5. Both human and animal play contain substantial components of aggression, and this is particularly true of the play of males of all species that have been investigated (Reynolds, 1981).

An examination of the similarities in the play of the various mammalian species leads us to a number of tentative conclusions. First, play is a normal activity for mammals, and particularly for those who are young. It is not an aberration. It is not something that animals do only because they have no more serious business to keep them occupied. Perhaps the animal research might be useful for those who sometimes find it necessary to argue that play is a normal activity for a human child. Unfortunately it is not so unusual to have to make such an argument in an age in which children are encouraged too early to take up the mantle of adulthood (Elkind, 1981, 1987) and in which nursery schools are often designed to start their pupils on the path toward Ivy League universities.

Second, the fact that children play is a reflection on their flexibility, their adaptability, and their creativity. In play they are distorting reality to suit their purposes, a phenomenon Jean Piaget (1962) described as the dominance of intellectual assimilation over accommodation. Such distortions of reality constitute a valuable intellectual exercise, and one that demonstrates the intellectual sophistication of the human organism.

Third, while this is not its sole purpose, play clearly seems to provide opportunities for the practice of skills that may be of use in other areas of life. Fourth, play in mammals is obviously related to socialization; in children, play promotes social development and may have an important role in teaching developmentally appropriate social skills (Athey, 1984). Finally, play allows children to display aggressive behaviors in a "safe" setting. Are such aggressive behaviors normal for human beings? Should they be encouraged, discouraged, or simply accepted for what they are? No one knows for certain, but aggressive behaviors are typical in young children, and if nothing else, play may provide a socially acceptable arena in which these behaviors can be demonstrated.

Cultural Differences in Play

Play has been observed in virtually every human culture, past and present. It is a true cultural universal. The appeal of play for a child must be considerable, because even in societies in which there is little time for play, children somehow manage to make the time by integrating play into their work routines. For example, in the Kipsigis community in Kenya, children have numerous chores, yet they discover ingenious ways to make play of their work. Harkness and Super (1983) described the practice common among Kipsigis children of playing tag while they watched the cows or of climbing trees while they supervised their younger siblings. It is a common and erroneous belief that a child needs extensive amounts of time in order to play (Schwartzman, 1986).

On the other hand, there are vast differences in both the amount and types of human play that have been observed both cross-culturally and within cultures. In some societies, children engage in highly complex and elaborate games; in some, the games are remarkably simple; in still others competitive games of any sort are nearly non-existent.

Competition is an essential ingredient in the play of many children, and yet there are societies in which competitive play is almost totally unknown. In complex societies like ours there is a considerable amount of individual and subcultural variation in competitive play. Some children's games require a substantial amount of intellectual skill, whereas in many cultures it is physical and not intellectual strategy that determines who will win and who will lose.

The emphasis of this section of the chapter will be on patterns of and reasons for cultural variations in children's play. The value of studying cultural differences, beyond the obvious social benefit of learning about the customs of societies other than our own, is that we cannot fully understand the play of American children unless we look also at the play of other peoples. Simply put, the play of children tells us much about the values of the culture they live in. As we shall see, the play of U.S. children mirrors the complexity of our cultural institutions, our particular approaches to childrearing, and our political and social philosophies.

Cultural Differences in Competitive Games

The competitive game is a form of play in which participants follow established rules as they compete against one another with the intent of winning. Such games have been observed in virtually every culture ever studied, although they vary considerably in type. The outcome of some competitive games depends solely on the physical skills of the players, in others the outcome is influenced by chance factors over which the players have little control, while in a third group it is the ability to make rational decisions that determines who will win and who will lose.

One of the clearest relationships between play and culture is the link between the types of competitive games that occur and the degree of cultural complexity, as defined by such factors as the extent of social stratification within a culture and the sophistication of its political and social organizations. The United States, for example, would be described as a highly complex culture because of our considerable socioeconomic diversity and our complicated political system, with its variety of rules pertaining to the selection of our leaders, the making of our laws, and the governance of our society.

The pattern observed repeatedly in the research literature is that children, or adults for that matter, who live in the most complex cultures are likely to play the most complex competitive games (Sutton-Smith & Roberts, 1981). It appears that the competitive games of a culture reflect, and perhaps offer opportunities for the practice of, skills that are necessary for success in life. Let us now examine the various types of competitive games that have been identified by anthropologists and the relationship of these games to cultural complexity.

Games of Physical Skill

In **games of physical skill** the outcome, be it a win, a loss, or a tie, is determined totally by the physical skills of the players (Sutton-Smith & Roberts, 1981). A foot race is an example, as is a weightlifting competition. The outcome in both cases depends not on chance or on mental strategy, but totally on the physical prowess of the competitors.

Games of physical skill are generally the only forms of competition found in simple cultures of limited technological sophistication, in which day-to-day survival depends on the possession of specific motor skills. In hunting-and-gathering societies, for example, the ability to use weapons effectively is essential, as is among jungle-dwelling peoples a certain proficiency at using sharp instruments to cut through the dense undergrowth. The element of play comes in when the same skills used in work are demonstrated in playful competition. For example, the games of hunting societies include foot races, competitive tracking, and spear-throwing contests. The play of tropical jungle dwellers often involves demonstrations of speed and skill in the use of a machete knife or similar instrument. In other words, it appears that the games rely upon the same physical skills, with minor variations, that are needed in work; the difference is that in play the skills are exhibited in an atmosphere of enjoyment and relaxation.

Games of Chance

The outcome of **games of chance** is determined only by sheer blind luck. Whether a player wins or loses may depend upon the roll of a die or the spin of a wheel. In what type of culture might one be likely to find an emphasis on games of chance? As could be expected, such games are typical of societies in which fate plays a large role in everyday life. These are highly diverse and geographically widespread peoples whose common characteristic is that their fortunes depend on factors they cannot control (Sutton-Smith, 1981). Thus, they learn to live with a high degree of individual, social, and environmental uncertainty.

Cultures that emphasize in play the element of chance that dominates their lives include nomadic peoples who wander in search of an uncertain livelihood and whose very existence is determined by uncontrollable variables, such as weather conditions. Since rationality seems to be of little use, such peoples often turn to religious rituals and divination in making decisions about the future; prophecies based upon a "reading" of the entrails of an animal may be as valid a method of decision making as any other.

Games of Strategy

Games of strategy are those whose outcomes are determined by the rational choices made by the players, and such games require a degree of intellectual skill. Consistent with the pattern that seems to emerge from a cross-cultural analysis of types of competitive games, games of strategy also reflect the general characteristics of the cultures in which they are found. These cultures are technologically advanced and

Highly organized sports are games that require a considerable amount of strategy as well as depend on chance and physical skill.

highly complex. Survival, or perhaps we should say success, depends on a person's ability to make correct rational choices, and not to any considerable degree on physical skills or on the whims of fate.

Included in the category of games of strategy are board games (e.g., Monopoly, checkers, chess), card games, computer games, and a wide variety of games that involve guesswork or memory (e.g., Twenty Questions, Charades, Concentration). Included also are highly organized sports that, although obviously dependent upon the physical skills of the participants, also require creativity, planfulness, strategy, and the ability to imagine oneself in the role of one's opponent.

The three types of games can be arranged in a hierarchy that is reflective of cultural complexity, with games of physical skill at the bottom and games of strategy at the top. That is not to say, however, that one type of competitive game is better than another in an absolute sense or that people who engage only in games of physical skill are less intelligent than those who play games of strategy. The hierarchy is based only on cultural complexity and tells us more about environmental conditions in which a society finds itself than about the basic abilities of individual society members. As Sutton-Smith and Roberts (1970), who have extensively studied cultural differences in competitive games, concluded, "In games, children learn all those necessary arts of trickery, deception, harassment, divination, and foul play that their teachers won't teach them, but that are most important in successful human relationships, in marriage, business, and war."

A thought-provoking analysis of the relationship between a culture's competitive games and its basic values was provided by Montague and Morais (1976) in their discussion of the values of American football. The game of football, they argued, bears a striking resemblance to life in the business world. Both football and business emphasize hard work, dedication, teamwork, and competition. Both involve strict hierarchical socialization; players must know their places and status rankings, and must carry out the roles assigned to them. Football and business are both team efforts, although in both cases individual accomplishments may be singled out either for praise or for blame.

Perhaps what is most disturbing is that both football and business involve an element of sneakiness, mistrust, and dishonesty, as players attempt to "psych out" their opponents. U.S. adults may be perfectly justified in forbidding children to participate in some of the organized games of our society. They might want to realize, however, that our games are not invented by chance but may reflect our culture's values more accurately than we like to admit. If the organized sports available to children are highly competitive, perhaps it is because we value competition—not only in sports, but in the classroom and in the world of work as well. If we dislike the aggression that we witness on the playing field, perhaps we might ask ourselves whether we are similarly disturbed by aggressive behaviors in other areas of our children's lives, and in our own lives as well.

Finally, we should point out that the three categories of competitive games are not exclusive to particular types of cultures, as it may at first appear. Primitive cultures do indeed tend to compete only in games of physical skill, but such games are also found in cultures that emphasize games of chance, and while children in technologically advanced cultures may accentuate gam̶e̶s̶ ̶o̶f̶ ̶s̶t̶r̶a̶t̶e̶g̶y, they engage in the other two types of games as well.

The Competition–Cooperation Balance

U.S. parents often complain that their children are encouraged at too early an age to become involved in competitive play. If we were less competitive, these parents argue, children would instead [...] point of view are that (1) competition [...] ries of play, (2) competitive play is in[...] and (3) if competitive play did not [...] cooperation. In fact, all of these assu[...]

In the first place, it is inaccur[...] mutually exclusive categories. There certainly are cultural differences in the proportions of the two forms of play, with children in some societies playing more competitively than those in others. Neverth eless, few cultures are either exclusively cooperative or exclusively competitive in their play. Most children in the world's societies play both competitively and cooperatively, and often within the same game. In fact, in some societies, such as the Soviet Union, group competition is encouraged precisely because it encourages cooperation and group loyalty (Bronfenbrenner, 1972, L[...]mann, 1970; Seymour, 1981). To understand this apparent contradiction, consider the example of a baseball player, who is competing with members of the opposing team to win the game but is at the same time intensely involved in cooperation with his or her teammates. The perception of a common enemy can foster cooperation, and as games become increasingly complex, the players' willingness to cooperate in fulfilling their interdependent roles becomes increasingly essential (Parker, 1984).

Is competitive play psychologically damaging to children? Apparently it need not be, since children who compete do not usually forget how to cooperate. What is more, since children's play to some degree reflects the values of their culture, it is likely that when children are highly competitive in their play, their elders are highly competitive as well. Indeed, one could argue that competitive play can help to prepare a child for the necessary competition of the adult world. U.S. children, as we shall see, engage in a considerable amount of competitive play, but they also live in a society in which individual self-determination and individual achievement are valued adult characteristics, and the ability to compete for success is a necessity.

Economic Factors in Competition

Cultures that are affluent, technologically advanced, and highly complex are likely to have the highest levels of competition in the play of their children. Those that are poorly developed and dependent upon a subsistence economy in which people seem to live from hand to mouth are the least likely to tolerate competition in play (Kagan & Madsen, 1972; Knight & Kagan, 1977; Shapira, 1976; Sutton-Smith, 1980).

What might be the reasons for the influence of economics on children's play? It seems that in simpler, more primitive cultures, people must cooperate within their

[Handwritten note overlaid:] α page 35: 'most children play both compet. coop + equally. + often within the same game.

family units in order to guarantee their very survival. When resources are scarce, it is adaptive to share. If a child in such a culture were to compete for a larger portion of food, such an effort would be criticized by adults on the grounds that if one person earns more, other family members must receive less. Thus, competition is selfish, has little adaptive significance, and is tolerated neither in play nor in any of the other activities of daily life.

In more complex, more advanced cultures, however, there is less sense of community, and individuals are expected to compete to ensure the economic survival of their families. The term *breadwinner* suggests that competition is involved in the process of making a living. If there are winners, there must also be losers. Competition is valued among adults, therefore, and is also valued, or tolerated at least, in the child's world of play (Madsen, 1971).

Political and Philosophical Variables

While economic conditions may predict the level of competitive play in a culture, they are obviously not the only predictor since cultures that are at similar levels of affluence and technological advancement still differ greatly in their acceptance of competitive play. Attitudes toward competition, during both childhood and adulthood, also reflect a society's beliefs about the ideal relationship between the individual and the group.

Some societies emphasize **collectivism,** stressing the importance of group goals, group loyalty, and group identification; they also encourage communal labor and communal property, and discourage the formation of potentially divisive allegiances to subgroups like the family. An emphasis on **individualism,** on the other hand, is characterized by a belief that loyalty to self comes before group loyalty, that people should develop their own individual identities rather than identifying with the group, that the purpose of work is more to benefit individual workers and their families than it is to benefit the state, and that individuals have a right to own property (Mead, 1937).

It should be pointed out that individualism and collectivism are matters of degree. They should be thought of as points on a continuum rather than mutually exclusive categories. While there is usually a connection between the general attitudes of a culture and the specific attitudes of individuals, this is not always the case. In many cultures that are characterized by a high degree of institutionalized competition, there still exists a considerable amount of cooperation on an individual level, and the reverse is also true (Seymour, 1981).

To illustrate the collective and individualistic societal emphases, let us look at some of the ways in which Soviet and U.S. philosophical differences are mirrored by differences in Soviet and U.S. children's play. In the Soviet Union there is a sense in which children belong to the community rather than to their biological parents alone. While walking on a Moscow street with his family, U.S. psychologist Urie Bronfenbrenner (1972) had an experience that would certainly be unusual in the United States: His four-year-old son was a few paces ahead of the rest of the family when the child was noticed by a group of teen-age boys. One of the teen-agers picked up the little boy, hugged and kissed him, and then passed him around for all of his friends to hold. Such an incident illustrates the Soviet attitude that a child is not a personal possession of its parents, but in a way belongs to the entire community.

Unlike U.S. mothers, Soviet mothers are willing to share the responsibility for raising their children with relatives, friends, and even to some extent with strangers. It would not be unusual in Moscow for a stranger on a public bus to offer you her infant or toddler to hold on your lap, nor is it unusual for adult strangers routinely to start up conversations with young children. Consequently the Soviet child is usually not fearful of strangers. In fact, many Soviet children spend a considerable amount of time in the care of people other than their parents: One of every ten children aged two or younger is raised in a collective setting, and one in five of those between the ages of three and six. Five percent of school-age children attend either boarding schools or what are called schools of the prolonged day, where they stay from early morning until six o'clock in the evening (Bronfenbrenner, 1972).

In a Soviet day-care center the emphasis on collectivism is readily apparent (Bronfenbrenner, 1972). Children are taught, for example, that there is no individual ownership of property. A commonly heard phrase, in English translation, is "Mine is

---

Play in a Soviet Childrearing Facility

When psychologist Urie Bronfenbrenner studied child development in the Soviet Union, he noticed a huge number of Soviet–American differences in attitude about the goals of childrearing. He also noticed differences in the ways in which Soviet and U.S. children play. This should not be surprising, since play so often reflects the political and social philosophy of a culture.

In the following passage, Bronfenbrenner (1972) describes preschoolers' play in the type of communal setting in which one in five Soviet children is raised:

From the very beginning stress is placed on teaching children to share and to engage in joint activity. Frequent reference is made to common ownership: "Moe eto nashe; nashe moe (mine is ours; ours is mine.)" Collective play is emphasized. Not only group games, but special complex toys are designed which require the cooperation of two or three children to make them work. As soon as children are able to express themselves, they are given training in evaluating and criticizing each other's behavior from the point of view of the group. Gradually, the adult begins to withdraw from the role of leader or coordinator in order to forge a "self-reliant collective," in which the children cooperate and discipline themselves, at meal times and in play activities too. Play often takes the form of role-playing in real-life stituations, which gradually increase in complexity. Beginning in the second year of nursery and continuing through kindergarten, children are expected to take on ever-increasing communal reponsibilities, such as helping at table, serving others, cleaning up. The effects of these socializing experiences are reflected in the youngster's behavior, with many children giving an impression of self-confidence, competence, and camaraderie.

SOURCE: Bronfenbrenner, U. (1972). *Two worlds of childhood: U.S. and U.S.S.R.* (pp. 23–25). New York: Simon and Schuster.

ours; ours is mine." Almost as soon as they are beginning to speak, children are encouraged to analyze and criticize their own behaviors from the perspective of other members of the group. In play every effort is made to cultivate an attitude of cooperation. Special toys are designed not to work properly if only one child is playing with them; they function only through the combined efforts of two or more children. Musical activities are structured to foster a sense of group belonging, rather than to showcase the talents of the individual child. Role playing is encouraged as soon as the child is ready, in order to help the players see the world from the vantage points of other people.

In the United States, the emphasis is on individualism rather than collectivism. Children are raised by one set of parents; outsiders may help, but the ultimate childrearing responsibility belongs to the parents alone. U.S. children may indeed spend time in day care, since half of the mothers of school-age children are now in the work force, but we still believe that the child's basic values should be taught by parents. Our goal is to raise human beings who have a sense of individual autonomy and individual initiative. Our children have their own possessions; sharing may be encouraged, but there is no question that it is *their* property that they are being asked to share. Cooperation is valued, but so is competition, and it is through their competitive efforts that children can demonstrate their individual accomplishments and enhance their personal status (Sutton-Smith & Roberts, 1981).

Is the U.S. sense of individualism represented in the play of U.S. children? To answer that question, Madsen (1967, 1971) developed an interesting technique to measure cooperative and competitive efforts in children's play: the Madsen Cooperation Board (see Figure 2.1). Four children sit at a table around an eighteen-inch square board, one child at each corner. The board is covered with paper, on which four target circles are drawn; at its center is a weight, attached to which is a pen with the point facing down and touching the board. Four strings are connected to the weight, each running to a separate corner of the board, through an eyelet hook, and into the hands of one of the players. The children are able, therefore, to draw on the paper with the pen by simply pulling on the strings. Actually it is not so simple a task at all, depending on the extent to which the players are willing to cooperate with one another.

In a cooperation condition, the four children are told to work together to draw lines across each of the four circles in numerical order. They are promised that every time a circle is crossed, each of them will receive a piece of candy, but they are warned that no one will receive a reward unless everybody else does. Children typically have little difficulty earning their rewards after being given this set of instructions.

In the competition condition, some groups of players have a much more difficult time of it. The children are told that a circle has been designated for each of them, with his or her own name on it, and that a child will get a reward only if the pen crosses his or her circle.

It is obvious that, even in the competition condition, the strategy that will earn the greatest rewards on the Madsen Cooperation Board is cooperation (Seymour, 1981). If all the children pull their strings at the same time, no player will be able to move the pen in the direction of his or her circle. If, on the other hand, the children decide to cooperate, each of them can easily earn a reward; they can simply agree to

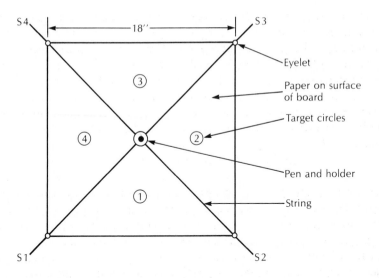

FIGURE 2.1   The Madsen Cooperation Board.

From "Cooperative and Competitive Behavior of Urban Afro-American, Anglo-American, Mexican-American, and Mexican Village Children" by M. C. Madsen & A. Shapira, 1970. *Developmental Psychology, 3,* 6–20. © 1970 by the American Psychological Association. Reprinted by permission.

take turns at winning, with one child at a time being allowed to pull the pen in his or her direction while the other three willingly release their strings.

A vast amount of cross-cultural research using the Madsen Cooperation Board or similar devices suggests that there are dramatic cultural differences in children's ability to cooperate when they play. For example, rural children seem to cooperate better than children who live in cities; children from cultures that are less technologically advanced cooperate better than those from more sophisticated Westernized cultures; Mexicans, and even Mexican-Americans, display a greater amount of cooperation than do Anglo-Americans (Kagan & Madsen, 1971, 1972; Madsen & Shapira, 1970; Shapira & Madsen, 1974).

American children tend to be extremely competitive as a group when compared to children in other cultures, even when such competition is clearly counterproductive. To understand why, let us look at differences in the attitudes of U.S. and Mexican mothers toward the performance of their children. Mexican mothers appear to be more likely than U.S. mothers to reward their children even for failure, to praise them because at least they tried. They are also more likely to actively discourage aggression toward peers. U.S. mothers choose more difficult goals for their children and are less willing to lower their expectations if their children fail to meet those goals; they tend to encourage their children to keep trying rather than admit defeat. It seems that the Mexican mothers responded more to how their children were feeling than to the child's level of accomplishment, whereas for the U.S. mothers the pattern was reversed (Kagan & Madsen, 1972; Knight & Kagan, 1977).

The relationship between levels of competition in the play of U.S. children and the individualistic, rather than collectivistic, attitude that characterizes the U.S. world view is only that: a relationship. It would be unfair to say that we specifically train our children to be competitive, since many U.S. parents and teachers work very hard to discourage childhood competition. In addition, as was alluded to earlier in this section, general societal attitudes are not always reflected in the thinking or the behaviors of individual society members. It may be reasonable to speak of a "U.S." perspective on the relationship between individuals and groups, but in a culture as diverse as ours, we would expect a substantial amount of diversity in individual points of view.

In fact, even within our competitive society, there is considerable variation in the amount of competitiveness found among children, or among adults for that matter. For example, research on U.S. children raised in communal settings, in which there is an emphasis on group ownership of property and on group rather than individual achievements, indicates that such children rarely get involved in competitive play (Plattner & Minturn, 1975). Similarly, U.S. college students who opt for communally oriented living arrangements seem to be more cooperative in outlook than students who live in traditional sorority or fraternity houses (Rappaport, Bernstein, Hogan, Kane, Plunk, & Sholder, 1972). Again, these data are only suggestive. We do not know whether communal living encourages cooperation, whether cooperative people are more likely to choose to live in a commune, or, as is probable, whether both of these possibilities are operating. We do know, however, that it is unwise to generalize from group to individual behavior, even when it seems appropriate to generalize about the underlying philosophical and political perspectives of a particular cultural group.

Cultural Differences in Symbolic Play

There has been a considerable amount of research on the effects of culture on children's symbolic, or make-believe, play, with an emphasis on social class differences within a culture as well as on cross-cultural comparisons. The findings have been fairly consistent: Children from cultures that are less technologically advanced or from the lower socioeconomic classes within a particular culture seem to experience what are sometimes regarded as symbolic play deficits. They engage in less frequent, less complex, and less sophisticated make-believe play, possibly because there is little opportunity for play in their lives (Ammar, 1954; Feitelson, 1979; Fortes, 1970; LeVine & LeVine, 1963; Mead, 1975; Schiller, 1954).

Perhaps the most frequently cited study of cultural differences in sociodramatic play is Smilansky's (1968) analysis of two groups of Israeli children aged three to six. One group was of European descent and was identified as middle-class; the second group, of North African parentage, was categorized as lower-class. Smilansky found that among the lower-class children there was significantly less sociodramatic play, defined as imitative role play, make-believe play with objects, social interaction, and verbal communication. She suggested in explanation that lower-class parents may provide less direct training in and offer less encouragement for pretend play, and that lower-class childrearing techniques may inhibit the verbal, social, and cognitive skills that promote the development of fantasy in children.

Results similar to Smilansky's have been found in studies of both American (Fein & Stork, 1981; Griffing, 1980; Rubin, Maioni, & Hornung, 1976) and British children (Smith & Dodsworth, 1976). To be sure, there have been studies (e.g., Golomb, 1979; Stern, Bragdon, & Gordon, 1976) that arrived at the opposite conclusion, that there were no measurable social class differences in pretend play, but these results constituted a definite minority opinion.

In summary, the research to date is characterized by a fairly consistent pattern of cultural differences in make-abelieve play. What is not known, however, is why these differences exist, and there is much disagreement as to whether these differences should be thought of as deficits in need of correction. One major criticism of many of the studies in this area is that the situational effects of testing were not properly considered. Schwartzman (1984) pointed out, for example, that children's imaginative skills are usually tested in a school or laboratory setting and rarely if ever looked at in children's natural surroundings. School may be a more natural and comfortable environment for a middle-class than for a lower-class child, however, and one in which a middle-class child will more easily display his or her imaginative skills. In fact, it has been found that lower-class children display a larger variety of verbal and social skills outside school than within it (Labov, 1972; Schwartzman, 1984).

There are other aspects of the conditions of testing that need to be considered as well. A child from a poor family probably has fewer toys and when asked to use toys as props in pretend play, may not know what to do with them (McLoyd, 1983). Perhaps, as Smith (1983) suggested, teachers should familiarize their pupils of low socioeconomic status with a variety of toys and play materials before testing their proficiency at symbolic play. In other words, the competence may actually be there, but children may not perform as well as they are able if the testing materials are strange to them. An interesting note along these lines is that in Griffing's (1980) study social class differences were found in children's ability to play a "mommy and daddy" game, but 83% of the children from the lower-class group lived in single-parent families, while 83% of the middle-class children had both a mother and father living at home! Is it surprising that the lower-class children were less capable of acting out their assigned make-believe roles?

Beyond the questions about conditions of testing, it should be mentioned that, since social class is a broad and complex construct, even if socioeconomic differences in make-believe play really do exist, it may still not be clear what these differences mean. Can symbolic play variations be attributed to ethnic, racial, or economic factors or perhaps to differences in patterns of childrearing? In much of the research, these variables have not been analyzed separately. In the Smilansky (1968) study, for example, it will be remembered that the children differed not only in social class, but in ethnic origin as well. Perhaps the differences she found could have been attributed as easily to ethnic background as to social class.

Do socioeconomic differences result from differences in the school curricula that middle- and lower-class groups of children are exposed to? In some of the research, efforts were made to compare children of different socioeconomic status who were

Symbolic play depends on children's levels of fantasy predisposition but also requires familiarity with the props used and the scenes that are enacted.

enrolled in the same schools, but such efforts do not characterize the majority of the research on the subject. Why should the question of which school a child attends be so important? Consider the findings of Gouldner (1978), who compared a middle-class, white, suburban school environment with that of lower-class, black, inner-city children. The differences in teaching approaches were striking: Teachers in the latter group were more likely to stress obedience, discipline, silence, and order in their pupils, while the teachers in suburbia put a greater emphasis on children's creative expression. It is likely that the encouragement of creativity would have a positive impact on the quality and quantity of children's make-believe play.

Since all the specific causal variables have not yet been identified, psychologist Vonnie McLoyd (1983, 1986) has argued that the evidence pertaining to cultural differences in symbolic play is still inconclusive. She further suggested that in much of the research on socioeconomic status differences in pretend play no clear and consistent definition of social class was established. In some cases, a variety of factors, including occupational status, family income, and educational attainment, were used to determine a child's social class, but in others, class was determined simply by asking the parents of the children involved to categorize themselves. Until there can be consistent definitions of the concept of social class, it will be difficult to arrive at any firm conclusions about the effects of culture on children's symbolic play.

Summary

Animal play is found only among those animals who occupy the highest positions on the phylogenetic ladder and typically only occurs among the immature of the species. Adults rarely play. The major characteristic of the play of animals is that it involves simulation, in that behaviors are applied in out-of-context situations. This pretend component of animal play requires a high degree of flexibility on the part of the player and resembles the nonliteral element in human play.

Play in animals resembles but differs from aggression in a number of ways. It is, first of all, a joyful experience, which aggression typically is not. Play also involves a withholding of strength in order to protect the players from harm. Finally, play differs from aggression in that there are pauses and even complete role changes in play, which are not found in acts of aggression. Play is also related to animal socialization; the most socially oriented animals are also the most likely to play. Play appears at just about the time that the animal is beginning to establish its position within the social hierarchy and may have a function in providing valuable social experience and defining social roles within the peer group.

Play has been observed in virtually every culture studied, although there is considerable variation in the amount of play and in the extent to which it involves competition or cooperation. The greatest amount of competitive play is found in technologically advanced and affluent cultures, while competition is rare in underdeveloped societies, in which survival is a day-to-day affair. The type of competitive game that is played reflects the values of the particular culture, and the skills required in play resemble the skills that are necessary for success in life. Games of physical skill are most evident in societies in which physical prowess is necessary for work and survival. Games of chance depend on luck or fate, and are emphasized in a variety of cultures that have in common a high degree of individual, social, and environmental uncertainty. The outcome of games of strategy depends on the ability of the players to make rational choices, and are found in complex and sophisticated cultures in which intellectual strategies are required to achieve success.

Cooperation and competition are not mutually exclusive categories of games. Most children play both competitively and cooperatively, even within the same game. Nevertheless, competition is emphasized over cooperation in some cultures: those that are well-to-do and in which individual identity and achievement are valued more than group identity, loyalty, and dependence. Cultures that emphasize cooperation are either poor and underdeveloped or proponents of a collectivist philosophy, placing responsibility to the group ahead of individual identity and achievement.

Cross-cultural, and particularly subcultural, differences have been found repeatedly in research on children's symbolic, or make-believe, play. Lower-class children typically engage in less of this type of play than do middle-class children. It is still not known, however, which particular variables associated with socioeconomic status are responsible for the observed differences in the children's performance. Do they stem from differences in education, ethnic background, approaches to parenting, or familiarity with the props that are used to stimulate imaginative play? In fact, the research is characterized by a failure even to provide clear and consistent definitions of social class.

Key Terms

Collectivism
Games of Physical Skill
Games of Strategy

Games of Chance
Individualism

CHAPTER THREE

The First
Two Years
of Life

At five months of age, Lauren seemed to have a great deal of curiosity about the world around her, so her father decided to see if she had any interest in play. He held a piece of paper in front of her, crumpled it noisily, and then offered it to Lauren to see what she would do with it. She immediately reached out and grasped the paper, and brought it to her mouth. Is this an example of infant play?

The next day, Lauren's father tried the same little experiment, and this time the child reacted, not by reaching for the paper, but by simply staring at it. Is this play? On another occasion Lauren was offered a crumpled piece of paper, and she reacted by grasping it and crumpling and rattling it herself. Can we now conclude that Lauren is able to play?

Answers to our questions about Lauren's behaviors should become obvious as we proceed through this chapter, which deals with the play of infants. There are several important points to be made here. The first is the rather obvious one that infants really do play, even during the first half year of life. A second point is that a degree of interpretation is often required to know exactly when a baby is playing and when it is not, because play is defined not by specific behaviors but by the purposes that they serve. It is easy to know what an infant is doing at a given moment but more difficult to understand the reasons why. As an illustration of this point, when we attempt to distinguish between play and exploration, it will be seen that the behaviors involved in these theoretically distinguishable activities are often remarkably similar.

A third major emphasis of this chapter will be on an examination of the various, often related, types of play that occur during infancy; these include visual play, motor play involving one's own body, play with objects, and the emergence of representational, or symbolic play. We shall describe the many forms of play, chart the progression of their development, and discuss the implications of their appearance for the process of child development in general.

Exploration and Play

Much has been written about the relationship of play to exploration during infancy. In actuality, the behavior of young children cannot be fragmented into isolated segments, since play, exploration, and a variety of other activities continuously flow from one another. An adult watching a preschool child might be hard-pressed to determine exactly when one type of activity ends and another begins. Exploration quickly evolves into play, and play often leads to further exploration of the world.

There are ways in which play and exploration can be said to differ, however, just as there are ways in which they are similar. In particular, the differences have most often been described in three areas: the children's affective state, the amount of stereotypy in their behavior, and the focus of the children's attention (Wohlwill, 1984).

In terms of the child's affective state, exploration is often characterized as either a neutral or a mildly negative emotional experience, while play is seen as joyful and highly positive. When children are exploring their surroundings, they are cautious and serious. The mildly negative affect is said to result from the uncertainty they are feeling or the tension that goes with directing their undivided attention to a phenomenon (Hughes & Hutt, 1979).

When children are exploring, they behave in stereotypical ways (Hughes & Hutt, 1979). A child exploring the contents of her mother's purse, for example, might examine each item she finds by smelling it, tasting it, rubbing it against her cheek in a manner almost ritualistic. In play, however, children are more flexible and more relaxed. They easily jump from one idea or activity to another, and play activities seem to be almost totally devoid of rigidity and stereotypy.

Finally, when children explore, they devote their attention wholeheartedly to the object of their exploration. They appear to be intense, their heart rates are steady, and they are unwilling to be interrupted. In play, however, the children's heart rates are variable, and they are less intensely concentrated on what they are doing (Hughes & Hutt, 1979; Hughes, 1978; Hutt, 1979). Parents of young children easily recognize the behavioral differences between play and exploration, as indicated by the often-heard remark, "When I can hear them, I know that everything's all right. When they're quiet, I begin to worry."

When do children explore and when do they prefer to play? The answer depends on the familiarity of the situation or the materials at hand. Exploration comes before play. In unfamiliar surroundings a child first explores, but gradually, as the setting becomes familiar and comfortable, exploration gives way to play. It seems that the child's attention is dominated by external stimuli that are unfamiliar and complex, but as the surroundings become familiar, the child increasingly dominates: The environment is increasingly likely to be mastered in play (Rubin, Fein, & Vandenberg, 1983).

Types of Infant Play

Turning now to a discussion of the various types of play that occur during infancy, we shall highlight three forms of infant play. *Sensorimotor,* or *practice, play* begins with the infant's accidental discovery of an activity that is inherently satisfying, and consists of the continuous repetition of that activity for the sheer joy of doing so. *Play with objects* involves the intentional manipulation of objects, with a definite interest on the part of the player in the results of the manipulation. *Symbolic,* or *make-believe, play* is characterized by the use of mental representation, in which one object is allowed to stand for, or represent, another.

Sensorimotor play and symbolic play are different in terms of their developmental levels; the former is limited to activities of a physical nature, while the latter involves the use of mental representation (Piaget, 1962). Object play, on the other hand, is described in terms of the materials used by the players rather than as a particular stage of cognitive sophistication. In fact, objects are used in both sensorimotor and symbolic play, although in different ways, of course, and from tennis balls to Trivial Pursuit cards, objects are also used in the play of adults. The developmental significance of object play is that the ways in which objects are used in play tell us much about the player's level of intellectual, physical, social, and emotional sophistication.

Sensorimotor Play
Much of a child's play in the first year of life consists of what cognitive theorist Jean Piaget called **sensorimotor play** or practice play. (Piaget, 1962), the repetition of

TABLE 3.1   Piaget's Substages of Sensorimotor Development and the Types of Play Associated with Each

Stage	Intellectual Characteristics	Type of Play
1. (Birth to 1 month)	The dominant activity is the simple exercise of reflexes.	There is little in the way of play that can be said to occur during this substage.
2. (1–4 months)	Primary circular reactions appear. Individual action sequences, such as sucking or grasping, begin to be coordinated.	Play occurs as the child repeats, for the sheer enjoyment of doing so, an activity that is oriented toward its own body.
3. (4–8 months)	Secondary circular reactions appear, involving the repetition of activities not specifically oriented toward one's own body. There is a definite interest in the effects of one's actions on the external world.	In play the child repeats behaviors, such as crumpling a piece of paper or banging on a table, that have a pleasing or satisfying effect on the environment.
4. (8–12 months)	There is the appearance of intentional, goal-directed activity, as when a child pushes aside a pillow in order to obtain a toy that is behind it.	The goal-directed infant often abandons the end in order simply to play with the means itself. For example, the very act of pushing aside the pillow becomes a joyful game, and the child seems to forget about the hidden toy.
5. (12–18 months)	Rather than precisely repeating interesting events, the child now intentionally *varies* them to make them more exciting. This behavior is known as a tertiary circular reaction.	There is considerable variation in the action sequences of sensori-motor play, as the child immediately and intentionally complicates play experiences to make them more interesting.
6. (Over 18 months)	Symbolization emerges—the child's ability to let one thing stand for, or represent, something else.	Sensorimotor play is increasingly replaced by symbolic, or make-believe play, which will dominate the preschool years.

Information is from *Play, Dreams, and Imitation in Childhood* by J. Piaget, 1962. New York: Norton. *The Origins of Intelligence in Children* by J. Piaget, © Copyright 1952, by International Universities Press, Inc.

already assimilated sensory or motor activities for the sheer pleasure of doing so. As can be seen in Table 3.1, Piaget (1962) suggested that such play reflects the child's gradual intellectual progress through a variety of substages of sensorimotor development and thus develops gradually during the first eighteen months before giving way to more sophisticated play involving make-believe.

The developmental transitions in sensorimotor play are nicely illustrated by the behaviors that Piaget called circular reactions, which appear in three increasingly sophisticated forms.

Primary Circular Reactions

Among the earliest forms of sensorimotor play to appear is the **primary circular reaction:** A baby accidentally discovers an interesting sensory or motor experience related to its own body, apparently enjoys it, and later continues to repeat it. The primary circular reaction, a typical occurrence within the age range of one to four months, is illustrated in Piaget's description of the behavior of his own eight-week-old son: Laurent "scratches and tries to grasp, lets go, scratches and grasps again, etc. . . . At first, this can only be observed during feeding. Laurent gently scratches his mother's bare shoulder. [The next day] . . . Laurent scratches the sheet which is folded over the blankets, then grasps and holds it for a moment, then lets it go, scratches it again, and recommences without interruption" (Piaget, 1963, p. 191).

Laurent's actions may appear at first to be play with objects rather than play centered on the child's own body, but actually this is not the case. The play is the physical action: the grasping, scratching, and letting go. Laurent appears to be fascinated by the actions themselves but has little interest in the objects he is performing the actions on. In fact, he will initiate the same scratching routine with *any* object that happens to be placed in his hand. This is the sense in which, even early in the first year of life, babies will manipulate objects; however, they will do so only if those objects are placed directly in their hands. Put a rattle in the hand of a three-month-old and the child will "play" with it by shaking, chewing, or simply looking at this interesting thing it has been given (Bayley, 1969). As will soon be apparent, however, such behaviors lack the elements of intellectual awareness and intentionality that characterize genuine object play.

Secondary Circular Reactions

After the age of four months, children continue to engage in circular reactions, but of a noticeably different type (Piaget, 1962). Now they become interested in the external results that their actions produce. They perform what Piaget called **secondary circular reactions,** the repetition of behaviors that bring about pleasing effects on their surrounding world. Notice the difference between the following circular reaction performed by Laurent Piaget at four months and his two-month-old behavior described above. Lying in his crib, the child is looking up at some rattles tied to a string stretched above him. His father then attaches a watch chain to the rattles. "Laurent pulls . . . the chain or the string in order to shake the rattle and make it sound: the intention is clear. . . . The same day I attach a new toy half as high as the string. . . . Laurent begins by shaking himself while looking at it, then waves his arms in the air and finally takes hold of the rubber doll which he shakes while looking at the toy" (Piaget, 1963, p. 164). Thus, we can see that Laurent's interest has now shifted, at least slightly, from his own actions to their environmental consequences.

Tertiary Circular Reactions

While the infant between eight and twelve months would have repeated an action in an attempt to prolong an interesting environmental result, the young one-year-old goes a step further. Now the repetition of the previous stage is accompanied by an attempt to vary the activity instead of repeating it precisely, a new behavior referred to as a **tertiary circular reaction.** The playful element in this type of circular reaction is very clear, as the child appears to enjoy novelty and actively looks for new ways of producing interesting experiences. Consider the experimental approach of Piaget's 13-month-old daughter Jacqueline in her bath: "Jacqueline engages in many experiments with celluloid toys floating on the water. . . . Not only does she drop her toys from a height to see the water splash or displace them with her hand in order to make them swim, but she pushes them halfway down in order to see them rise to the surface. Between the ages of a year and a year and a half, she amuses herself by filling with water pails, flasks, watering cans, etc. . . . by filling her sponge with water and pressing it against her chest, by running water from the faucet . . . along her arm, etc." (Piaget, 1963, p. 273).

Play with Objects

Once the focus of a child's attention moves from the activities of its own body to the events of the outside world, the stage is set for the appearance of play with objects. In addition to the player's interest in its surroundings, however, there is another obvious requirement for object play: the motor skills needed to grasp and handle play materials. This interest will also appear in the second trimester of the child's first year.

Perhaps it is obvious that many of the objects that infants have contact with are toys, even though a child does not discriminate between toys and nontoys during the first year. Parents often report, in fact, that their infants' favorite playthings were pots and pans taken from the cupboard, or raw potatoes or onions that the children came across in their exploration of the kitchen. Nevertheless, it is likely that infants will have a variety of toys to play with; it has been estimated that the average U.S. infant has 28 different toys by the time it is a year old (Rheingold & Cook, 1975).

Since toys are often the objects that infants are given to play with, and since the most successful toys for a child of any age are those that are developmentally appropriate, our discussion of object play will incorporate information about the preferred and most appropriate toys for the first two years of a child's life (see Table 3.2).

Birth to Three Months

There is little to say about intentional object play during the first three months, since the young infant spends much of its time lying on its back. It cannot sit erect, even with full support, until the age of nine or ten weeks and does not yet have even a primitive grasp (Bayley, 1969). While these developmental limitations do not preclude a discussion of appropriate toys for this age period, they would indicate that the primary value of toys for young infants is to stimulate the senses. Toys are for looking at, hearing, and feeling and not yet for physically manipulating.

Parents might wish to string colorful objects across an infant's crib, to surround the child with eye-catching pictures, and to provide bells and rattles for sound production. Intentional, premeditated sound production will not be observed until the age of six months, but the younger infant will ring a bell or shake a rattle if the object is placed in its hand, or by its movements in the crib it will cause a dangling object to

TABLE 3.2   Appropriate Toys for the First Two Years of Life

Age	Play Materials
Birth to 3 months	Toys that are primarily for sensory stimulation, since the infant is not yet ready to grasp objects: rattles, bells, colorful pictures and wallpaper, crib ornaments, mobiles, music boxes, and other musical toys.
3–6 months	Now that a primitive grasp has been acquired, toys for grasping, squeezing, feeling, and mouthing should be added. Included might be cloth balls, soft blocks, teething toys.
6–12 months	Colorful picture books, stacking toys, nesting toys, sponges for water play, mirrors, toy telephones with dials that move. Toys that react to the child's activity.
12–18 months	Push toys, pull toys, balls to throw, plain and interlocking blocks, simple puzzles with large, easy-to-handle pieces, form boards, peg boards, stacking toys, riding toys with wheels low to the ground.
18–24 months	Toys for the sandbox and for water play: spoons, shovels, pails of various sizes. Storybooks, blocks in a variety of sizes, dolls, stuffed animals, puppets, miniature life toys.

sound. At first these actions will be accidental, but because of their pleasing consequences the child will make efforts to repeat them (a circular reaction).

Three to Six Months

By the time they are four-and-one-half months old, infants begin to show signs of eye-hand coordination when reaching. It is also at about this time that, if seated at a table on the lap of an adult, they will begin to manipulate the table edge with their hands. Play with objects begins in earnest at five months, however. Now infants are able to reach out and pick up a block that is set in front of them, and they will soon begin to pass objects back and forth from one hand to the other. The five-month-old will play with a piece of string or a piece of paper (by crumpling it) and will, sometimes to the annoyance of its parents, playfully bang a spoon or other object on a table.

The functions of play materials change as the infant begins to manipulate objects actively. Toys are now to be grasped and manipulated, as well as merely listened to or looked at. Is there such a thing as an ideal toy for a three- to six-month-old? A good toy obviously must be safe and have no sharp edges or small parts that can fit into the child's mouth. It must be sturdy and small enough to be grasped in one hand but large enough so that it cannot be swallowed (Hartley & Goldenson, 1963). A good toy will also stimulate as many of the child's senses as possible. Adults are quick to recognize the value of visual stimulation but often fail to take account of the sound or the feel of a toy. Variety is a key element in the selection of a toy. Does the toy itself have much variety, and to what extent does it add variety in color, size, shape, sound, and texture to the child's existing toy collection?

Six Months to One Year

Children in the second half of the first year become quite mobile. By six-and-one-half months they will sit alone, and they will creep or crawl a distance of nine inches or more by the time they are in their eighth month. They will pull themselves to a standing position by holding onto furniture by the middle of the ninth month, and will walk with help as they approach 10 months of age (Bayley, 1969).

Prehension skills continue to improve, and by the age of nine months they are able to pick up objects using only the thumb and forefinger. In addition, they will be able to bring objects together in play. If an adult holds a block in each hand and bangs them together in front of his or her body, the eight-month-old infant will attempt to imitate this behavior—a forerunner of the "pat-a-cake" game that will make its appearance a month later (Bayley, 1969).

Despite the refinement in motor skills that allows the child to play easily with a variety of objects, early object play is somewhat unsophisticated. Infants from five to eight months of age still seem to be less interested in play objects themselves than they are in the actions they perform upon them. This focus on one's own actions over objects is illustrated by the fact that six-month-olds treat all objects of the same size in exactly the same way; they bang them in play, for example, or shake them or put them in their mouths (Fenson, Kagan, Kearsley, & Zelazo, 1976). Give the baby a spoon, and the spoon will be banged on the table; replace the spoon with a crayon, and the baby will bang the crayon on the table; offer instead a small doll, and the doll is immediately banged on the table. All objects, new or old, familiar or unfamiliar, seem to serve the purpose of being assimilated into what is the child's preferred activity at the moment (Rubenstein, 1976).

By the age of nine months, new developments are taking place in the realm of object play. In the first place, infants attend carefully to the properties of the objects themselves, rather than using them only as props in their repetitive action sequences. Now the baby takes note when a plaything is unfamiliar; there is more initial interest in a new object than in a familiar one, and an unfamiliar toy will hold the child's interest for a longer time. In addition, the child attends to the specific features of objects when handling them and no longer behaves as if all objects are the same (Rubenstein, 1976). Psychologist Holly Ruff (1984) observed the various manipulation techniques of babies aged six to twelve months as, seated on their mothers' laps, they were presented with a series of objects one at a time. She found that younger babies engaged in a lot of mouthing, looking, and passing things from one hand to the other, but that all three of these activities decreased with age. By way of contrast, older babies tended to run their fingers across the surfaces of objects, and, a finding of even greater significance, they changed their patterns of manipulation to accommodate the article in hand. When an object was followed by another that differed in texture, the babies did a lot of fingering; if successive objects differed in shape, the babies would rotate them in their hands, and pass them from hand to hand, looking at them from different angles.

Ruff (1984) suggested that the older baby is more sensitive to the features of specific objects, and handles them in ways that are appropriate for learning as much about them as possible. Fingering seems to inform the child about texture differences, while rotating objects to view them from different angles offers information about shape.

What do the refinements in motor skill suggest about appropriate toys for infants in the latter part of the first year? Babies of this age love banging and manipulating objects. They seem particularly to enjoy putting things into one another and taking them out again. Stacking or nesting toys appeal to them, as do plastic pop beads, sponges for play in the tub, and "toys" like pots and pans of different sizes or spoons to stir in plastic cups.

By the age of 10 months, a child will look at the individual pictures in a book rather than simply regard the book in its entirety as a thing to be played with; two months later the child knows how to turn the pages of a book. It seems clear that the first year of life is a suitable time to begin reading storybooks to children and drawing their attention to the individual pictures within them. Such activities can increase children's attention span, inform them at a very young age of the wonders that books contain, and provide opportunities for quiet, intimate contact between parent and child.

Children in the second half of the first year are likely to play longer with a toy that reacts to their own actions (Fenson, 1986). A relevant question to ask, therefore, when making a purchase is "What kind of a response will the child get from this toy?" For example, a toy that can be squeezed and will then recover its shape is more interesting than one that is rigid. A toy that produces an interesting sound or visual display *in response to* the child's pushing a button or turning a dial is more appealing than one that either does not respond at all or provides an interesting sensory display regardless of how the child plays with it. It seems that even at this young age, children derive satisfaction from having an effect on the world around them, and the ability to influence their surroundings may be important in the development of self-confidence—of a sense of self in general. Some toys allow the child to achieve this sense of satisfaction, while others clearly do not.

Object Play in the Second Year

During the second year of life, object play changes in three ways. First, there is a decline in behaviors involving only one object at a time. Ninety percent of the object play of infants between the ages of seven and nine months involves the use of only one object at a time; by the age of 18 months, single-object play activities are relatively rare. At that age, only one in five episodes of object play involves a single plaything; the rest are characterized by the bringing together of two or more objects in play (Fein & Apfel, 1979; Rubin, Fein, & Vandenberg, 1983; Zelazo & Kearsley, 1980). Even by the age of 12 or 13 months, parents will notice the combining of objects in play. Children will begin, for example, to put beads into a cup, to put a cup on a saucer, to place a shape into a form board, or to build a tower of two blocks (Bayley, 1969).

A second trend in object play in the second year has to do with the appropriate uses of playthings. Children now begin to realize the functions of objects. They know, for example, that a ball is to be thrown or that blocks are to be stacked, and this realization makes playthings all the more interesting to them (Fenson, 1986).

In distinguishing between appropriate and inappropriate uses of objects, Rosenblatt (1977) described three types of behaviors that are found in infant object play, the first two of which we have already discussed. *Indiscriminate* behaviors are those in which the child reacts to all objects in the same way, regardless of their individual properties: Steven is given a toy telephone and immediately puts the receiver into his mouth and begins to suck on it. *Investigative* behaviors involve the exploration of the specific features of objects: Stephanie is given a toy telephone, and examines it carefully, looking at it from different angles and fingering its various parts. Finally, *appropriate* behaviors involve the use of objects in the ways they were intended to be used: Todd is given a toy telephone and he holds the receiver to his ear and begins to dial with his finger. As for the developmental trend in these three types of behaviors, perhaps it will not be surprising that indiscriminate and investigative behaviors in object play decline throughout the second year and appropriate behaviors increase in frequency (Rosenblatt, 1977).

The third change in object play that occurs between the ages of one and two is a dramatic increase in the representational use of objects, which is characterized by the mental substitution of one object for another (Fenson, 1986). For example, when Sean was just a year old, he loved to play with old magazines, looking at the pictures and tearing out the pages; when he was 20 months old, he still liked to play with magazines, but now he used them in a representational way: He rolled up the torn pages and offered them as "meatballs" to his stuffed animals. Thus, the representational use of objects refers to their use by children in make-believe, or symbolic, play, about which we shall have considerably more to say later in this chapter.

In summary, object play in the second year of life becomes increasingly resourceful, increasingly complex, and increasingly well-organized. These changes reflect increases in the sophistication of the child's level of intellectual functioning (Fenson, 1986).

Refinements in object play during the second year provide useful information about developmentally appropriate toys. For example, early in the second year, the child is motorically sophisticated enough easily to combine objects in play. Even by the age of 13 months children on the average can place a peg in a pegboard, and by 14 months they are able to place pieces in form boards; they can build a tower of two blocks by the age of 14 months, and by 17 months they are able to balance a third block on the tower.

Appropriate toys for the 12- to 18-month-old are those that capitalize on the development of children's large muscles, allow children to manipulate combinations of small objects, promote interaction between parent and toddler, and do these things in such a way as to help children develop a sense of competence. Children might appreciate balls to throw (which they can do even at 13 months of age), pull toys that can be used when walking, peg boards (and later in the year, hammers to go with them),

Children in the second year of life appreciate play materials, such as pull toys, that capitalize on their level of large muscle development.

plain and interlocking blocks, puzzles with large, easy-to-handle pieces, musical toys, stuffed animals, and books with colorful illustrations.

In the latter half of the second year, children often become negative and stubborn as they strive to develop a sense of self that is different from that of their caretakers. They often insist on doing things for themselves, but unfortunately they have a difficult time coping with delay or failure (Ames, Gillespie, Haines, & Ilg, 1979).

Motor skills continue to improve, but the major development in this period is in the use of language. By 18 months, toddlers can use words instead of gestures to make their wishes known. By 20 or 21 months they can name objects that an adult points to, and they are beginning to put together original two-word phrases, a major turning point in the acquisition of language (Ames, Gillespie, Haines, & Ilg, 1979; Bayley, 1969).

The sandbox becomes an extremely popular place to play, especially if it is equipped with various utensils for shoveling, scooping, sifting, pouring, and molding the sand. The primary interest of sandbox play is sensory exploration, however, and children under the age of two are far from being ready to intentionally create products. A child's block collection should now be added to, with an increase in both the number of blocks and the variety of shapes. Books continue to be favorite playthings, and they capitalize on children's developing linguistic skills. Dolls and stuffed animals become objects of attachment, as well as affording children the opportunity to engage in simple forms of make-believe play. Crayons and paper might be added at this time because even by the age of 18 months, children can imitate a crayon stroke, and by 20 months they can differentiate between scribbles and strokes.

Symbolic Play

Peter was 16-months old, and his father was accustomed to seeing him engaged in a variety of rough-and-tumble play activities. One day, however, a new element appeared in Peter's play. As his father sat on the sofa reading the newspaper, Peter stood on the other side of the room, one hand cupped, and repeatedly dipped his free hand into the cupped one, retrieved something, and brought it to his mouth. "What are you eating?" Peter's father asked. The child just shook his head. Again his father asked what he was eating, and this time Peter approached, reached into his cupped hand, and held something up for his father to taste. What was it? Nothing at all. Both of Peter's hands were empty.

Peter's behavior illustrates the fact that in the second year of life a new type of play is emerging. Children are beginning to represent reality to themselves through the use of symbols to let one thing stand for another. This can be seen in the child's use of language, which involves the representation of objects and people through the use of words. And it can also be seen in children's **symbolic play.** In symbolic, or make-believe, play a child might pretend that an empty dish has food on it, that a cardboard box is a rocket, or that a few sticks or wooden blocks are a fortress.

Let us now turn to an in-depth examination of symbolic play, looking first at the development of the individual cognitive elements that it is composed of and then at its intellectual, social, and emotional benefits for the child.

The Developmental Progression of Pretend Play

Symbolic play first appears early in the second year of a child's life, usually at around the age of 12 or 13 months; its appearance is rather sudden, as indicated by month-to-month percentage increases of such play observed in children from 10 to 14 months of age (Rubin, Fein, & Vandenberg, 1983). However, although its earliest signs seem to appear quite suddenly, the development of symbolic play follows a gradual and fairly predictable path, which is often characterized as a series of increasingly sophisticated levels (Fenson, 1986; Piaget, 1962; Watson & Jackowitz, 1984). Perhaps the best way to describe the developmental progression of symbolic play is to examine the development of the three underlying elements (see Table 3.3) upon which it is based: decentration, decontextualization, and integration (Bretherton, 1984; Fenson, 1986; McCune-Nicolich & Fenson, 1984; Piaget, 1962; Werner & Kaplan, 1963).

TABLE 3.3   Developmental Trends in Symbolic Play During the Second Year of Life

Stage	Decentration	Decontextualization	Integration
12 months	Make-believe actions are centered on the self, usually occur when the child is alone, and involve familiar rituals from everyday life.	Realistic substitute objects are used in a realistic manner.	Little evidence of a connection among the various symbolic play activities.
18 months	Pretense involves inanimate objects as recipients of make-believe actions initiated by the child.	Substitute objects are less realistic in terms of appearance and function.	Pairing up of related activities in single-scheme combinations.
24 months	Inanimate objects are now the initiators as well as the recipients of make-believe actions.	Substitute objects may bear no physical resemblance to what they represent and are used in a way that is far removed from their original function.	Multischeme combinations: Two or more activities, each of which involves a different theme.

Information is from "Representing the Social World in Symbolic Play: Reality and Fantasy," by I. Bretherton. In *Symbolic Play: The Development of Social Understanding* (pp. 3–41) edited by I. Bretherton, 1984. New York: Academic Press. "The Developmental Progression of Play," by L. Fenson. In *Play Interactions: The Contribution of Play Materials and Parental Involvement to Children's Development* (pp. 53–66) edited by A. W. Gottfried & C. C. Brown, 1986. Lexington, MA: Heath. "Methodological Issues in Studying Early Pretend Play," by L. McCune-Nicolich & L. Fenson. In *Child's Play: Developmental and Applied* (pp. 81–104) edited by T. D. Yawkey & A. D. Pellegrini, 1984. Hillsdale, NJ: Erlbaum. *Play, Dreams, and Imitation in Childhood* by J. Piaget, 1962. New York: Norton. *Symbol Formation* by H. Werner & B. Kaplan, 1983. New York: Wiley.

Decentration

When we speak of centration and **decentration,** we refer to the degree to which children focus, or center, on themselves in pretend play; the normal developmental progression is from self-to other-centeredness. The earliest pretend play, which appears at about the age of 12 months, consists of make-believe acts that are directed toward the self (Piaget, 1962). Children, usually when alone, will act out familiar rituals from their everyday life experiences, as when they pretend to eat, drink, or go to sleep. Pretense is involved because the action is not related to the child's real needs at the time; a child may pretend to eat, for example, when not actually hungry. When Piaget's daughter Jacqueline was just a year old, she would often pick up a piece of cloth and pretend it was her pillow. She would lie down with it and act as if she were sleeping, although she wasn't tired at the time and didn't actually fall asleep. Such play illustrates the concept of centration in the sense that it is totally self-focused. The child both initiates and is the object of the make-believe action.

Within a few months after the earliest pretend play has appeared, children begin to show signs of decentering (Fenson & Ramsay, 1980). They now incorporate inanimate objects into their pretend play, and they initiate make-believe actions directed, not at themselves, but at other objects (Fenson, 1986). For example, instead of pretending to wash his own face as he often did when he was younger, Joshua began at 16 months to pretend he was washing the face of his teddy bear. Although he was still the initiator of the make-believe action, the object of the action was no longer Joshua himself but was now his teddy bear.

Toward the end of the second year of life, decentration reaches a new level of maturity. Now the dolls or teddy bears or other inanimate objects, which had for several months been an integral part of the child's pretend play, begin to assume new roles. They, and not the children who play with them, become the initiators as well as the recipients of make-believe actions (Corrigan, 1982; Fenson, 1986). The sophistication of children's pretend activities is that now they are able to inject make-believe actors into their own make-believe action sequences. For example, two-year-old Kristen would arrange her stuffed animals around a table, put empty plates and spoons in front of them, and allow them to enjoy their meal. Consider the sophistication of this form of pretense, especially as compared to the symbolic play of a 12-month-old: Kristen's make-believe characters were expected to initiate the make-believe activity of eating make-believe food!

Decontextualization

The second element of make-believe play, **decontextualization,** refers to the use of one object to substitute for another (Fenson, 1986). The earliest, least sophisticated form of decontextualization occurs at about 12 months of age, when children use realistic substitute objects in a realistic, appropriate manner. A piece of cloth, for example, might represent a sheet when a child pretends to go to bed. The point is that the cloth actually *does* resemble a sheet, and so the child's play with it is quite realistic.

As children mature, however, their substitutions become further and further removed from reality. A substitute play object for a three-year-old may in no way resemble the real thing, and the manner of play with the make-believe object may be far different from the appropriate use of the object being represented. Pederson, Rook-Green, and Elder (1981) found, for example, that three-year-olds were able to pretend that a ball was a comb and would go through the motions of combing their hair with it, whereas younger children could not easily do so. The younger child would often simply bounce the ball and, when asked to pretend that it was a comb, respond, "I can't. It's a ball."

Integration

The third element in symbolic play is referred to as **integration** (Fenson, 1986). This means that as children develop, their play becomes increasingly organized into patterns. Fenson (1986) pointed out that during most of the first two years of life there is a "piecemeal" quality to children's play. They drift from one activity to another, with little in the way of any connection between activities. Then, late in the second year, there is evidence of linkages between successive actions. First, there is the simple pairing up of related activities, initially seen at around the age of 18 or 19 months (Belsky & Most, 1980; Fenson & Ramsay, 1980). For example, Jonathan has his teddy bear "climb" to the top of a tower of blocks and jump off the other side; the teddy bear is followed in this same activity by several of Jonathan's other stuffed animals. Thus, a single theme—jumping off—unites a succession of activities, in "single-scheme combinations" (Nicolich, 1977).

By the time a child is approaching his or her second birthday, integration is becoming increasingly complex (Fenson & Ramsay, 1981). Now there is the appearance of "multischeme combinations" (Nicolich, 1977), which are made up of two or more activities, each involving a different theme. Jonathan, now going on two, involves his stuffed animals in a game of (1) jumping off a tower, followed by (2) crawling through a tunnel. This combining of two, but rarely more than two, successive acts by the child of about 24 months is highly significant in the development of symbolic play, according to Fenson (1986). Play is moving from being an uncoordinated collection of activities to one that is coordinated and schematic, a trend that parallels the transition at the end of the second year from one-word utterances to original, two-word combinations in speech. This parallel is more than coincidental. Both language and symbolic play require the ability to represent reality to oneself through the use of symbols, the substitution of one thing for another; it is, therefore, not surprising to see developmental parallels between the two (Fenson, 1986).

Social Aspects of Infant and Toddler Play

Children's play, even in the first year of life, cannot help but involve the other people in their environment, and most typically those playmates are parents and siblings. In recent years, it is increasingly probable that a young child's playmates come from outside the family as well; included in this group are teachers, child-care workers, and extrafamilial peers. Let us look first at the ways in which adults influence the play of infants and toddlers, and then at the play of very young children with their peers, which is surprising both in its extent and in its level of sophistication.

Play with Adults

It is a joyful moment in parents' lives when their infants begin to play with them. Most parents love to play with their babies, but they may not realize that such play is more than simply enjoyable; it is also extremely beneficial for the child. The role of the parent, or other adult, is to initiate and structure infant play, with the result that the child is offered a richer and more varied experience than he or she could possibly obtain if left to play alone. Let us look now at some of the benefits of infant-adult play.

Benefits of Infant-Parent Play

More than 20 years ago, psychologist Sibylle Escalona (1968) carried out what has become a classic study of the play behaviors of 128 infants and their mothers. Her main interest was to find out if infants played differently when left alone than when they had their mothers as social partners and playmates. Escalona's major finding was that, even if they had a large variety of toys to play with, the sensorimotor play of babies playing alone was less complex and less sustained than that of babies who had an adult to interact with. What was it exactly that the mothers in Escalona's study were contributing to their children's play? They seemed to be skilled social directors. They tended to adapt the play activities to the immediate needs of the children by varying their own activities in response to what their child was doing. For example, mothers would vary the rate at which they offered new play materials, they would introduce variations or increase the intensity of play when the child seemed to be losing interest, they would reduce their own level of activity if the child became overly excited, they would offer reassurance if their babies were having a difficult time, and they would reinforce them when they did something well. As a result, the mothers were able to sustain their children's interest in the various play activities and thereby increase the length of their attention spans.

More recent research offers support for Escalona's conclusion that infant play is facilitated and encouraged by the parent's structuring role and that the play that results is more sophisticated than would be found in infants with limited access to adult play partners (Power & Parke, 1980; Ross & Kay, 1980; Stern, 1977; Stevenson, Leavitt, Thompson, & Roach, 1988). The value of such play includes the following:

1. It keeps the infant at an optimal level of arousal, so it is neither bored nor overly excited (Power & Parke, 1980).
2. It provides the infant with a feeling of control over its environment, thereby fostering self-confidence and promoting intellectual growth (Watson & Ramey, 1972).
3. It exposes the infant to intense social interaction with its parents and so facilitates the process of parent-infant attachment (Stern, 1977).
4. It encourages the infant to explore its surroundings.
5. It causes the infant to attend more closely to the social aspects of language (Ratner & Bruner, 1978).

Mother–Father Differences in Play with Infants
The father's role is an increasingly visible one in today's society, and, more than ever before, the U.S. father seems to realize the importance of his influence on the life of his baby (Bronstein, 1988). Fathers, like mothers, enjoy playing with their infants, although mothers are the primary playmates until the child is about 20 months of age; fathers and mothers share the playmate role equally for approximately one year after that, and beyond the age of two-and-a-half, more play periods are initiated by the father than by the mother during the young child's day (Clarke-Stewart, 1978). Mothers spend considerably more time overall with their young children, but at all ages during infancy the largest percentage of the time a father does spend with his baby is play time (Power, 1985).

Are there differences in the ways in which mothers and fathers play with their infants? A considerable amount of research in recent years has been devoted to trying to find an answer to that question, and perhaps it is not too surprising to find that there are indeed gender differences in parent-infant play. However, before we describe those differences, we should point out that, on balance, mothers and fathers are more alike than different when they play with their babies. Mothers and fathers seem to be equally sensitive to their babies' developmental changes; they both make the appropriate adjustments in play as their babies develop (Belsky, Gilstrap, & Rovine, 1984; Belsky & Volling, 1985; Hunter, McCarthy, MacTurk, & Vietze, 1987). For example, during the first year, there is much physical play, but as the child moves into its second year the emphasis of the parent changes from physical to make-believe play, which, in keeping with what we discussed earlier in this chapter, is an appropriate developmental transition (Crawley & Sherrod, 1984; Power, 1985; Stevenson, Leavitt, Thompson, & Roach, 1988). There is also a developmentally appropriate expectation in the second year that parent and infant can take turns in play (Ross & Kay, 1980), as well as an attempt, again quite reasonable, to get the infant to coordinate play materials in a complex manner (Power & Parke, 1986).

Despite the overall similarity, however, there are some fairly consistent mother–father differences in play with their babies. One is that fathers engage in more rousing physical play, defined as rough-and-tumble activities and run-and-chase types of games, than mothers do (MacDonald & Parke, 1986; Power, 1985; Parke & Tinsley, 1987; Stevenson, Leavitt, Thompson, & Roach, 1988). A second finding is that mothers seem more closely attuned to their infants' interests and are more likely than fathers to follow a child's lead; for example, mothers typically allow their babies to explore as they wish and to choose their own activities. Fathers, on the other hand, seem to be more obtrusive social directors. They are likely to disregard their babies' interests and to steer the play activity in the direction they would prefer it to go (Power & Parke, 1983, 1986; Schaffer & Crook, 1979). It is not known why this parental sex difference in directiveness appears. Perhaps it is that fathers are less sensitive than mothers to their children's interests, or it may be that fathers are more likely than mothers to see actively directing their babies' play as their responsibility (Power & Parke, 1986).

A final major parental difference is that mothers tend to engage in more instructive play with infants than fathers do (Pedersen, 1980; Stevenson, Leavitt, Thompson, & Roach, 1988). In other words, the play of mothers is more likely than the play of fathers to contain a teaching emphasis. Mothers will make a point, for example, of naming objects or colors or numbers and then asking the infant to demonstrate that they have learned the label by looking directly at the object as the mother names it, by pointing to it when asked, or, in the case of an older child, by responding correctly when mother says, "What do we call this?" In general, fathers are more tactile in play, relying heavily on the sense of touch, while mothers are more verbal in their interactions with their infants (Parke & Tinsley, 1987).

Before leaving the issue of parental gender differences in play with infants, we should mention that this pattern is not a universal one. For example, mother-father comparisons in Sweden (Lamb, Frodi, Hwang, Frodi & Steinberg, 1982) and in the Israeli kibbutz (Sagi, et al., 1985) reveal no gender differences in parental play with infants. There is no certainty as to why gender differences would appear in one particular culture and not in another, but it has been suggested that both Swedish culture and that of the Israeli kibbutz are characterized by more egalitarian attitudes toward gender roles than are found in the United States; differences in mothers' and fathers' styles of play with infants may reflect general cultural attitudes about the appropriate roles of male and female parents in a child's upbringing (Parke & Tinsley, 1985; Sagi et al., 1985).

Parents Versus Siblings as Playmates

It is obvious that in many families the parent is not the only social partner available to an infant or toddler. Except in the case of a first-born child, an infant will have older siblings to share its play activities. Research on play with older siblings, however, serves primarily to highlight the importance of parent-infant play. Why? Because infant play with siblings seems to differ considerably from play with parents. The unique and very special quality of parent-infant play is lacking in sibling play, according to University of Wisconsin psychologist Marguerite Stevenson, in the sense that the structure or direction that a parent provides is rarely provided by a sibling. In fact, when infants are playing with their siblings, they are not likely to be involved in the types of activities that require social partners, but instead will play with their toys or simply watch their older brothers and sisters. For their part, the older siblings tend to ignore their infant brothers and sisters in play situations (Lamb, 1978; Stevenson, Leavitt, Thompson, & Roach, 1988; Vandell & Wilson, 1983).

It should not be concluded, however, that sibling play is of little value for infants, because this is not the case. In all likelihood, parent-infant and sibling-infant play serve different purposes; it appears that parents stimulate their babies to develop new skills while siblings help the child to consolidate those skills that have already been learned (Dunn, 1983). If this is true, there is an obvious value in having multiple play partners available, each of whom might take on a slightly different role in promoting optimal infant development (Stevenson, Leavitt, Thompson, & Roach, 1988).

Infant Social Games

Between the ages of 9 and 18 months, infants acquire the skills needed to play simple cooperative games (Ross & Lollis, 1987). Beginning at nine months, they are able to coordinate their activities to a sufficient extent that they can engage in games that are initiated by adults, and even take an active role in such games (Gustafson, Green, & West, 1979; Ratner & Bruner, 1978; Sugarman-Bell, 1978). By the age of 18 months, they are able to play games without any adult structuring at all, as evidenced by the fact that in the middle of the second year simple cooperative games with peers make their appearance (Ross & Kay, 1980).

What is involved in these early social games between parents and their children? There are several elements, but, as might be expected, the rules are fairly simple. One element is the taking of turns; the parent engages in an action, then stops and waits for the baby to act. There is repetition of roles at the end of each understood round of activity. For example, the parent may build a tower of three blocks; the baby waits until it is completed and then knocks it over; the parent builds again while the baby waits, then the baby knocks the tower over again, and so forth. These games are characterized also by the offering of toys to one's partner, by careful observation of one's partner while awaiting one's turn, and by signaling to one's partner that his or her involvement is required (Ross & Lollis, 1987).

The benefits of parent-infant games are readily apparent. The baby learns how to wait for its turn, a useful skill at any age in life, and how to adapt to the schedule of another person. Awareness of others is reinforced in such games because careful attention to a partner's actions is a necessity. Parent-infant play is often so delightful an experience for both parties that it can facilitate the process of attachment between parent and child. And finally, since these early social games involve a considerable amount of verbalization, it has been suggested that such play encourages the development of language in children (Bruner, 1983). Although the direction of cause-and-effect is difficult to establish, a positive relationship has been found between the frequency of mother-infant games and the sophistication of the child's speech production (Shatz, 1983).

The fact that parent-infant games appear much earlier than peer games indicates the importance of the adult's structuring role in infant play. The adult provides the structure, the scaffold as it were upon which the game is built, and as the infant matures, the adult can become less and less involved in the structuring process (Hodapp, Goldfield, & Boyatzis, 1984). Since the adult's role in the early social play of the infant is so directive, however, some psychologists maintain that it is difficult to know what the baby is really able to do (Bruner, 1983; Ross & Lollis, 1987). In other words, how much of the play is the baby's and how much of it is Mom's or Dad's? In an attempt to answer that question, Ross and Lollis (1987) observed babies ranging from 9 to 18 months of age playing simple turn-taking games (e.g., peek-a-boo, stack-and-topple, ball) with an adult partner. To measure the extent of the child's involvement in the play, the adult would occasionally fail to take her turn, and the child's reaction to the interruption would be observed. It was found that babies in all age groups, even the youngest, made efforts to signal the adult that it was time to take her turn. They would vocalize, look back and forth between the game toy and the adult's face, touch her, offer her a toy, and even repeat their own turn—in case she missed her cue. The authors concluded that, although younger infants cannot initiate social games and must rely on adult structuring, their level of involvement in social play cannot be questioned. In fact, the extent of their involvement may be even greater than was previously believed.

Peer Play

We have made reference to the fact that it is beneficial to have multiple play partners available to infants, and we have pointed out the differences between the features of infant play with parents and play with older siblings. Parents and siblings are not the only playmates available to an infant, however. Half the mothers of our preschool children hold jobs outside the home (Hoffman, 1979), and between 20 and 40 percent of infants in the United States who are between the ages of 6 and 12 months make contact with other infants more than once a week; thus, it seems that very early peer interaction is the norm for a considerable percentage of our children (Geismar-Ryan, 1986; Hartup, 1982).

Not only do infants and toddlers have peers available to them as playmates, but there are clear, unmistakable signs of interest in peers even during the first few months of life. Babies make efforts to communicate with one another, and by the second year they are showing rudimentary signs of cooperative peer play. It is simply not true, as is often believed, that infants and toddlers are so completely self-centered that they are unable to have meaningful interactions with their peers.

Let us now examine the quality of peer interactions from the early months of the first year of life through the child's second birthday, paying particular attention to the indications of early peer play.

Communication with Peers

One of the more interesting studies of infant peer interaction was carried out by psychologist Alan Fogel (1979), who observed babies ranging in age from 5 to 14 weeks in three social settings. In one condition, the children were alone, in another, they were observed while they watched their mothers, and in a third, the children were seated on their mothers' laps and facing another infant of the same age. When they were alone for a brief period of time, the infants seemed to be relaxed and content. When they saw their mothers, they would smile, sometimes stick out their tongues, and gesture with their arms and legs. The sight of another infant, however, produced reactions that were qualitatively different: the babies would stare intently, often leaning forward as if to get a closer look. They would also make jerky head and arm movements, almost as if they were very excited. There can be little doubt, therefore, that infants are interested in one another even as early as the second month after birth.

The social gestures of the infant in its first year are admittedly unsophisticated, and, in fact, they are limited in two important ways. First, they are of very short duration, although the time spent on social gestures will increase throughout the first two years. Second, they are relatively simple at first, in the sense that they consist of only one or two behaviors at a time (e.g., waving one's arms and vocalizing, smiling and leaning forward). Such simple behaviors are eventually combined into more complex patterns in the second year, with the result that social interaction becomes more controlled and more predictable (Brownell, 1982, 1986; Hay, Pederson, & Nash, 1982).

By the middle of the second year, the amount and variety of infant communication is quite extensive. Children at play will show their toys to one another, offer and give one another toys, invite peers to play with them, protest a playmate's actions, and in general communicate their feelings effectively to one another. As was discussed earlier in this chapter, they are now capable of initiating social games of their own without the necessity of adult structuring.

Early Forms of Cooperation

As communication becomes more sophisticated in the second year, there appear the first glimmers of cooperative play. Brenner and Mueller (1982) described what they called **shared meanings** in the play of young toddlers, and these are themes that organize their social interactions. Included are social games like run-and-chase, peek-a-boo, stack and topple, and motor-copy, in which one child simply imitates the motor activity of another. It has even been suggested that a child's social competence during the second year of life can be equated with his or her ability to engage in complementary and reciprocal play (Howes, 1988). Complementary activities are those in which each child does something different, but the two roles complement one another, and reciprocal play refers to the ability to take turns. Howes (1988) also discovered that such activities increase significantly from age one to age three, and that one-year-olds who are skilled at reciprocal and complementary play grow into two-year-olds who are skilled at social pretend play.

Finally, it should be noted that social play seems to be easier for a young child than social *pretend* play because the former involves only the ability to communicate effectively with a partner, while the latter also involves the intellectual skill of manipulating symbolic transformations. Howes, Unger, and Seidner (1989) have proposed a series of successive levels of social pretend play that correspond to the levels of social play in children aged one to three; and these are contained in Table 3.4. As shown in the table, developments in social play (e.g., social exchanges, integration of actions, differentiation of roles) seem to precede parallel developments in social pretend play.

Summary

Play and exploration often resemble one another, but they also differ in three areas: the affective state of the child, the amount of stereotypy in the child's behavior, and the focus of the child's attention. In exploring, children appear to be serious, they attend very closely to what they are doing, and they engage in stereotypical, almost ritualistic, behaviors. Children at play are more joyful, more willing to be distracted, and more diverse in their behavior.

Throughout the first year of life, children engage in a good deal of sensorimotor play: the repetition of an already learned sensory or motor activity for the sheer pleasure of doing it. At about the age of five months, infants begin to play with objects, but early object play is somewhat unsophisticated in the sense that infants are less interested in the properties of objects themselves than they are in their own actions upon them. By the age of 9 or 10 months, however, they begin to differentiate among objects; they prefer new to familiar objects, and they handle different objects differently, in such a way as to extract as much information from them as possible. Finally, object play in the second year is even more mature in that the child now combines objects in play, uses objects appropriately, and begins to incorporate objects into symbolic, or make-believe, play.

Symbolic play appears rather suddenly early in the second year, and its further development is characterized by a series of increasingly sophisticated levels. Development can be seen in each of the underlying elements of symbolic play: decentration, referring to the degree to which the child is able to shift the focus of its interest from self to external objects, decontextualization, the use of one object as a substitute for another, and integration, the organization of play into increasingly complex patterns.

The major function of adults in the play of infants is to be skilled social directors, initiating play routines, controlling the frequency with which new playthings are introduced, varying the intensity of play in response to the child's behavior, and providing support and encouragement. Mothers are less directive than fathers, they

TABLE 3.4   Levels of Social Play and Social Pretend Play from the Ages of 12 to 36 Months

Social Play	Social Pretend Play
1. 12–15 months Parallel play, with eye contact and/or exchanges of social behavior, such as smiling or vocalizing. One child recognizes another as a potential play partner.	Pretend activities are performed near another child, but the second child makes no response to the first child's play.
2. 15–20 months Children engage in social exchanges while engaged in the same social activity. For example, they smile or vocalize while playing together in the sandbox.	Children engage in similar or identical pretend acts while making eye contact. For example, both of them push dolls in doll carriages.
3. 20–24 months Children integrate their actions in such a way that they have a common goal, but the goal is suggested by the activity itself. These actions are shared meanings, such as run-and-chase, stack-and-topple.	Similar or identical pretend acts now involve social exchanges. For example, both children smile at one another as they push their dolls in carriages, or one offers a doll to the other.
4. 24–30 months Children engage in joint activities with common goals, but now the goals and the themes of play are invented by the children themselves. For example, two children work together to make a block structure for a truck to drive through.	Children share a common pretend theme but make no effort to integrate their own activities with another's. For example, two children play "tea party," but *each* pours tea, adds sugar, and so forth.
5. 30–36 months There is now a clear differentiation of complementary roles. For example, one child is the leader in an activity, and one is a follower. One child directs the building project, and the other gets the blocks.	There is joint pretend activity, with complementary roles. For example, instead of both pouring tea, now one child may pour and the other one may add the sugar. Games like mother–baby and doctor–patient begin to emerge.

Adapted from "Social Pretend Play in Toddlers: Parallels with Social Play and with Solitary Pretend" by C. Howes, O. Unger, & L. B. Siedner, 1989. *Child Development, 60,* pp. 77–84.

engage in more verbal and more instructive play than fathers do, and they engage in less rousing physical play with their infants. Parent-infant play is more sustained and more active than is solitary play or play with siblings, and it is more likely to teach the infant new skills.

Babies have a definite interest in peers, even during the first few months of life. It is not until the middle of the second year, however, that there is an extensive amount and variety of infant communication and that the first signs of cooperative peer play make their appearance. Social games with adults precede social games with peers because the adult is the initiator who provides the structure for the game. By the middle of the second year, however, infants are able to provide their own structure, and so peer games become possible.

Key Terms

Decentration

Decontextualization

Integration

Primary Circular Reaction

Secondary Circular Reaction

Sensorimotor Play

Shared Meanings

Symbolic Play

Tertiary Circular Reaction

CHAPTER FOUR

The Preschool Years: From Two to Five

Every year in a young child's life brings with it substantial changes. This chapter will examine the processes of development from the age of two to the age of five. The more typically observed attributes of children at each of the different ages will be presented, but it is important to keep in mind, of course, that human development at any age is characterized by a high degree of diversity. (The behavioral norms presented here are based on extensive research on the typical behaviors of young children that has been carried out over the past 60 years at the Gesell Institute, much of it the work of Arnold Gesell, Louise Bates Ames, and Frances Ilg.)

Appropriate toys and play activities for children at each age will be discussed, because play and development are inseparably connected and because age appropriateness is perhaps the most essential feature of any toy (see Table 4.1).

The second section of this chapter will consist of a description of the general developmental trends in play from age two to age five. Specifically there will be an examination of the ways in which changes in play mirror the changes in the child's level of intellectual, social, and emotional maturity, and much will be said about the type of play that is clearly predominant during the preschool years: symbolic, or make-believe, play.

TABLE 4.1   General Characteristics and Appropriate Play Materials for the Preschool Child

Age	General Characteristics	Appropriate Play Materials
2	Uses language effectively. Large muscle skills developing, but limited in the use of small muscle skills. Energetic, vigorous, and enthusiastic, with a strong need to demonstrate independence and self-control.	Large muscle play materials: Swing sets, outdoor blocks, toys to ride on, pull toys, push toys. Sensory play materials: Clay, fingerpaints, materials for water play, blocks, books, dolls and stuffed animals.
3	Expanded fantasy life, with unrealistic fears. Fascination with adult roles. Still stubborn, negative, but better able to adapt to peers than at age two. Early signs of product orientation in play.	Props for imaginative play (e.g., old clothes). Miniature life toys. Puzzles, simple board games, art materials that allow for a sense of accomplishment (e.g., paintbrushes, easels, marker pens, crayons).
4	Secure, self-confident. Need for adult attention and approval—showing off, clowning around, taking risks. More planful than threes, but products often accidental. Sophisticated small muscle control allows for cutting, pasting, sewing, imaginative block building with smaller blocks.	Vehicles (e.g., tricycles, Big Wheels). Materials for painting, coloring, drawing, woodworking, sewing, stringing beads. Books with themes that extend well beyond the child's real world.
5	Early signs of logical thinking. Stable, predictable, reliable. Less self-centered than at four. Relaxed, friendly, willing to share and cooperate with peers. Realistic, practical, responsible.	Cut-and-paste and artistic activities with models to work from. Simple card games (e.g., Old Maid), table games (e.g., Bingo), and board games (e.g., Lotto), in which there are few rules and the outcomes are based more on chance than on strategy. Elaborate props for dramatic play.

Finally, this chapter will include discussion of a variety of environmental factors that influence preschool play: childrearing patterns, peer interactions, exposure to day-care settings, physical characteristics of the play environment, and the effects on play of the electronic media, and specifically the medium of television.

The Two-Year-Old

What happened to our pleasant, easily controllable little boy, the Steins wondered as they watched two-year-old Jason throw another of his increasingly frequent temper tantrums, this one because his mother gave him a peanut butter sandwich cut into small squares instead of the triangles he had asked for. It seemed that lately Jason had become more and more stubborn; when he didn't refuse outright, he was slow in following his parents' directions. As in the incident of the peanut butter sandwich, he seemed to want everything in his life to go in a certain predetermined way and would complain bitterly when variations were introduced. He often said "No" to a parental request even before his mother or father had completed the sentence, and he would refuse to eat what had once been his favorite foods for no reason that was apparent to anyone.

Actually, Jason's behaviors are not terribly unusual for a two-year-old. The stubbornness, negativism, and striving for independence are fairly typical, and might even be seen as positive characteristics in that they represent the assertion of the child's newly forming sense of self. This is small consolation, however, to the Steins as they fight the battle of the peanut butter sandwiches! Let us look at some general characteristics of two-year-olds and then at the play materials that are particularly appropriate for this age group.

General Characteristics

As children enter the third year of life, a number of developments directly influence the quality of their play. In terms of sensory and motor development, the two-year-old can get around easily. Not only can they walk and run, but now they easily climb up and down stairs. In addition, they can work with simple puzzles that have large pieces, they can string beads, and they can manipulate clay or Play Doh (Ames, Gillespie, Haines, & Ilg, 1979). They are still somewhat limited, however, in the development of fine motor skills, such as those required for cutting, pasting, or using a pencil or paintbrush effectively. Large muscle play activities are definitely preferred.

The child of two is also quite interested in sensory exploration; the feel of play materials like paints, clay, or sand is more important for a two-year-old than is the possibility of creating a product.

Two-year-olds are also beginning to use language effectively. For example, they combine two words into phrases by the age of 21 to 24 months (e.g., "Want milk," "Push car"), and they are increasingly likely to become frustrated if an adult fails to understand what they are trying to say; at 18 months they showed no such frustration. During the third year, they typically speak in simple three-word sentences, and their

*The feel of play materials such as paints or clay is more important
to a two-year-old than the possibility of creating a product.*

vocabulary expands dramatically. They can tell you their names, and whether they are
boy or girl. And they absolutely love to be read to (Ames, Gillespie, Haines, &
Ilg, 1979).

The increasing linguistic proficiency of the two-year-old has a decidedly positive
effect on the child's social maturity because it makes communication more efficient.
The young two is likely to give affection to adults and other children and in general to
do things to please people. And because of their greater ability to communicate, they
are more likely than a younger child to make attempts to play cooperatively with peers.
Social contact among two-year-olds is brief and fleeting, however. They enjoy being
near other children but are still quite limited in their ability to share and to cooperate.

In their personalities, two-year-olds are energetic, vigorous, and enthusiastic.
They are at a stage in which the need is strong to demonstrate independence, to show
that they are capable of doing things for themselves—what psychoanalytic theorist
Erik Erikson referred to as the crisis of autonomy versus doubt. In effect, children of
this age are saying to their caretakers: "I am myself. I am separate from and different
from you." The ability to demonstrate control over their own bodies is all important,
and twos will take great pride in physical accomplishments like climbing up a jungle
gym, turning a light on or off, sliding down a slide, or developing a measure of bowel or
bladder control.

The need of two-year-olds to assert their independence can be manifested in
stubbornness, rigidity, and negativism. There is often an unwillingness to make any
sort of compromise. Parents will comment, for example, that their two-year-old likes

to have the same story read over and over again and in exactly the same way. If a page is skipped, or if the reader introduces variations of any sort, the child may complain loudly. Another frequently heard adult complaint is that children of this age refuse on principle to do what is asked of them. Tell them to stay outside, and they will want to come in; tell them to come indoors, and they will insist on staying outside. Such negative attitudes are not necessarily indicators of impending juvenile delinquency; instead, they serve to indicate the extent of the two-year-old's need for autonomy.

Play Materials

The best play materials for a two-year-old, as for a child of any age, are those that capitalize on the child's developmental needs. For example, play materials that develop large muscle skills are most appropriate. For outdoor play, a two-year-old could benefit from parallel bars to hang on, ladders to climb, wagons to pull and toy lawn mowers to push, outdoor blocks to drag around and to stack, and small spaces to crawl in and out of. Toys that the child can ride on are also favorites, and help to develop strength and large muscle coordination. For sensory exploration, clay and its many variations provide wonderful opportunities for squeezing, squishing, and molding (but not for product creation at this age). Finger paints serve much the same purpose, and water play (e.g., squeezing and dipping sponges, pouring water from one container to another, blowing bubbles, sailing boats in the bathtub) becomes a highly enjoyable activity.

Two-year-olds are now stacking blocks, and they enjoy playing with things that can be put together and taken apart, so the block collection that was begun in the second year can be added to. Blocks in the basic shapes (squares, rectangles, triangles) are the most appropriate since twos are more interested in manipulating the blocks and combining them in different ways than in making things with them. Similarly, additions might be made to the library since children of this age enjoy books and love being read to—even if it is the same story read over and over again in exactly the same way. Finally, two-year-olds often develop the habit of clinging to a favorite doll or stuffed animal, and such toys are now considerably more appreciated that they were the year before.

The Three-Year-Old

When Jessica Allen was three years old, she developed a terrible fear of the dark. Her mother was surprised at first because Jessica had always been remarkably fearless and adventuresome. Until recently, she had gone to bed without a night light and with the door closed; now she would not sleep unless her door was left open, and she demanded that every night her mother check her closet and under her bed for monsters. This development seemed regressive to Mrs. Allen. A child was supposed to become less fearful with age, not more so.

Mrs. Allen noticed at about the same time that Jessica had begun to take a strong interest in her; the child wanted to wear her makeup and asked repeated questions about mommies and daddies and what they were supposed to be like. Mrs. Allen was gratified by her daughter's interest in her and efforts to imitate her, but she also wondered if this development might be related to Jessica's fear of the dark. Was Jessica troubled by the fact that she had no father living in her home? Was her interest in adult roles an effort to understand why some of her playmates had two parents and she had only one? Were her fears of the dark a symptom of insecurity about her family status?

General Characteristics

Mrs. Allen might appreciate knowing that she is the mother of a typical three-year-old child. Like Jessica, the average child of three is highly imaginative. There is significant expansion in their fantasy lives, which sets the stage for great strides in imaginative play and, on the negative side, explains the appearance of unrealistic fears, such as fear of the dark, of monsters, or of loud noises.

As for Jessica's new-found fascination with the roles of mommy and daddy, this too is typical. There are clear indications that threes, unlike twos, begin to identify strongly with adults—to become increasingly interested in what adults do and to imagine themselves doing the same things. Perhaps as a result, threes become interested in dramatic play, in which they have an opportunity to act out adult roles for themselves.

Dramatic play reflects the social maturity of the three-year-old as compared with the two, not only because such play requires an appreciation of the roles of others, but because the success of role-playing games depends upon the cooperation of the players: each child must act out his or her individual part or the play will not work. The social component of dramatic play becomes evident when one realizes that 70% of all such play among three-year-olds occurs in a group setting (Johnson & Ershler, 1981).

Social maturity is relative, of course. Like the two-year-old, the child at three can still be very stubborn and negative. However, at three there is at least a slightly greater willingness to conform to the expectations of others. It is obvious that the child of three is moving into a world of increasing social interaction, because three-year-olds are better able to share, to await their turns, and to cooperate with adults and with peers. People are more important to a three-year-old than they were a year ago, and the three seeks out social interaction and recognizes the value of membership in a group (Ames, Gillespie, Haines, & Ilg, 1979).

Finally, compared to a two-year-old, threes are more interested in the effects of their behaviors on the surrounding world. In their orientation they are beginning to move from process to product, from actions to their end results. Unlike the two, the three-year-old is able to draw satisfaction from making things that they can show to others. We should point out, however, that the three-year-old is not planful in the sense of deciding on goals and following through; such abilities will not appear until the age of four or five (Hartley, Frank, & Goldenson, 1952). Many of the products that three-year-olds are so proud of were accidental rather than intentional creations.

Play Materials

Play materials for three-year-olds should reflect their increasing social maturity, their emerging interest in adult roles, and the expansion of the child's imagination compared to that of a two-year-old. A major addition to the supply of playthings, therefore, would be props for imaginative play: articles of adult clothing no longer used, eyeglasses, a plastic or wooden shaving kit, a doctor kit, makeup, and other props that allow children to be just like Mom or Dad or other adult figures. For the same purposes, three-year-olds appreciate miniature toys that represent adult models: toy trucks, gas stations, dolls, doll houses, space ships, and so forth.

The expansion of the child's imagination affects the ways in which children use play materials that are already familiar to them. For example, threes, like two-year-olds, continue to enjoy block play, but blocks can be used differently now. At three, children will incorporate blocks into fantasy play rather than simply stacking or arranging them in interesting combinations. Three-year-olds will use blocks to further their interest in the world of adults. They will create structures, such as buildings, streets, and tunnels, that represent the adult world in miniature, and they will use these structures to play imaginatively. The time is right, therefore, for the adult to increase the supply of available blocks, both of the indoor and the outdoor variety and, in doing so, to make certain that the blocks are varied enough to facilitate make-believe play; square blocks may make fine small buildings, but long rectangular blocks and ramps will suggest the building of roads, arches raise the possibility of bridge building, and large outdoor blocks can be transformed into habitable structures, such as forts, houses, or boats.

Finally, the preliminary signs of product-orientation that are seen in some three-year-olds should be taken into account when play materials are selected. Certainly adults should not demand or even expect a product from such a young child. Nevertheless, whether they be puzzles, simple games, interlocking blocks, or art materials, toys should be selected with the possibility of a child's accomplishment in mind. Let us look at art materials as an example. Whereas the two-year-old is process oriented, and enjoys art materials like fingerpaints and clay primarily for their sensory appeal, threes are interested as well in the results, however unintentional, that their efforts produce. Now there is a joy in accomplishment and an interest in showing off one's creations, and fingerpaints may be too formless to capitalize on that interest. Art materials should be provided, therefore, that allow children to demonstrate their skills and to produce something, even if accidentally, that can be shown to others. Included might be paintbrushes, easels, marker pens, and crayons.

The Four-Year-Old

When Mr. and Mrs. Petrillo gave Alan a Big Wheel vehicle for his fourth birthday, they didn't realize that he might decide to use it in some rather inventive ways. Eager for adult attention, Alan loved to show off, and many times he would engage in activities, such as racing with the neighborhood children or "jumping" his Big Wheel off the sidewalk onto the street, that led his parents to worry about his safety. Alan wanted to be like the motorcycle stunt riders he had seen on a recent television program, and he had little awareness of the potential dangers in such activities.

Mr. Petrillo wondered if perhaps the Big Wheel had been a bad idea because it encouraged Alan to show off and to behave recklessly. Mrs. Petrillo insisted that the problem was that their son had been allowed to watch television programs that encouraged the reckless use of motor vehicles. Another opinion was offered by Alan's grandmother, who suggested that it was the neighborhood children who were encouraging the boy's displays of bravado. Whose interpretation was correct? Any of them might have been, but in fact, Alan's emulation of adult roles, his bursting self-confidence, his recklessness, and his showing off are typical characteristics of four-year-olds, as will now be described.

General Characteristics

Compared to three-year-olds, four-year-olds appear to be more secure and self-confident. Their bodies are considerably more efficient than they were a year ago. They can balance themselves by standing on one foot, can roller skate, and can ride a small bicycle with training wheels (Ames, Gillespie, Haines, & Ilg, 1979).

Their small muscle control is more sophisticated also, so they button large buttons and even tie their shoelaces. In addition, they are able to engage in many play activities that were difficult and frustrating the year before. They enjoy drawing, cutting things out of paper, painting, coloring, woodworking, and imaginative block building with smaller blocks of various shapes. When working with such materials, the four-year-old is more product oriented than the three; still, the products are often

The sophisticated small muscle control of this four-year-old girl allows her to engage successfully in activities such as drawing, coloring, and using a pair of scissors.

unintentional in that they evolve as the project develops. In other words, fours are more likely than threes to make plans at the outset, but the plans may change continuously as the play material changes in appearance.

Four-year-olds are more thoroughly involved than threes in the process of identification with adults. They are becoming keenly aware of their own masculinity or femininity and may go to great efforts to demonstrate their similarity to the same-sex parent. Nevertheless, gender lines are still somewhat indistinct at this age; children do not yet see gender as a fixed and unchanging characteristic of a person's being and may ascribe gender differences to such surface features as hair length or type of clothing (Kohlberg, 1966).

The focus on adults may cause the four-year-old to engage in many socially immature behaviors designed to elicit adult attention and approval: showing off, clowning around, bragging (Hartley, Frank, & Goldenson, 1952; Hartley & Goldenson, 1963). Parents may find themselves constantly enjoined, "Watch me," or "See what I can do." Parents also discover that their children's new-found self-confidence can lead them into risky and dangerous behaviors, as Alan Petrillo demonstrated when he rode his Big Wheel around the neighborhood.

Play Materials

Play materials for the four-year-old should reflect their increasing sociability and the fact that they simply cover a lot more territory in their daily wanderings. It is appropriate, therefore, to provide them with vehicles, such as tricycles, Big Wheels, or wagons, that will facilitate social interaction and allow them to demonstrate their large muscle skills both for peers and for adults. In addition, children at four need play materials that help them develop their small muscle skills, and these might include materials for sewing, woodworking, stringing beads, coloring, painting, and drawing. A question to keep in mind when selecting materials is whether an activity allows children to extend the range of implements they use in play—beyond the ordinary pencils, brushes, and scissors to include items like pick-up sticks, jacks, and even computer keyboards. Finally, books continue to have high interest value, and now an adult might look for those that capitalize on the child's sense of adventure, with themes and locales that extend far beyond the child's everyday world.

The Five-Year-Old

When she was four, Lora could never be depended upon to pick up her room; now at five she did so regularly and often without having to be reminded. When she was four, she fought constantly with her two-year-old sister, whom she generally regarded as a little pest; now at five Lora was becoming increasingly protective of little Jennifer, helping to tuck her into bed at night, showing her picture books, telling her all about the grown-up world of kindergarten, and even asking their mother if she could babysit for her at some time! When she was four, Lora needed almost constant supervision when she played with her friends because she was a headstrong child and liked to have things her way; now at five she seemed to have developed an understanding of give-and-take in interpersonal relationships. She was better able to share, take turns, and cooperate than she had been before.

What miracle, her parents wondered, had brought about the dramatic changes in their little girl? It is likely that it was only the miracle of normal human development. Let us look now at the characteristics of the average five-year-old child, who stands at the end of the period of early childhood.

General Characteristics

From an intellectual standpoint, five-year-olds are already showing signs of logical thinking as they begin the transition to what cognitive psychologist Jean Piaget referred to as concrete operations. Their thinking is better organized than before; as a result, they tend to see the world as being a rational and orderly place.

They are more stable, predictable, and reliable than they were when younger, and they are less self-centered. As a result, they are often perceived by adults as relaxed and friendly, and when they play with peers, there is usually a willingness to share, take turns, and cooperate.

This same spirit of reliability and cooperation is seen in the home. The parents, particularly the mother, occupy a central place in the child's life. Fives like to please their parents, and they demonstrate a willingness to take on new responsibilities in caring for themselves and their belongings. They are often willing to help in caring for their younger siblings, even though they typically get along better with children outside the home (Ames, Gillespie, Haines, & Ilg, 1979). It is at five that children begin to appreciate their "babies," as they often refer to younger brothers or sisters, become protective of them, and, like Lora, take pride in being able to help care for them.

It will be remembered that the three-year-old was entering a world in which there was a significant expansion of fantasy and a blurring of the distinction between fantasy and reality. By the age of five, however, children are considerably more realistic. Their fears, for example, are based more in reality (e.g., fear of physical dangers, accidents, illnesses, war, death) than are the fantasy-world fears of the younger child, who may really believe there is a monster in the closet! The realism of five-year-olds can be seen also in their dramatic play. No longer satisfied with the minimal props used by threes and fours (e.g., sticks for swords or a red paper hat to indicate that one is a firefighter), they want the entire costume, or they argue the need for realistic store-bought props instead of miscellaneous items found around the home.

Play Materials

Like the four-year-old, the child at five enjoys activities like drawing, painting, coloring, and working with scissors, but the five-year-old is more interested in precision and realism. The child now seeks direction from adults and often appreciates having a model to work from. Unfortunately, at five there is often an excessive concern with making things correctly and a tendency to compare one's work with that of others. The child may be extremely judgmental about the quality of his or her own work, even if adults go to great efforts to discourage such self-criticism.

Skill-oriented play materials that allow the child to plan an activity and to work it through should contain appropriate directions and allow for the possibility for children and adults to work together, at least occasionally. Art materials continue to be valued playthings and should be both structured in terms of an expected product (e.g., coloring books, a paint- or color-by-numbers set) or unstructured (e.g., paints and brushes, crayons, marker pens, glue, scissors, stencils, sequins and glitter, clay, play-dough). Some adults may complain that such "structured" art materials may inhibit the development of a child's creative expression, but they should realize that artistic production involves skill as well as creative expression, and children at five are particularly interested in developing and displaying their skills. For these reasons, a five-year-old might also appreciate receiving toys like a workbench with realistic tools, playing cards, table games and board games with dice (e.g., Candyland, Chutes and Ladders, Lotto, Bingo). A necessary feature of games for this age group is that they should emphasize the element of chance, rather than demanding a high degree of strategy for success.

General Patterns of Play

Increasing Social Play

More than 50 years ago, psychologist Mildred Parten (1933) carefully recorded the changing nature of children's play from the age of two to the age of five, and her observations were so perceptive that her categories of play are still seen as a meaning-ful framework within which to examine the increasing social maturity of the child. That is not to say, however, that all of Parten's conclusions are accepted without question. They are not. For example, it is likely that she underestimated the abilities of young children to play cooperatively, in part because she observed their behavior in the context of nursery school groups that ranged in size from 2 to 15; many of the children in these groups, particularly among the two-year-olds, were not well known to one another. Researchers today agree with Parten that communication and cooperation occur rarely when two-year-olds play in unfamiliar groups, but they suggest that the very same children will play communicatively and cooperatively if paired with a familiar peer. In other words, while Parten's observations were accurate, the setting in which she worked prevented her from seeing the children at their social best.

Parten described the transition from the solitary play that is so typical of one- and two-year-olds to the highly interactive cooperative play of the average four-year-old. In doing so, she outlined a series of stages of play that increase in their level of social sophis-tication. Let us now describe those stages and their implications for children's development.

Categories of Social Play

Typical of two-year-olds, **solitary play** is the lowest level of social play. The child is playing while totally alone in his or her own world, even if surrounded by other children. Approximately half of the separate observations of two-year-olds in Parten's study found them engaged in solitary play. Two-year-olds also engaged in a considerable amount of **onlooker play,** which occurs when a child watches another child or children at play, is definitely involved as a spectator, even to the point of asking questions or offering suggestions, but does not become an active participant.

Next comes the form of play most commonly observed in all age groups in the Parten study; **parallel play,** in which children play separately at the same activity at the same time and in the same place. They are aware of the presence of peers, and, in fact, the presence of others obviously has some meaning for them, but each child is still playing separately. Parents or teachers will often comment on how nicely a group of children are playing together in the sandbox, but upon careful inspection they discover that the children may be playing in the same place and with similar materials, but each is involved in a separate and distinct play routine. Parallel play seems to represent a point of transition between the socially immature level of solitary play and the socially sophisticated level of genuine cooperation. Interestingly enough, parallel play often draws children into cooperative activities, but it is rarely followed by the less mature solitary play, leading some psychologists to suggest that playing in parallel is a safe way to set the stage for more intense group interaction (Bakeman & Brownlee, 1980; Damon, 1983).

Associative play, common among three- and particularly among four-year-olds, resembles parallel play in that each child is still focused on a separate activity, but now there is a considerable amount of sharing, lending, taking turns, attending to the activities of one's peers, and expansive communication. Two children may be painting at adjacent easels, for example, and while each is producing a separate work of art, there is much discussion about their paintings (or about anything else), there is sharing of materials ("I'll lend you some of my red if you lend me your blue"), and there is a genuine interest in socializing that may be more compelling than the act of painting a picture.

Finally, four-year-olds engage in **cooperative play,** which represents the highest level of social maturity. Cooperative play occurs when two or more children are engaged in a play activity that has a common goal, one that can be realized only if all of the participants carry out their individual assigned roles. A group of children in the sandbox decide, for example, that they will build a city; one child works on the road, two others on a bridge, and others dig a tunnel. Many adults remember tunneling through a mound of dirt or sand with their bare hands while a playmate worked from the other side, with the hope that the two hands would eventually meet in the middle, and many remember the feeling of accomplishment that such a meeting engendered. This is the essence of cooperative play.

Developmental Trends in Social Play

Parten noticed that as children developed from age two to four, there was a significant decline in solitary activities, as well as in passive watching while others played. She also noticed that the size of children's play groups was related to age; in all age groups except the oldest (four-and-a-half to five-year-olds), the most popular group size was two, but in the oldest group, the most popular size was in the range of three to five children. The tendency to play in groups of five or more definitely increased with age.

In analyzing the preferred play materials and activities of the children in her sample, Parten again found some interesting developmental trends. Children between two and two-and-a-half seemed to prefer, in order, the following activities: sandbox play, trains, "kiddie" cars, idly looking, and idly sitting. The preferred activities—again, in rank order—of the four-year-olds were paper cutting, clay, family (house, dolls), sandbox, and swings. This information should not be taken to indicate that these are the preferred activities in *all* nursery school or day-care settings; preferences depend upon what is available and what is encouraged by adults and by peers. However, the preferences of Parten's children make some interesting points about child development. The preference for solitary activities among the younger children, compared to the older ones, is striking. The older children are more likely to be involved in social play ("family") as well as in small muscle activities (paper cutting). What is more, even when the same activity appeared in both preference lists, the form of the play often differed. For example, when younger children played in the sand box, they typically played by themselves, feeling the sand, pouring it back and forth from one container to another, or making molds of it. The older children showed signs of cooperative play in the sand box, working in groups to construct roads, tunnels, or bridges. Similarly, when the younger children played with trains, they attached the cars and pulled them around for long periods of time, whereas the older preschoolers would work in pairs or groups to build tracks, train stations, and so forth. Again, these differences attest to the increasing social maturity of the child throughout the preschool years; cooperation becomes increasingly common, as does the tendency in play to identify with the world of adults, as children are doing when they try out the roles of mother or father, construction worker or train engineer.

The Expansion of Make-Believe

Developmental Trends in Pretend Play

The years from three to six are generally recognized as the golden years of pretend, or make-believe, play; at no other time in life is a human being so thoroughly involved in the world of fantasy. But what is pretend play? Actually it is found in many varieties, corresponding roughly to the types of play first described by Parten in 1933. Pretend play can be a solitary activity, as when a child shares a personal fantasy world with dolls, other miniature life toys, or imaginary companions. Jean Piaget (1962) described solitary pretend play as the first, and least mature, stage of symbolic play, although it should not be forgotten that a good deal of highly creative activity can result from solitary make-believe.

Pretend play can occur in parallel, when two or more children are ostensibly playing together, but each is under the spell of a separate fantasy. Finally, pretend play can involve intense group interaction, with each group member taking a role that complements the roles played by all others in the group. Such group pretend play, which is also referred to as dramatic or **sociodramatic play,** comprises approximately two-thirds of all the pretend play of preschool children (Rubin, 1982, 1986).

The ratio of activities involving make-believe to *all* episodes of free play

Computers in the Preschool:
What Is the Effect on Play?

In recent years there has been a dramatic increase in the availability of microcomputers in educational settings, and more and more of these symbols of advanced technology are finding their way into preschool classrooms (Fein, Campbell, & Schwartz, 1987; Simon, 1985). The arrival of the computer has not been greeted with total enthusiasm, however. In fact, many teachers and parents are extremely worried about the availability of these machines.

Some teachers fear that the presence of microcomputers will encourage children to play alone and thus keep them from developing a variety of much needed social skills. In the sense that they could encourage detachment, microcomputers have been attacked as "dehumanizing influences" (Burg, 1984; Tan, 1985). Others fear that children in the presence of computers will emphasize symbolic activities to the neglect of those that require hands-on work with concrete objects or that teachers will overly structure the young child's activities to the point that child-organized activities will all but disappear (Fein, Campbell, & Schwartz, 1987). Finally, the concern has been raised that the presence of the microcomputer in the preschool reflects society's emphasis on computer literacy as a goal of education; the computer is seen as a tool for work, and its presence represents an erosion of the principle that young children should be allowed to play (Tan, 1985).

What effect does the presence of a computer have on young children's play? In terms of the impact on social interaction, some researchers have discovered that the arrival of a new computer has little effect on peer play (Fein, Campbell, & Schwartz, 1987; Strein & Kachman, 1984), while others have offered evidence that social encounters actually increase when a computer is present (Borgh & Dickson, 1986; Hawkins, Sheingold, Gearhart, & Berger, 1982; Wright & Samaras, 1986; Zaijka, 1983). A typical pattern is that children become obsessed with a computer only in the beginning, but once the novelty wears off, they become quite willing to share and take turns at the keyboard, and life in the preschool soon returns to normal (Simon, 1985). This initial obsession and gradual return to life as usual is similar to the pattern of video game play that is seen among older children (Creasey & Myers, 1986). And even when a preschooler *is* playing at the computer, the play is likely to be parallel rather than solitary. While only one child at a time can control the keyboard, others typically watch and offer suggestions (Tan, 1985).

On the positive side, young children develop a feeling of accomplishment from mastering computers and find in them a variety of opportunities for play with language, imaginative experimentation, and problem solving (Piazza & Riggs, 1984; Tan, 1985). More importantly, computer play is fun. If one's reason for making them available to preschoolers is to produce a generation of adults who are computer literate, then so be it, but to a young child a computer is no more a work machine than is a tricycle or a set of blocks.

increases significantly from the age of three to the age of six (Hetherington, Cox, & Cox, 1979; Johnson & Ershler, 1981; Rubin, Fein, & Vandenberg, 1983), and this increase is due primarily to increases in the number of episodes of group-oriented sociodramatic play (Connolly, 1980; Hetherington, Cox, & Cox, 1979; Rubin, Fein, & Vandenberg, 1983). Solitary and parallel pretend play episodes remain fairly stable throughout the preschool years. This gradual transition from solitary to social pretense was described by Piaget (1962) as a normal developmental progression that indicated the increasing social maturity of the child.

Is it fair to characterize solitary pretense as inherently less sophisticated than group pretense requiring cooperation and the assumption of complementary roles? From a practical standpoint, should a parent or teacher be concerned if an older preschooler still enjoys solitary pretend play? There is, indeed, a sense in which solitary pretense is less mature than social pretense, but we must point out that judgments about children's social maturity should never be made on the basis of individual make-believe play episodes. Because Paul is playing Star Wars by himself while Brooke is playing house with four other children, it should not be concluded that Brooke is a more mature five-year-old than Paul, or even that Brooke's particular play episode is inherently more sophisticated than Paul's. Instances of solitary pretend play occur throughout the preschool years and even beyond, and their appearance should not be a cause for concern.

On the other hand, solitary and parallel pretend play activities constitute a distinct minority of the pretend play activities of preschoolers, approximately 13 and 17 percent, respectively; as was pointed out earlier, most of the pretend activities of preschoolers occur in the context of group interaction. Children who engage in a *disproportionate* amount of solitary and parallel pretense, and thereby deviate significantly from the observed norms, may indeed be displaying signs of social immaturity. As psychologist Kenneth Rubin (1982, 1986) discovered, young children who engage in abnormally high percentages of solitary and parallel pretense, as compared to social pretense, tend to be rejected by their peers, have difficulty solving social problems, and be rated by their teachers as socially maladjusted. Thus we need not be concerned at all if Paul enjoys a solitary game of Star Wars, but if most of Paul's pretend play occurs when he is alone (assuming that playmates are available to him), and sociodramatic play within a group is a rare occurrence, then we might wish to ask questions about the child's social maturity.

Dramatic Play Roles

Dramatic play roles have been extensively analyzed, and it has been found that most roles fall into three categories, depending on the extent to which the roleplaying involves simply being a character of one's choice or is defined by the performance of a specific action sequence. There are family roles, character roles, and functional roles.

Family roles, which are those most likely to be played out by the preschool child, are the roles of mother, father, brother, sister, baby, and even that of a family pet. The youngest preschool children limit themselves to the roles of mother, father, and baby, while older children are the more likely to include siblings, grandparents, and other relatives. Not surprisingly, family roles tend to come in pairs; that is, when a mother character appears in sociodramatic play, it is likely that a father character will appear as well (Garvey, 1977).

Character roles are based on characters that are either stereotyped or fictional. Stereotyped characters are defined by their occupations or by their habitual actions, mannerisms, or personality characteristics. Fictional character roles, on the other hands are based on specific individuals from the various media—Tom Sawyer, Princess Leia, Superman, or Wonder Woman. Character roles, which tend to be somewhat flat and one-dimensional in nature, are like family roles in the sense that they need not be expressed in terms of specific action plans. A child may play at simply being an alien from outer space, a wicked witch, a cowboy, or a princess, without following any predetermined course of action.

Unlike family and character roles, which are possible to play simply by *being* a particular character, the **functional role** is always defined in terms of a specific plan of action—preparer of dinner, firefighter, monster, victim, train conductor, passenger on the train. The functional role defines the behavior, but not the permanent identity of the character (Bretherton, 1986). A family or character role can become functional at times, as when a father protects the children by chasing away the monster or a cowboy circles the wagons in preparation for an Indian attack. However, family and character roles require no specific action plans because they can be defined by who the character is as well as by what the character does.

Garvey (1977) found that the family role is the most central of all roles and the most complex, perhaps because it is the one that children are the most familiar with. The centrality of family roles is illustrated by the pattern of role transformation that is seen in sociodramatic play. Children will typically use the family role as a base out of which one or more functional roles will evolve, but the base will be returned to periodically during the play episode. For example, a father in a dramatic play situation may be transformed into a firefighter, a monster-chaser, a chauffeur, or a carpenter, but between transformations he returns regularly to his original father role. In that sense, the family role is a core role from which a variety of functional roles may emanate.

Props for Dramatic Play

Children's dramatic play is obviously facilitated by the availability of props to stimulate them in one direction or another, and one of the questions adults most frequently ask is "How realistic should props for dramatic play be?" Will a child's imagination be as easily stimulated by a rag doll or a "truck" that is only an empty cardboard box with headlights painted on it as by toys that are realistic to the smallest detail? In fact, there is research to suggest that the child will play more imaginatively with the toy that is less realistic. Pulaski (1973) found that kindergarten, first-, and second-grade children played more inventively with toys that were less structured in terms of an obvious intended purpose (rag dolls, empty cartons, bolts of fabric) than with those that were highly realistic.

The pattern of results for research on prop realism seems to depend, however, on such variables as age and familiarity with dramatic play (Fein, 1981). For example, Fields (1979) discovered that preschoolers played more imaginatively and in a more sustained manner with toys that seemed to have specific purposes (e.g., a cardboard box painted like a car or truck) than with those that were more abstract (e.g., a cardboard box painted in an abstract design), a finding that was in direct contrast to those of Pulaski (1973). How might these apparent inconsistencies be resolved? Fein (1981) suggested that variables of age and social class may have been at work: The children in the Fields study were younger than those in the Pulaski study, and were more likely to come from a lower-class background. It would seem that children need to have some familiarity with play materials if they are to use them imaginatively, and yet if the intended uses of toys are too obvious and too specific, the imaginations of the players might be constrained.

Perhaps the apparent inconsistencies in the earlier research might be explained by the results of a study by B. L. Mann (1984), who had 40 children ranging in age from three-and-a-half to five-and-a-half listen to a story about the adventures of "Mole" and "Troll." They were then told to act out the story, some given realistic props that resembled the story's characters and events, others given unrealistic props. Finally, the children were asked questions about the story.

It was found that the children who had the realistic props acted out the story line in more realistic detail and had a better memory of the story when they were asked questions about it. However, those with unrealistic props seemed to rely on cognitive activities requiring a greater degree of creative imagination; their renditions of the story were less technically accurate but more creative. B. L. Mann (1984) concluded that children may need realistic props to get them started and to sustain their play in the early stages, but that as they become comfortable in the exercise of their powers of make-believe, unrealistic props suffice and serve to stimulate their creativity.

Functions of Dramatic Play

Psychologist Ruth E. Hartley, a pioneer researcher in the area of children's play, has described a number of important functions for preschool children. The first major function is *simple imitation of adults:* The child can play out scenes that he or she may have witnessed adults engaged in, and by doing so may come to a better understanding of what the world of adulthood is all about. A second function is *intensification of a real-life role:* The child plays a role that he or she is accustomed to in everyday life and is familiar with, such as the role of the victim, the dependent role of a baby, or the role of a boss or leader of other children. While conducting research at a day-care center, the author noticed a small boy who came repeatedly to the teacher to complain that the other children were hurting him in play. Closer examination revealed the child's habit of constantly placing himself in the victim role; at one point, the children were playing race cars and the little boy dared them to run him over. They did, and, of course, he immediately rushed to find the teacher and seek her sympathy. His roles in dramatic play seemed to reflect a real-life need to be a victim and to gain as a result the attention and sympathy of a caring adult.

Dramatic play may serve the function of *reflecting home relationships and life experiences,* when simple imitation of what they have seen adults do is combined with intense emotion. Children in dramatic play may unwittingly reveal a good deal of information about their home lives and about the people who live with them. Hartley, Frank, and Goldenson (1952) described the case of three-year-old Mary, the child of an anxious and controlling mother. Mary and her mother ordinarily related well, but the mother seemed overly concerned about neatness and often slapped Mary for touching things she wasn't supposed to or for getting her clothes dirty. In dramatic play Mary became a gross exaggeration of her own mother: She slapped her "children" regularly, yelled at them, and complained about the messes they made.

Another function of dramatic play is to allow children to *express urgent needs.* As an example, consider the case of three-year-old David, the youngest of four children and the "baby" of the family, who received much love from his parents and older siblings but who wanted to have someone *he* could be protective of and nurturant toward. In dramatic play, David almost always assumed a parent role, holding, cuddling, calming, and reassuring a variety of dolls, stuffed animals, and even other children.

Dramatic play serves as an *outlet for forbidden impulses.* The child who fears the expression of aggressive impulses in real life might in play take the role of a highly aggressive character, or the child who is curious about the body's sexual parts and functions might express that curiosity by playing the role of doctor or nurse. The point is that in play the impulse is safe because it is acceptable, while in the child's everyday world it is not.

Finally, dramatic play also allows for the *reversal of roles*: a child who ordinarily feels helpless in the family situation may assume the role of parent, and therefore become the source of power rather than the victim of it. By reversing roles, children can learn much about the points of view of other people and can thereby expand their own self-concepts. In the case of the parent-child role reversal, the child might also learn that parenting is more of a challenge than it ordinarily appears!

Benefits of Dramatic Play

The benefits of symbolic play can be thought of in three general areas of development: the affective, the intellectual, and the social. The affective benefits include the development of self-awareness, self-confidence, and self-control (Singer, 1973). In pretend play children have an opportunity to master an environment that is bounded only by the limits of their fantasy. They can extend themselves beyond the real world in which they often feel powerless into a world in which they can experience the pleasure of exercising their powers of mastery. In doing so, they are often able to reduce conflicts in their lives, to compensate for unpleasant experiences by "undoing" them and playing them out with happier endings and by taking revenge on reality (Bretherton, 1986; Freud, 1974; Piaget & Inhelder, 1969).

The intellectual benefits of dramatic play are many. Such play, by allowing children to create alternative worlds, encourages them to engage in subjunctive representation of reality (Bretherton, 1986). That is, it stimulates the "what if" type of thinking that forms the basis for mature hypothetical reasoning and problem solving. Dramatic play stimulates children to think creatively and, in fact, has been found to predict later creativity (Dansky, 1980). In addition, extensive involvement in dramatic play seems to improve children's memory, language development, and cognitive perspective-taking abilities (Burns & Brainerd, 1979; Dansky, 1980; Rubin, Fein, & Vandenberg, 1983; Saltz, Dixon, & Johnson, 1977).

Finally, dramatic play has been described as the form of play that is the most social and has the greatest impact on the development of social awareness in children (Hartley, Frank, & Goldenson, 1952). Involvement in dramatic play seems to improve children's ability to cooperate in group settings, to participate in social activities, and to understand human relationships (Fink, 1976; Smith, Dagleish, & Herzmark, 1983; Smith & Syddall, 1978).

Factors That Influence Preschool Play

Family Influences

Maria was four years old when her parents decided to separate, and Maria's nursery school teacher, Mrs. Jensen, watched carefully to see if the separation and eventual divorce would have an effect on the child's behavior in the classroom. Mrs. Jensen expected to see problems like excessive dependency, negativism, and overwhelming sadness, but none of these behaviors was evident. However, the teacher did begin to notice differences in the quality of Maria's play. Specifically, the child seemed to less and less time in dramatic play, the themes of her pretense were less flexible, and she seemed to be engaging in increased amounts of solitary and parallel play, a trend in the direction opposite to what might be expected of a four-year-old.

Maria's behavior was not at all unusual, because the play of a preschool child outside the home can be influenced by a variety of factors in the child's home life, and most especially by the quality of the relationships within the family. Most of the research on familial influences on play has consisted of examinations of the relationship between play and the degree of parent-child attachment and on the effects of marital disruption on children's play.

Play and Attachment

It has long been recognized that there is considerable individual variation in the quality of parent-child attachment in our society (Ainsworth, 1977; Ainsworth, Blehar, Waters, & Wall, 1978), and the quality of attachment is related to the quality of children's play. (In fact, play has been found to *facilitate* attachment between parent and child, a point that will receive further attention in Chapter Nine.)

Children appear to be the most closely attached to parents who tend to be secure, and who are confident in their parenting skills. Such parents make themselves readily available to their children from infancy onward and appear to be sensitive to their children's needs. They handle their children with affection, are interested in the various aspects of their lives, and truly enjoy spending time with them. On the other hand, the profile of the parent whose children are less closely attached is that of an anxious, irritable person with little interest in his or her children; such parents feed and handle their young children in a mechanical way and only as necessary (Egeland & Farber, 1984).

Attachment predicts the quality of play throughout the preschool years. Securely attached infants are more likely to explore the physical environment when in the presence of their mothers and are more likely to discover the appropriate uses of objects, as when they realize that a ball is to be rolled or a toy car to be pushed across the floor (Bakeman & Brownlee, 1980; Sutton-Smith, 1979). Securely attached toddlers are more sociable and more likely to engage in rudimentary cooperative games with peers (Lieberman, 1977). Finally, preschoolers who are the most closely attached to their parents are the most likely to engage in fantasy play with objects, and their make-believe play is more sustained and more complex than that of insecure children (Slade, 1987). They are more likely to function independently at the age of two, and by the age of five they seem to have a greater amount of curiosity and behavioral flexibility and are more environmentally oriented in free play (Belsky, Garduque, & Hrncir, 1984; Joffe & Vaughn, 1982).

Play and Marital Disruption

Much of the research on the effects of divorce on the play of children was conducted by psychologist E. Mavis Hetherington and her associates. In one of the most often cited studies, Hetherington, Cox, & Cox (1979) examined the play of two groups of preschool children: one from intact families and one whose parents had been divorced. They found that girls from disrupted families engaged in less dramatic play than did those from intact families at two months and at one year after the divorce; when observed two years after the divorce, however, the differences between the two groups of girls had disappeared. Boys from disrupted families, on the other hand, engaged in fewer episodes of dramatic play at all three time periods studied, and when dramatic play did occur, these boys appeared to be more rigid and less imaginative in their roles than were their counterparts from intact families. Furthermore, sons of divorced parents engaged in more of the relatively immature solitary and parallel functional play, involving the simple repetition of motor behaviors, than did the boys from intact families.

It appears that the stresses of marital disruption can significantly affect the quality and the degree of maturity of children's play. It also appears that boys' play is affected more noticeably than is the play of girls. This gender difference indicates, perhaps, that the effects of divorce may be more pronounced for boys than they are for girls (Rubin, Fein, & Vandenberg, 1983).

Peer Influences

Psychologists have long regarded the childhood peer relationship as the context in which a variety of important social skills emerge (Damon, 1983; Hartup, 1986). In a relationship between a child and an adult, it is the adult who typically determines the rules for interaction. The childhood peer relationship is a mutual one, in that the children themselves must establish the rules by which they will interact; in doing so, they are stimulated to develop an understanding of cooperation and mutual respect, characteristics that are essential to the maintenance of successful social relationships of any kind (Smollar & Youniss, 1982).

Considering the overwhelming significance of peer interactions for children's social development, one would expect to find that peers, like adults, would have a substantial influence on children's play. In fact, they do, and the research indicates the presence of peer influence on play in three specific areas: peer familiarity, sex of playmate, and age of playmate.

Peer Familiarity

In general, the presence of stable, consistent peer relationships is related to a greater degree of overall social competence in preschool children, a greater likelihood of their being accepted by others, and a broader range of mature cooperative social play. Children who have been in the same day-care setting over a period of time, having a fairly stable group of peers to interact with, play in a more mature manner than do children of the *same* age who have not been exposed to a stable and consistent peer group (Howes, 1988). Perhaps it is not surprising, therefore, that children who enter kindergarten with a group of peers they knew in nursery school the year before seem to like school better and to display fewer symptoms of school-related anxiety (Ladd & Price, 1987).

Peer familiarity influences children's play in other, more specific, ways. For example, children are more willing to engage in dramatic play when they are with familiar rather than unfamiliar peers. As they become more comfortable with the particular peer group, their fantasy play becomes more complex and reflects a higher level of cognitive functioning (Doyle, Connolly, & Rivest, 1980; Rubenstein & Howes, 1976).

Sex of Playmates

The sex of a child's playmate also seems to influence the quality of social play. On the one hand, children are more likely to explore new objects and spend less time with familiar toys when playing with a same-sex playmate (Rabinowitz, Moely, Finkel, & McClinton, 1975). On the other hand, however, when boys play only with boys and girls only with girls, they are more likely to engage in forms of play that are traditionally gender-typed (Serbin, Conner, Burchardt, & Citron, 1979). In other words, same-sex play seems to broaden a child's horizons in one sense but to limit them in another, indicating the value of *both* same- and mixed-sex play for young children.

Children tend to seek out same-sex playmates and do so even as early as the age of two in many cases (La Freniere, Strayer, & Gauthier, 1984). Are there ways in which mixed-sex play can be encouraged as well? Indeed, there are. Mixed-sex play is more likely to occur if teachers comment approvingly on it in their classrooms (Serbin, Tonick, & Sternglanz, 1977), if the school curriculum emphasizes the teaching of nonstereotyped values regarding gender roles (Bianchi & Bakeman, 1978; Lockheed, 1986), and even if the room is designed so that boys and girls are more likely to interact. Kinsman and Berk (1979) found, for example, that if a wall of shelving between the block and the housekeeping corner—traditionally "masculine" and "feminine" play areas—was removed, boys and girls were more likely to play together.

Age of Playmates

Young preschoolers, aged two and three, are likely to interact with playmates of almost any age, but as children develop, they are increasingly likely to select playmates of their own age. By the time they enter elementary school, children typically prefer same-age playmates over younger or older ones (Berk, 1989; Lederberg, Chapin, Rosenblatt, & Vandell, 1986; Roopnarine & Johnson, 1984).

Play with same-aged peers differs from play in mixed-age groups in several ways. Same-age interaction tends to be more positive in general, there tends to be a greater incidence of verbal interaction, and cooperative play is more likely to occur in mixed-age groups (Lederberg, Chapin, Rosenblatt, & Vandell, 1986; Roopnarine & Johnson, 1984). In addition, imitation of the behavior of peers is more likely to occur if peers are the same age or older, but it is unlikely if peers are younger (Berk, 1989; Brody & Stoneman, 1981). Finally, children are drawn more easily into social interaction by older playmates than by same-age or younger ones, perhaps because the older child tends to assume the role of social director, as it were, in structuring the play (Brody, Graziano, & Musser, 1983).

Group Day-Care Experience

The need for day care for children is rapidly growing in U.S. society, and in the year 1990 there were approximately 10.5 million U.S. preschool children who required nonparental care (Children's Defense Fund, 1990). As a result, the day-care setting is increasingly likely to be the environment in which children find the time to play.

Day care comes in many forms, of course (see Table 4.2). Most such arrangements involve home care, in which a child or children are supervised in their own home or in the home of another person. However, as the table indicates, a sizable minority of preschoolers attend organized day-care centers (Berk, 1989; U.S. Bureau of the Census, 1987), and most children in day-care centers spend 30 or more hours a week there (Travers, Goodson, Singer, & Connell, 1980).

TABLE 4.2   Child-Care Arrangements in the United States in 1987

Age of Child	Percentage of Children of Working Mothers in Different Types of Child-Care Arrangements			
	Home-based Care*	Child-Care Centers	On-the-Job by Parent	Child Self-Care
2 years and under	75.5	16.3	8.2	—
3–4 years	58.0	33.9	8.1	—
5–14 years	66.6	7.6	5.8	20.0†

Adapted from *Child Development* by L. E. Berk, 1989. Boston: Allyn and Bacon. Used by permission of the publisher and the author. Data are from *Who's minding the kids? Current population reports*, Series P-70, by U.S. Bureau of the Census, 1987. Washington, DC: U.S. Government Printing Office.

*In the children's own home or in someone else's. Thirty-four percent of all children two and under, 27.1% of all three- and four-year-olds, and 41.6% of all children aged 5 to 14 were cared for in their own homes.

†Self-care children are sometimes referred to as latchkey children. The figures presented here would suggest that 1 million U.S. children fit into this category, although some researchers suggest that the actual figure is substantially higher (Berk, 1989).

What are the effects of exposure to day care on children's development, and more specifically on children's play? For the past 30 years, educators and psychologists have put considerable effort into seeking answers to these questions, but simple answers have yet to be discovered. In fact, there is little to report about the overall effects of home-based day care, since arrangements of this type are difficult to study. And even when researchers focus specifically on organized day-care centers, they often find themselves "comparing apples and oranges" because the qualifications of care-givers and their access to material resources are so varied.

Perhaps it should not be surprising that inconsistent and even contradictory findings have emerged from research conducted in child-care centers: the general finding is that exposure to such environments may indeed influence the maturity of children's social interaction and social play, *but* the influence can be either negative or positive.

On the negative side, extensive group care involvement has been associated with negative affect, displays of aggression, and resistance to adult authority (Clarke-Stewart, 1984; Howes & Olenick, 1986; Phillips, McCartney, & Scarr, 1987). On the positive side, experience in child-care centers is related to advanced levels of social play, characterized by a greater degree of sophistication in children's social interactions (Belsky & Steinberg, 1978; Howes, 1988; McCutcheon & Calhoun, 1976; Phillips, McCartney, & Scarr, 1987; Rubenstein & Howes, 1979; Smith & Bain, 1978).

Illustrative of such positive findings were those of Schindler, Moely, and Frank (1987), who looked at the relationship between time spent in day care and social maturity of play in terms of Mildred Parten's (1933) classification system. Children ranging in age from two to five were grouped according to (1) the number of months they had been in day care, and (2) the number of hours a week they spent at a day care center. It was found that children who had spent and were spending the greatest amount of time in a day-care setting were more likely to engage in socially mature associative play, as well as in constructive play, and less likely to engage in solitary play, onlooker play, or what is termed unoccupied behavior.

Interestingly enough, time spent in day care was not related to the amount of cooperative play observed by these particular researchers, although other researchers (e.g., Howes, 1988) have reported that children who begin day care at an earlier rather than at a later age, such as age one as opposed to age three, engage in more cooperative social pretend play, and have an easier time relating to their peers in general.

How can the apparent contradiction between the positive and negative social influences of group child care be explained? Much seems to depend on the quality of the centers themselves. For example, Phillips, McCartney, and Scarr (1987) found that positive social outcomes were most likely to occur when (1) the child-care environment was verbally stimulating, in that adults and children regularly engaged in conversation, (2) the director of the center was relatively experienced in her or his role, and (3) the staff-to-child ratio in the center was high.

In summary, the group child-care experience can enhance social maturity and lead to increasingly sophisticated levels of social interaction and social play. However, the effect depends upon the characteristics of the setting that children are placed in, and, unfortunately, considerable variation exists in the quality of child care in the United States today (Phillips, McCartney, & Scarr, 1987).

Play Space Density

Visitors to a nursery school or child-care center quickly notice that the space is usually divided into specific play areas of varying sizes and degrees of seclusion. There might be a block area, an art area, a large muscle area, a housekeeping corner, and so forth. In fact, parents in the process of selecting programs for their children should be suspicious if "learning centers" are not obvious in a child care facility, because experienced caretakers of young children realize the wisdom of dividing overall play space into activity areas of different sizes.

The major reason for the partition of play space is to maximize the flexibility and enhance the overall quality of play, since children have been found to play differently in different physical settings. For example, in smaller spaces there is less running around, and less rough-and-tumble play, although there is more actual physical contact among the children (McGrew, 1972; Smith & Connolly, 1976). Furthermore, in smaller spaces, the child's attention can be focused on the activity that the space was designed for, whether constructive play in the block area, dramatic play in the housekeeping corner, or creative play with paints or clay in the art area.

There is an important caution to be observed, however, in the designing of small play spaces: If the space becomes overly crowded, children's play can be interfered with, rather than facilitated. In small crowded areas, some children feel a loss of the privacy that everyone needs on occasion, and some display increases in aggressive behavior, a natural consequence of overcrowding in human beings and lower animals alike (Bailey & Wolery, 1984).

Large open spaces, on the other hand, seem to suggest to children that large muscle activities (e.g., running, jumping, general roughhousing) are appropriate, and they may discourage the quieter, more creative forms of play. A large undivided room might contain exactly the same play materials as a room divided into theme areas, but a child in the open room is more likely to be distracted from a particular activity by other children, other play materials, and other ongoing play activities. Perhaps it is not surprising that children are more likely to engage in imaginative play when in smaller spaces with flexible boundaries than when in larger ones (Peck & Goldman, 1978).

A final, more practical, reason for the division of play space is to help the teacher maintain a degree of organization and structure over both materials and time. Materials are less likely to be misplaced or used inappropriately if their use is restricted to a theme area, and it is difficult to schedule activities for particular times of the day if the materials are scattered throughout the room rather than housed in specific places.

The Influence of Television

The Harrises jokingly referred to their five-year-old daughter Stacy as a TV-holic, but actually they were concerned about the fact that, if they allowed her to do so, she could spend hours on end in front of the television set. Mr. Harris believed that Stacy should be playing instead, and that her addiction to television would inhibit the development of her own powers of imagination. Did he have any reason for concern? Perhaps he did. It has been found, in fact, that children who spend a lot of time watching television play less imaginatively than those who do not (Singer & Singer, 1979). This is not because that television *suppresses* imaginative play, but because the more time children spend in front of their television sets, the less time there will be for other activities, including the exercise of their imagination in fantasy play.

The effects of television on children's play, and particularly on children's fantasy play, is not a simple and direct one, however. In fact, the research findings have been somewhat inconsistent (Rubin, Fein, & Vandenberg, 1983). There are several possible reasons for the inconsistency, not the least of which is that there is huge variety of programming for children to watch on television, and the positive and negative influences of television depend to a large extent on the programs that are watched (Salomon, 1977).

In addition to program variation, there is also variation in the conditions under which children watch television. For example, television watching can range all the way from a solitary passive experience to one that is active and interactive. In some families parents help their children select programs to watch, and occasionally watch with their children and discuss the program content. At the opposite extreme are families in which the television set is a substitute babysitter and the parents are often totally unaware of what their children are watching. In a study that demonstrated the significance of adult-child interaction in television watching, Singer and Singer (1976) examined the imaginary play skills of a group of children and then exposed them to one of four conditions. The first group worked with a live adult who taught them a variety of make-believe games. The second group watched "Mr. Rogers' Neighborhood" in the presence of a live adult mediator, who directed their attention to certain of the program's features and discussed the program with them. A third group watched "Mr. Rogers" alone, while a fourth group, serving as a control, was exposed to no specific experimental treatment. The most dramatic increases in fantasy play occurred in the group that watched no television, but instead worked with a live adult teacher. Second in terms of fantasy play increases was the group who watched the television program with an adult mediator, while no changes were seen either in the control group or in the group that watched television without the company of the adult.

The inconsistent findings regarding television's effects on fantasy play might be attributed to another factor: the initial level of imaginative skill that the viewer possesses. Television is often regarded as a destructive force in children's lives, under the assumption that if children could not watch the tube, they would be engaged in a variety of activities that are more intellectually stimulating. Indeed, some children might; others probably would not. Excessive television watching could inhibit the imaginative play of normally imaginative children, but the results of one study seemed to indicate the child who is less imaginative to begin with may benefit from watching intellectually stimulating programs. Tower, Singer, Singer, and Biggs (1979) found that a two-week exposure to either "Mr. Rogers" or "Sesame Street" had a significant positive effect on the imaginative behavior of a group of preschoolers who had initially been rated as poor in their imaginative skills. Perhaps children who would not ordinarily involve themselves in imaginative play can be encouraged to do so by a stimulating television program, while a child who already has a rich fantasy life needs no such encouragement and is therefore unaffected by it.

Summary

The years from two to five are characterized by a decrease in rigidity and stubbornness, by increasing degrees of stability, reliability, and predictability, and by a move from primarily large muscle play to that involving small muscle activities. Sensory exploration during play is on the decline, and increases occur in play that is social and reflects children's interest in and identification with adults.

Between the ages of two and five, children move from solitary and onlooker play to parallel play, and then to associative and cooperative forms of play. The size of the play group increases with age, and the same play materials are used differently at different ages, with younger children typically playing with them in isolation and older ones integrating them into cooperative social activities.

Pretend play can be a solitary activity, it can occur in parallel, or it can involve extensive cooperation, as in the case of sociodramatic play. Solitary and parallel pretend play can be found among children of all ages, but a disproportionate amount of solitary, as opposed to cooperative, pretense is thought to be a sign of social immaturity.

The central roles in dramatic play are family roles, but children typically assume a variety of character and functional roles as well. The dramatic play props most likely to stimulate the processes of creative thinking are those that are the least structured. However, if props leave *too* much to the imagination, many children, and particularly very young ones or older ones with little experience at dramatic play, may not know what to do with them. The functions of dramatic play are many and include simple imitation of adults, intensification of real-life roles, reflection of home relationships, expression of pressing needs and forbidden impulses, and the reversal of roles. Finally, dramatic play appears to have a number of affective, intellectual, and social benefits for the preschool child.

The play of preschoolers is influenced by family factors, such as the security of parent-child attachment and the stability of the marriage, by the familiarity of the child's peer group, and by the amount of experience the child has had in a group setting, such as a day-care center. The quality of play is affected also by such elements in the physical environment as the size of the play space and the extent to which it is organized into definable activity areas. Finally, excessive television watching can inhibit the play of the average preschooler, but children who are initially less imaginative appear to benefit from exposure to intellectually stimulating television programs.

Key Terms

Associative Play

Character Roles

Cooperative Play

Functional Roles

Family Roles

Onlooker Play

Parallel Play

Sociodramatic Play

Solitary Play

CHAPTER FIVE

Play in Later Childhood and Adolescence

I s there play after kindergarten? Judging from the relative number of studies of school-age and adolescent play as compared to play during the preschool years, one might come to the conclusion that children stop playing after they enter the first grade (Glickman, 1984). In fact, many psychologists (e.g., Garvey, 1977; Rubin, Fein, & Vandenberg, 1983) suggest that the organized games of older children should not be thought of as play at all, a point with which we are only in partial agreement. As will be indicated throughout this chapter, play continues to be an important element in the lives of children beyond the preschool years and it continues to mirror their overall pattern of intellectual, social, and personality development.

The first half of the chapter will be devoted to a discussion of some of the general intellectual, social, and personality characteristics of the school-age child and the adolescent. For obvious reasons, an exhaustive treatment of the principles of child and adolescent development will not be presented. Only the more general features of these phases of life will be examined, with particular emphasis on the relationship between development and trends in children's play.

In the remainder of the chapter trends in play during later childhood and adolescence will be discussed, and the ways in which play both reflects the internal processes of human development and enhances them. For example, it will be seen that as children become more logical in their thinking, their play becomes more orderly and more rule dominated. As children socialize with one another in increasingly mature ways, their play becomes a vehicle by which they can better understand the perspectives of others and the hierarchical structures of their specific peer groups; such social awareness is often a prerequisite for entrance into the "culture of childhood."

General Characteristics of the School-Age Child

There are three general characteristics that capture the essence of the period of middle childhood, corresponding to trends in the areas of intellectual, social, and personality development.

From an intellectual standpoint, the major development is that the child's thinking is becoming more orderly, more structured, and more logical. Therefore, the school-age child at play will be more realistic and more rule-oriented than was the preschooler. Play will thus reflect a developing *need for order.*

The school-age child is more socially involved with age-mates than ever before, and the peer group provides support that formerly was offered only within the family. Acceptance by one's peers is of great importance to children in this age group, and their play reflects a sometimes overwhelming *need to belong.*

Finally, in the realm of personality development a major challenge to the emerging self-concepts of school-age children is to demonstrate to themselves and others that they are competent, that they have talents, skills, and abilities that they can be proud of. In their play there is reflected this *need for industry.*

The Emergence of Logical Thinking: A Need for Order

Even as early as the beginning of the second year of life, children are able to represent the world mentally to themselves. They are starting to use symbols in that they can let objects represent one another and can let words stand for objects, people, or events. Therefore, as was pointed out in Chapter Three, they can now begin to engage in make-believe play. In a sense, the preschooler's intelligence consists of mental activity, as compared to the sensory and motor intelligence of the younger infant (Flavell, 1985; Piaget, 1983; Piaget & Inhelder, 1969).

Preschoolers are limited, however, in that their mental representations of reality are not regulated by a consistent system of thought. They are easily distracted. When solving problems, they often focus on irrelevant aspects of the materials they are working with, while they ignore information that is highly relevant. They are influenced too easily by appearances and too often fail to attend to substance. A preschool child may conclude, for example, that a tall, thin glass of water contains more liquid than a wide bowl *even if* the child has watched the liquid being measured in exactly equal amounts beforehand into both containers. The tall glass looks bigger and so it must hold more liquid—never mind the fact that the taller glass is also wider. (See Chapter Eight for a discussion of the influence of play on the child's emerging awareness of the concept of quantity).

Children of five or six are entering a new stage in the development of thinking, what Piaget (1963, 1983) referred to as the stage of **concrete operations.** Now the child's mental representations of reality are organized into an overall system of related representations. The result is that thinking takes on a more logical, more orderly appearance. When asked to sort objects into groups, for example, the child in concrete operations sorts with reference to the logically defining properties of the objects. Thus, a collection of geometric forms might be sorted according to size, color, shape, or the number of straight lines they contain. By contrast, the preschool child would have sorted the geometric shapes perceptually rather than logically and arranged them into what Piaget referred to as **graphic collections,** which are pleasing perceptual arrays: The preschooler may have arranged the shapes into a circle to make a "necklace" or into a straight line to make a "choo-choo train" (Inhelder & Piaget, 1964).

The emergence of a logical system to govern one's thinking allows children to perceive the universe as an orderly place. In addition to acquiring the ability to classify materials logically, the child develops an understanding of cause-and-effect relationships, a mature understanding of the concepts of time and space, and an ability to reason by induction, which involves the postulation of general principles on the basis of particular observed instances.

Now, because the child's thinking is patterned and orderly, the universe assumes the patterns of the child's mind. As will be seen, children's play during the years of middle and later childhood reflects the transition from the stage of prelogical thinking to that of concrete operations, in the sense that play becomes increasingly realistic and increasingly characterized by a need for order.

The Childhood Peer Group: A Need to Belong

Preschool children, even if they spend considerable amounts of time in nursery school or day-care settings, are primarily home centered in orientation. That is, the family is the social unit around which most of their social activities are focused. By the age of five or six, however, children are becoming increasingly peer oriented and decreasingly family oriented (Hughes, Noppe, & Noppe, 1988; Minuchin, 1977; Williams & Stith, 1980). The reason for this transition is that school-age children spend a greater and greater proportion of their waking hours in the company of peers; when they are not actually in school they may be out roaming the neighborhood looking for playmates, and parents often comment that their child no longer wants to spend time in the company of Mom and Dad.

The actual composition of a childhood peer group is highly variable, with children drifting into and out of a circle of friends, sometimes on a week-to-week basis (Hartup, 1983). Nevertheless, the peer group is a close-knit society, with definite, if unwritten, rules for membership. Children who are different in any way, whether because of physical characteristics, personality traits, manner of dress, access to material possessions, or socioeconomic status, may be quickly excluded (Dodge, 1983).

The peer group is a major socializing agent in middle childhood. It is from their peers, not from parents or teachers, that children learn about the culture of childhood. Peers will teach a child quite effectively, and sometimes very harshly, about social rules and about the importance of obeying them. Peers establish a certain moral order that may differ somewhat from that established by adults (Hartup, 1983). For example, parents may teach their children to inform on a child who is misbehaving, but in the peer culture "ratting" may be a major crime that qualifies the child for exclusion from the group.

Socializing and working together with peers gives elementary school children a needed sense of belonging and helps them to understand and obey social rules.

Peers teach children a variety of physical and intellectual skills that are necessary for group acceptance. Parents may provide instruction in riding a bicycle, but rarely do they teach their children how to do "wheelies" on their bikes or how to jump them across ditches! Such education is usually provided by more experienced children in the peer group. Similarly, many of the jokes, stories, riddles, and slang expressions heard among the "coolest" of grade-school children were never taught to them by adults, but transmitted directly by the peer group (Williams & Stith, 1980).

The significance of the childhood peer group as a socializing agent cannot be overestimated, nor can the importance to grade-school children of being accepted by their age-mates. What is the context in which the transmission of peer culture takes place? What is the battleground on which children fight to gain acceptance and to avoid rejection by the group? It should not be surprising, considering the amount of free time that is spent in play, that the battleground is very often the playground—both figuratively and literally. Indeed, it would be surprising if the play of school-age children did not comprise a large portion of their socialization experience and did not enhance the socialization process. In fact, play serves that very function and is often used to satisfy the school-age child's preeminent need to belong.

The Developing Self-Concept: A Need for Industry

Mrs. Rourke, the third-grade teacher, was concerned because eight-year-old Amanda displayed little enthusiasm for school-related activities, and as the term progressed the child withdrew further and further into herself. The teacher recognized that Amanda had problems with her self-image, and so she praised and encouraged the child whenever appropriate. It required much creativity on the teacher's part, however, to find reasons to offer praise, because Amanda was at best a mediocre student and had little in the way of social skills or athletic ability. Then one day Mrs. Rourke made a discovery. It happened when the children were invited to submit designs that might be used on buttons to be worn by the entire school during "School Appreciation Week." Amanda took an interest in the project and submitted not one, but three designs to Mrs. Rourke; the designs were impressive, not because Amanda was a particularly talented artist, but because she was able to communicate effectively in her simple drawings a number of the themes that the contest organizers wanted to represent. Most of the other children, even those more skilled at drawing than Amanda, did not have Amanda's talent for communicating ideas graphically and as a result produced designs that were either pointless or meaningful but overly cluttered.

One of Amanda's designs reached the final level of competition for the official school button, and although she did not go on to win, Amanda actually won in another way. The reaction to her drawings made it clear to her that there *was* a particular talent that she had, an area in which she excelled. Mrs. Rourke thoughtfully pointed out that many adults, including artists, architects, and political cartoonists, are extremely successful in their professions precisely because they are blessed with such a skill. There followed a gradual but perceptible improvement in Amanda's interest in schoolwork, and more importantly there appeared to be improvements in the image the child had of herself.

Amanda's story illustrates the importance to the grade school child of what psychoanalytic theorist Erik Erikson (1963) called a sense of **industry**. As children develop, Erikson wrote, they come to realize that there is no future for them "within the womb of the family" (p. 259), and so they begin to apply themselves to a variety of skills and tasks that are necessary for success in the larger world of adults. They become eager to be productive, to achieve a sense of mastery and a feeling of accomplishment. In more traditional cultures, children's feelings of accomplishment were acquired by their learning to use the tools, utensils, and weapons that adults in their culture needed for survival; in the United States the "tools" are often acquired in the classroom.

Children who feel unsuccessful in the use of their "tools" or in their ability to achieve positions of status among their tool-using peers are likely to develop feelings of exclusion and inferiority, as did Amanda when she was unable to demonstrate skills in the classroom. When Amanda learned, however, that she did have certain talents that could be of use to her later on, she began to move toward the sense of industry that Erikson saw as a necessary component of healthy ego development.

It is clear that when Erikson spoke of the need for industry, he was referring to accomplishment in the world of work, however that may be defined. He was not speaking specifically of play, and, in fact, he even suggested that as children strive for industry, they leave behind the "whims of play" (p. 259). It seems, however, that an ego-building sense of mastery can be acquired in the performance of activities other than those that have as their specific purpose the acquisition of skills. Indeed, why could a sense of mastery not be acquired from the performance of activities that have no external purpose at all? From activities that fall under the definition of play? As will later be indicated, the need for industry is often reflected not only in the classroom activities of grade school children, but also in their play.

General Characteristics of the Adolescent

In discussing the characteristics of school-age children, we pointed out that exhaustive descriptions were not possible in a book specifically dealing with the topic of play but that it is possible to identify three general patterns that typify the middle childhood years. The same can be said for adolescence. Some general characteristics of the period of adolescence will be offered, again, referring to needs in the three areas of social, intellectual, and personality development, and we shall later attempt to relate these three types of needs to the forms of play that are often observed during the adolescent years.

In terms of intellectual development, the adolescent is experiencing a transition from the concrete form of reasoning that typifies the middle childhood years to a reasoning that is abstract and hypothetical. The intellectual need of the adolescent is a *need for abstract conceptualization*. In social terms, the adolescent needs more than simply to belong within the peer group; now there is a need to single out particular individuals with whom one can have an intimate relationship. In their social interactions and in their play adolescents express a compelling *need for communication*. Finally, the adolescent is engaged in a struggle to create a stable and permanent sense of self—to achieve a degree of self-awareness and self-acceptance. Again, play will be the context within which this *need for identity* can often be met.

Formal Operations: A Need for Abstract Conceptualization

The use of a logical system of thinking appears, as we have pointed out, at the beginning of the elementary school years and brings with it a passion for order that is seen in children's **games-with-rules.** As adolescence approaches, however, there is again a qualitative change in the processes of thought. The adolescent, according to Piaget (1983), is ready for a transition from thinking in concrete to thinking in **formal operations.**

The child who is using logic is still limited in terms of the types of issues and problems that can be reasoned about. Children can reason about the concrete (hence the name concrete operations), but they are not yet able to reason about abstractions. They can apply their logic to questions involving objects, people, places, and events, but they cannot reason about ideas, theories, and concepts. It is during adolescence, for example, that people are first able to scrutinize their own thought processes and personality characteristics, to question the meaning of political structures and religious ideologies, to analyze the nature of feelings, such as love and hate, and to attempt an understanding of the significance of life itself.

Formal operations allow the user to be more planful in problem solving. Instead of relying on trial-and-error approaches to problems, the formal thinker sets up a variety of hypotheses, or "if–then" statements, ranks them in order of probability, and then tests them out systematically in sequence. This is known as **hypothetico-deductive reasoning,** and it allows the formal thinker, in contrast to the child who is using concrete operations, to generate a universe of alternatives when dealing with a problem. Thus, formal thought is possibility oriented, while concrete reasoning is focused on the real rather than the possible.

The possibility orientation of formal reasoning also allows the adolescent to go beyond the world as it exists and to speculate about a world that might be or that might have been but never was. Indeed, young adolescents often become so absorbed in the realm of possibility that they forget the realistic limitations on their dreams. Most adults can remember being lost in fantasies about what their futures held and thinking that it was possible for them to do or be anything they wanted. In time, of course, reality intervened, and the budding neurosurgeon acknowledged the fact that her career probably lay in other directions since she was failing all her science courses!

The ability to consider numerous life possibilities other than those that actually exist often leads the adolescent to become overly idealistic. Why can't the world be different, they ask; adults reply that someday they will realize that an outcome's being theoretically possible does not mean that it is likely to occur. The adolescent is often seen as a dreamer, a foolish idealist, or even a threat to the status quo if adults do not take well to having their values questioned.

Finally, a characteristic of adolescent thinking that is relevant to a discussion of their play activities is adolescent egocentrism. The two major forms of egocentrism

Formal thought allows an adolescent to engage in hypothetico-deductive reasoning, a skill that is necessary for experimentation with problems in the natural sciences.

during the teen-age years have been referred to as the imaginary audience and the personal fable, and both result from the adolescent's failure to distinguish his or her thought processes from those of other people (Elkind, 1981).

The **imaginary audience** is the belief that what is of interest to oneself is of interest to others as well, and adolescents are often shocked to discover that their passion for a particular cause is not shared by other people; in fact, most people may be totally indifferent to an issue that an adolescent may be ready to die for. The issues that are of greatest concern to most people, of course, are those directly related to themselves: concerns about one's body, one's clothing, one's personality. Adults are likely to realize, however, that their interest in themselves is probably not shared by others; adolescents often feel, on the other hand, that other people are as interested in them as they are in themselves. The result is a sense of being always on center stage; because of this feeling, some adolescents play shamelessly to their imaginary audiences, while others are overcome by an excess of self-consciousness.

Adolescent egocentrism appears also in the form of the **personal fable**, the belief that one is unique and that no one else could possibly share or understand one's thoughts and feelings. The often tragic element in the personal fable is that a teen-ager may take frightening risks, secure in the belief that nothing bad could happen to him or her. Bad things happen only to other people.

We shall see later that the types of play engaged in by adolescents in our society reflect the transition to formal operational thinking, with its emphasis on abstraction, explorations of the realm of possibility, and the early confusion in reconciling one's own thoughts and those of other people. Play also enhances adolescents' thinking processes by offering an opportunity for them to indulge their need for abstract conceptualization.

The Redefinition of Friendship:
A Need for Communication

Ask a nine-year-old child to tell you the name of her best friend and why the two of them are friends. She is likely to describe her friend in a somewhat concrete way. She will tell you, for example, what her friend looks like, how she dresses, where she lives, and various other bits of information about her friend's external characteristics. Ask a teen-ager the same question, and you are likely to hear a description filled with references to the other person's personality characteristics, such as attitudes, values, worries, interests, and beliefs (Berndt, 1982; Diaz & Berndt, 1982).

Developmental changes occur not only in the types of knowledge people have about their friends, but also in basic definitions of friendship, in the expectations one has of one's friends, and in the perceived obligations of friendship, with the general trend being a shift from external, action-oriented conceptions to those that are internal and communication oriented (Bigelow, 1977; Ryan & Smollar, 1978; Smollar & Youniss, 1982). As an illustration of this pattern, Volpe (1976) reported that a 10-year-old boy, asked how one develops a friendship, answered, "Friends are easy to make. All you have to do is go up to a guy, and ask him if he wants to play ball; then he's a friend. If he don't want to play ball, then he's not a friend, unless you decide to play something else" (in Smollar & Youniss, 1982, p. 283). In contrast, 12- and 13-year-olds usually referred to the importance of personal qualities rather than shared activities, and they stressed the importance of really getting to know somebody intimately, with particular emphasis on their interests, likes, and dislikes.

Adolescents, then, see a relationship as an opportunity to satisfy their need to communicate, and they seek levels of intimacy with their peers that children do not require. Mere playmates—people whose preferred recreational activities are the same as one's own—are no longer sufficient, and shared personality characteristics replace shared activities as the basis for friendship. It should not be surprising, therefore, that a major function of play during adolescence is to satisfy this need for intimacy. We shall see that although much of adolescent play is less structured than that of children and often consists of simply "hanging out," such play is no less important developmentally than the games of childhood.

The Growth of Self-Awareness: A Need for Identity

As children enter their teen-age years, a number of circumstances occur that cause them to reevaluate their definitions of self. The first is a series of major physical changes attributable to the onset of puberty. Erikson (1963) maintained that as a result of pubertal changes "all samenesses and continuities relied on earlier are more or less questioned again" (p. 261). In other words, because the transitions of early adolescence are so rapid and so dramatic, children must, in a sense, reacquaint themselves with their own bodies.

A second major change at adolescence is the change in social roles and expectations; the adolescent is no longer expected or allowed to behave like a child and now must make serious plans for the future as an adult. As but one example of these changed social expectations, frivolous or unrealistic career goals are no longer seen as appropriate by adults, and the adolescent is encouraged to think seriously about future work roles. If a 9-year-old announces that when he grows up he wants to be a cowboy, parents will smile approvingly; if a 14-year-old still plans to be a cowboy, parents may send the child to a career guidance counselor. But how are adolescents to know which careers are appropriate for them? They must ask themselves what they like to do and what they dislike, what they are good at, what needs they expect to have fulfilled in the workplace. Do they need status, power, control over others? Do they feel the need to be of service to other people? Do they prefer to work alone? All of those are questions about the self, and the adolescent must attempt to answer those questions and thus define the self before a satisfactory career choice can be made.

Finally, as mentioned earlier, adolescents can reason in abstract terms, and are now able to analyze themselves, to stand back and assess themselves as others see them. In fact, Erikson (1963) believes that although the major concern of children is with what *they* feel they are, the concern shifts during adolescence; teen-agers become concerned with what they appear to be in the eyes of other people.

Rock Music and the Adolescent
Search for Identity

As adolescents strive to understand themselves better, they often turn to the world of music, as listeners, participants in the spectacle of a rock concert, or in the case of the young man whose words appear below, as producers of music. As you read this passage, notice the ways in which the performance of music is used to enhance the musician's image of himself.

If the dances [of today] are feminine, or at least bisexual, today's rock is highly masculine. Terms used to describe rock music are synonymous with those words that are heavily loaded with masculine connotations: "hard rock," powerful, strong, "heavy," solid. The rock band, as the instrument which projects this masculine music, is thus in the position of symbolic phallus. Guitars have always been recognized as phallic symbols, but it should be realized that the rock band as a whole may be seen as the ultimate potent male, stimulating his audience, particularly female, to collective orgasm. This conceptualization is obviously helpful to the rock musician in establishing his sexual identity. Being in a rock band will not solve sexual problems, but it can give greater ego strength, greater support to the formation of a positive self-concept. This role also explains one of the reasons for [my] joining a rock group.

From *Experiencing youth: First-person accounts* (2nd ed.) by G. W. Goethals & D. S. Klos, 1976. Boston: Little, Brown.

Physical changes, changed social roles and expectations, and the intellectual changes related to formal reasoning all combine to challenge the adolescent to integrate past, present, and future in such a way as to establish a stable and consistent sense of self. This is the crisis of **identity**. A stable identity will not be established quickly, however, and it is during the period of adolescence that there is a slow trial-and-error process of identity resolution. Teen-agers test themselves in a variety of ways as they seek deeper levels of self-awareness. They try out different jobs, different classes at school, different relationships. Quite often it is through relationships that adolescents come to understand themselves. Erikson noted, for example, that when adolescents fall in love, it is not entirely a sexual matter, but may also be an attempt to understand the self by seeing the self reflected in the loving eyes of another person.

When we speak of adolescent play, we should try to think of it in the context of the adolescent's attempts at identity resolution. While Erikson did not directly address the issue of play during the teen-age years, his conceptualization of ego development explains much about the play of adolescence. Adolescent play, as we shall see, is both a reflection of and an effort to satisfy the adolescent's *need for identity*.

Play in Middle Childhood

If we combine the trends we have described as characteristic of the elementary school child (the development of an orderly and logical system of thought, the increasing peer orientation and the effort to gain acceptance into the "culture of childhood," and the need to demonstrate one's skills, talents, and abilities), what types of play might we expect to see among children in this age category? One would expect the play of grade school children to be more patterned, logical, and orderly than that of the preschooler. It would be more realistic, less dominated by the world of fantasy, more adultlike. It would also be more intensely social, and often group focused in its orientation. Finally, it would be designed to allow children to demonstrate their newly emerging intellectual, physical, and social skills and to receive the approval of their peers for doing so.

As we now examine some of the characteristics of the play of school-age children, it will become obvious that their play does, in fact, reflect the general trends in social, intellectual, and personality development.

A Decline in Symbolic Play

Make-believe play occurs in children of all ages, and it is not unusual to find a child of 9 or 10 pretending to be Superman, Robocop, or Princess Diana. However, beginning at about the age of five, there is a significant decline in the prevalence of such play. How can we explain the child's loss of interest in the world of make-believe? Piaget (1962) suggested three reasons for the decline. The first is that children no longer need make-believe to serve their ego needs; as they come to feel more powerful and less helpless in the real world, they are less likely to use play to compensate for perceived inadequacies. Second, symbolic play naturally evolves into games that have rules whenever more than one player is involved. And finally, as children develop, they make greater and greater efforts to adapt to reality, rather than distorting reality, as in make-believe play.

Play and the Acquisition of Skills

The young elementary school child takes great pride in developing and refining a variety of motor and intellectual skills that, on the one hand, enhance the child's sense of industry and, on the other, are likely to promote acceptance by the peer group. Whether by skateboarding, shooting baskets, roller-skating, wrestling, jumping rope, performing stunts on a bicycle, throwing a Frisbee, or climbing a tree, each generation of children inherits or invents a wide assortment of motor activities that allow them to show off in front of peers and adults and establish their positions within the peer group.

Skills can be demonstrated intellectually as well, and elementary school children will take great satisfaction in demonstrating how well they can play a game of cards, read a book all by themselves, tell a joke, guess the answer to a riddle or ask one that no one else is able to guess, or negotiate their way through a tongue-twister. It appears sometimes that the surest way to encourage a grade-schooler to try something is to offer the challenge "I'll bet you can't _____."

To illustrate the multiple values of skill-oriented play activities, consider the case of eight-year-old Peter, who for several months had begged his parents to buy him a skateboard. Peter's parents had little understanding of their son's fascination with this toy until they had finally bought him one and began to realize its many functions. In the first place, Peter seemed to derive great satisfaction from practicing a variety of tricks on his skateboard, and he beamed with pride when he could show his parents, almost on a daily basis, how accomplished he had become. In addition, the possession of a skateboard gave Peter access to a new social group composed, naturally, of other children who also owned skateboards. Although his parents weren't aware of it, Peter had been somewhat of an outsider before, and now he had become a member of the "inner circle" of his second-grade class. Finally, when Peter and his friends played with their skateboards, they often made up elaborate games.

Sometimes the games of Peter and his friends involved the establishment of intricate rules and a high degree of competition (we shall have more to say about such games-with-rules). Sometimes they were noncompetitive. In either case, they always seemed to involve considerable stretches of the imagination, and Peter's parents had to admit that the acquisition of a skateboard had resulted in benefits for their son that they had not anticipated. At least that is how they felt until Peter began to argue that now he needed the baggy T-shirts and "jammer" shorts that all the other skateboarders were wearing!

The Child as Collector

Maybe it is because grade school children think in a more logical, orderly manner than they did when younger. Maybe it is because they are able to see the world in terms of logical classes and categories. Whatever the reason, children in elementary school often acquire a genuine passion for collecting (Williams & Stith, 1980). What do they collect? Almost anything that interests them: bubble gum cards, comic books, stickers, stamps, rocks, coins, Barbie dolls, leaves, or any of the assorted trinkets that may be found in Happy Meal boxes at fast-food restaurants. Collected materials may be used in play, as when collectors read their comic books or play with their dolls. Often, however, the play *is* the collecting itself, and the objects are not used at all, but are only taken out occasionally to be looked at.

Collections of any sort can be of great significance to the child's social, intellectual, and personality development. One social value is that they may enhance the child's popularity within the peer group if the collection is seen by peers as being of interest. For example, a large collection of bubble gum cards, particularly if it contains rare cards, may add to the status of the fortunate collector; on the other hand, a collection of bottle caps that the peer group has no interest in probably will not do so.

Another social value of collecting is that collectors often share or trade their possessions. Lending and borrowing can teach a child to be responsible and to respect the property of other people. Trading can teach negotiation skills as well as concepts of equivalence and fairness.

The intellectual value of collecting is that children can learn a good deal about the materials in their collections and may even need a certain amount of knowledge even to begin their collections. Through the experience of collecting, one child can gain a wealth of information about the players in the Natonal Football League, while another becomes the family expert on rock formations, and a third learns about world geography by assembling a collection of stamps from various countries.

Children who collect may also refine their counting skills. They may acquire more mature concepts of logical classification, as when they realize that their collectibles can be sorted into groups and subgroups in a variety of different dimensions. Finally, the experience of collecting often requires the collector to attend to the sometimes very minor distinguishing features of the objects within the collection; there is often little point in having two identical items in the collection, and so collectors must attend closely to notice exactly how a new rock or stamp or coin differs from the ones they already have.

Finally, a collection is an accomplishment, and as the collection enlarges, so does the magnitude of the accomplishment. The experience of collecting can, therefore, boost children's self-esteem by providing them with the sense of industry that is so important during the elementary school years.

Play Rituals

"If you step on a crack, you'll break your mother's back." "One potato, two potato, three potato, four . . ." "You can't hit a kid with glasses on." Such rhymes, counting rituals, and superstitions are familiar to everyone, regardless of where in the United States or even what part of the world one is from. They are an integral part of what is often regarded as the culture of childhood.

Children's play during the elementary school years is replete with such chants and rituals, and they reflect both the orderliness of children's thinking and the extent to which ritual is involved in the socialization process. The point is that the children usually take them very seriously. When children are told to come into the house and one calls out, "The last one in is a rotten egg," there begins a competition to avoid being last that may seem silly to adults but is certainly meaningful to the children involved. Many a parent has tried unsuccessfully to allay the genuine anguish of the child who ends up being the "rotten egg"!

Similarly, counting rules like "One potato, two potato" or "Eeny meeny miny mo" are not to be taken lightly; if a child attempts to cheat or refuses to accept the role determined by the count, that child will be harshly criticized by peers. Learning the rituals puts a child "in the know"; learning to abide by them teaches a child how to obey rules and follow a moral order.

Games-with-Rules

We noted earlier that as children become increasingly logical, they become increasingly likely to see the world as a logical and orderly place that is governed by a system of rules. This orderliness of thought finds its way into children's play in the form of what Piaget (1962) described as the major play activity of the civilized being, the game-with-rules.

Games-with-rules may be sensorimotor in nature, as in the case of marble or ball games, tag, hide-and-seek, hopscotch, blindman's buff, or jacks. They may also be of an intellectual variety, such as checkers, cards, or Monopoly and other board games. Whether they be sensorimotor or intellectual, however, they contain two essential characteristics. First, they involve competition between two or more players. Second, they are governed by a set of regulations agreed to *in advance* by all the players that may not be changed midgame unless the players have previously determined that modifications will be acceptable. The rules themselves may be handed down by code, as in a game of chess, or may exist in the form of a temporary agreement between players. In other words, children may either learn the rules from their older peers or establish their own rules at the outset of a particular game.

Piaget (1962) maintained that games-with-rules require (1) the ability to engage in rule-dominated forms of thinking and (2) the presence of two or more potential players. A prelogical child will not engage in such games, nor will an older child who is playing alone, for that matter. Consider the example of the play activities of a three-year-old girl observed by Piaget when she was offered some marbles. She did not engage in a rule game, but instead either initiated sensorimotor play with the marbles (e.g., by throwing them) or incorporated them into symbolic play: She pretended they were eggs in a bird's nest!

As was indicated earlier, the rules found in the games of older children may be either handed down intact from one generation to another or spontaneous. It was the spontaneous rules that were of the greatest interest to Piaget, because these are forged out of the intense socialization process that occurs during the elementary school years. The establishment of and adherence to a set of rules requires sensitivity to the viewpoints of other people, mutual understanding, willingness to delay gratification, and a high degree of cooperation. In a sense, mature socialization requires the adherence to a set of implicit or explicit rules for social interaction, although on the surface at least, adults who play by the social rules are not engaged in a competitive activity.

Were there no rules, then, in the cooperative make-believe play of preschool children? Indeed there were, although the rules of make-believe are quite different from those in the games of older children. The purpose of rules in symbolic play is to assign roles and sustain the make-believe plan of action. For example, children will often engage in complex negotiations about designated roles (e.g., "You can be the bus driver next time if you will be a passenger this time"), and such negotiations naturally involve a measure of give-and-take. However, the roles and themes of make-believe play may change continually, and thus the rules in symbolic play have none of the rigidity of the more mature games-with-rules. As we have already indicated, in genuine games-with-rules the rules are decided upon in advance, and changes may not be made during the course of the action unless all the players decide at the outset that such changes are allowable (Rubin, Fein, & Vandenberg, 1983).

Finally, we should point out that games-with-rules are seen by many psychologists as falling outside the definition of play (Garvey, 1977; Rubin, Fein, & Vandenberg, 1983). Play, it will be remembered from the opening chapter, is an activity engaged in for its own sake; it contains no external goals. Games-with-rules, however, involve competition and thus have an external goal: the goal of winning.

Why, then, should we consider game-with-rules as a topic in a book about children's play? It is because, the competitive element notwithstanding, much of the activity that occurs during a game-with-rules really *is* play, particularly for the young grade school child. A group of first- and second-graders playing soccer certainly realize that their purpose on the field is to win and not to lose, but they are also able to enjoy the activity simply as an end in itself; the game offers them a chance to run around and interact with friends, and in doing so they may even lose sight of their intended purpose. Unfortunately it seems that many of their overzealous parents and coaches cannot do as much.

Organized Sports

While games-with-rules can take many forms, a form that is increasingly in evidence throughout the childhood years is the highly organized sports activity. Organized sports for children have, in fact, increased in popularity over the past 15 years (Collins, 1984).

More than eight million U.S. children between the ages of 6 and 16 participate in such activities every year, with an average of three to four hours of sports involvement every week. For a typical first-grader, that is four times longer than is spent in doing homework! Looking at it in another way, involvement in sports takes up approximately 20 percent of the child's overall play time between the ages of 6 and 8, 25 percent between the ages of 8 and 10, and fully 40 percent of the time that 11- and 12-year-olds devote to play (Collins, 1984).

What are the benefits of sports participation during childhood? Presumably one would expect to discover benefits in three areas: in overall physical fitness, in self-esteem, and in the ability to get along with others and work cooperatively within a group.

Sports and Physical Fitness

Adults in the United States today are urged continually to incorporate exercise into their daily lives in order to reduce the likelihood of cardiovascular disease; in fact, the cardiovascular benefits of regular exercise have been repeatedly demonstrated in the adult population (Dawber, 1980; Glomset, 1980; Shonkoff, 1984). Are there short-range and long-range physical benefits for children who participate in sports? Unfortunately there are no simple answers to that question.

In the short term, common sense would indicate that athletic participation could improve the cardiovascular fitness of children as it does for adults. Such common sense is not supported by the research, however. Children are indeed more physically active than adults, since participation in physical fitness activities declines with age, and children also display higher levels of physical fitness. It has not been established, however, that age differences in activity levels actually *cause* age differences in health; children may be healthier than adults only because of genetically determined developmental changes in the physiological well-being of the human organism.

If we cannot learn about the cardiovascular benefits of sports involvement by making age comparisons, perhaps we can do so by examining activity and fitness differences within a population of children. Might there be differences in the fitness levels of children who are extremely active in sports (e.g., competitive swimmers) and those who are less active? In fact, such differences have been established, but again, the existence of a relationship tells us little about specific causal factors. It *may* be that intensive sports involvement causes children to be more physically fit than their peers, but it may also be the case that children who are initially more physically fit are the ones who seek out competitive sports activities.

Turning to the question of long-range physical benefits, it has never been demonstrated that sports involvement during childhood has any impact on the likelihood of cardiovascular disease later in life (Shonkoff, 1984).

In summary, an examination of the research leaves one wondering what physical benefits, if any, are to be gained from participation in sports during childhood. Perhaps there are benefits that we have not discussed. The general consensus among researchers is that there is indeed a significant long-range physical benefit to athletic participation during childhood: Children who learn to enjoy sports may carry with them into adult life a positive attitude toward such activities and may continue to incorporate physical exercise into their patterns of life.

Sports and Self-Esteem

Parents, teachers, and coaches often assert that encouraging children to participate in sports will positively affect their self-concepts. "Sports build confidence," they say. But is this really true? Does participation in sports help children to feel better about themselves? To answer that question, we must first refer to a growing body of opinion among psychologists that "self" is not a global concept at all, that children acquire images of themselves in a variety of different capacities. That is, they may develop a *self-schema* for their physical selves, their social selves, their intellectual selves, and so forth. These self-schemas, which typically begin to differentiate during the elementary school years, focus on the domains that are of lasting relevance, investment, and concern (Markus & Nurius, 1984). To discuss the effects of sports participation on the self, therefore, we need to specify which aspect of the self we are referring to.

A number of researchers in the past 15 years have discovered in children a relationship between successful athletic participation and a positive image of the self-as-athlete (Anshel, Muller, & Owens, 1986; Dowell, Badgett, & Landis, 1976; Guyot, Fairchild, & Hill, 1981; Magill & Ash, 1979; Smith, 1986), but we must be cautious in interpreting this not unexpected finding. In the first place, as is true of all correlational studies, the existence of a relationship says little or nothing about the direction of cause-and-effect: Does participation in sports cause children to feel better about their physical selves, or are the children who already have a positive physical self-image the most likely to go out for sports? Furthermore, there are no consistent indications that being a successful athlete improves a child's overall self-concept or that athletic success improves children's opinions of themselves from an intellectual or a social standpoint.

It should be mentioned also that athletic success will be of little consequence to a child who lacks a self-schema that pertains to athletics. In other words, if there is no investment in the athletic component of the self, then success or failure on the playing fields will have no effect on a person's self-image. Perhaps this explains why successful sports experience is related more clearly to the self-concept of a boy than to that of the average girl; Girls are less likely than boys to define themselves in terms of athletic prowess (Guyot, Fairchild, & Hill, 1981).

Finally, it is extremely unlikely that sports participation will enhance a self-image of any sort if the game leaves a child feeling frustrated and unsuccessful. A sensitive adult could minimize the possibility that children in sports will feel like losers by taking a number of steps. First, the child in sports should be taught the skills that are necessary to play the game. This point is rather obvious, but it is surprising how often skill training is overlooked and children are told instead that the way to learn is simply by playing. Second, the child should learn that winning is not all-important, that the goal of athletic participation is to play as well as you can. Third, the child should be exposed to a variety of sports, both of an individual and a team variety, so that if one sport is difficult or otherwise unappealing, others are available. Fourth, the child should not be forced to play if he or she chooses not to. Forced participation can make what should be a playful experience into a chore and can foster negative attitudes toward sports in general. Finally, adults must remember that the game belongs to the children and that it should not be contaminated by any hidden agenda the adults may have. Children should not have to prove their worth to parents or coaches, either in the sports arena or anywhere else!

Do Sports Build Character?
It is often said that involvement in sports builds character, in that children learn how to play fair, act responsibly, follow rules, and function as team players—all characteristics that might serve a child well in many other areas of life. Is it true that a child's "moral fiber" is built up by his or her sports participation? Apparently it is not!

Psychologists Brenda Bredemeier and David Shields have done extensive research on the relationship of sports participation to moral development, and their findings would probably disappoint those who argue that sports build character.

Bredemeier and Shields (1985) examined the moral reasoning skills of 120 high school and college students, some athletes and some nonathletes, asking them questions about moral situations related to and unrelated to the world of sports. As an example of a sports-related dilemma, students were told about Tom, a football player whose coach tells him to injure an opposing player deliberately in order to win the game. What should Tom do? A moral dilemma unrelated to sports included a question about whether a person should keep a promise to deliver a sum of money to a rich man or spend the money instead to help feed his or her own hungry relatives.

The researchers discovered that adolescent and young adult athletes and nonathletes alike believed that a different set of moral principles applied to sports than applied to everyday life situations. Specifically they expressed the view that a lower moral code may be followed in a sporting event. One high school girl commented that in sports it is often difficult to tell right from wrong, and so it is necessary to use "game sense." A male college basketball player noted that you can do what you want in sports because you are free to think only of yourself, while in everyday life you must be attentive to the feelings of other people. The general consensus seemed to be that in real life one should try to be considerate, while in sports, because of the emphasis on winning, one need not treat opposing players as they would like to be treated themselves.

It is important to recognize that Bredemeier and Shields did not suggest that playing in organized sports actually *causes* a player to function at a lower moral level; perhaps it is the case that people with a less well-developed moral sense are more easily attracted to highly aggressive sports. Many successful athletes, however, are morally mature people who apparently try to coordinate their everyday moral principles with their sports behaviors (Bredemeier & Shields, 1985). Nevertheless, this study and a number of others (Bredemeier & Shields, 1986; Bredemeier, Shields, Weiss, & Cooper, 1986; Romance, 1984) clearly indicate a relationship between interest in and/or participation in aggressive sports and level of moral reasoning—in children, adolescents, and adults. People who have the greatest interest in highly aggressive contact sports, or have participated in them for the longest amounts of time, tend to score lower on tests of moral reasoning; interestingly enough, athletes who *do* earn high moral reasoning scores are the least willing to display hostile aggression during a game.

In summary, it would be difficult to make the case that participation in sports, at least in those that involve high levels of aggression and physical contact, improves the moral character of a child. As long as anyone sees deliberate injury to another person as conceivable under *any* circumstances, involvement in high-contact sports may be counterproductive to the moral development of the grade school child (Bredemeier, Shields, Weiss, & Cooper, 1986).

It is difficult also to argue that sports involvement will build character in other ways. An analysis of personality characteristics of adult athletes does reveal a number of positive features (a high need to achieve, a tendency to set high goals for oneself and others, an organized approach to life, and a high degree of psychological endurance and self-control); on the other hand, adult athletes are likely to suffer from depression, hyperanxiety, and an exaggerated reaction to failure (Ogilvie & Tutko, 1971).

Parents, teachers, and coaches may encourage children to participate in sports for many reasons (for the health benefits, for the opportunity to socialize, for the sheer pleasure that is found in the activity), but if the reason for involvement is to build the child's character, adults may want to rethink their motives.

Adolescent Play

As children progress through the later years of childhood, there is a gradual decrease in the actual number of *different* play activities in a given week. Larger amounts of time are spent on the preferred forms of play as children's interests tend to stabilize.

In addition, there is a decrease in games-with-rules (Damon, 1983) and an increase in activities that are solitary in nature, including reading and television watching. The movement toward solitary forms of play does not indicate, however, that children are losing interest in their peers. Instead it is thought to be a reflection of a trend that will reach its culmination during the years of adolescence: an increasing understanding of the self and one's interests and abilities combined with an increasingly long attention span.

From Doing to Being

By the age of 12 and into the adolescent years the most popular recreational activities include many that reflect a need for self-awareness, heterosexual socialization, and intimate communication. For example, adolescents like to attend movies, watch television, read, go to dances and parties, and listen to music (or watch music videos). They also like just to "hang around" with friends, and much adolescent play is of this unstructured variety. Consistent with the transition from a concrete and action-oriented view of friendship to one that involves a greater degree of abstract conceptualization, socialization is defined less as *doing* something with friends and more as simply *being* together.

At the Movies

As an illustration of the extent to which the choice of play activities reflects the player's developmental needs, consider the experience for the adolescent of attending a movie. In the first place, moviegoing often provides an opportunity for heterosexual interaction. It is still, even in the 1990s, a relatively inexpensive date. It is also one that is stress reducing for a young adolescent who has difficulty making conversation with a member of the opposite sex; one need not talk during a movie, and a stimulating film might provide a wealth of material for conversation afterwards. Even if the adolescent is not on a date, movies provide socialization opportunities; teen-agers often attend movies in mixed groups, meet friends at the theater, or sit near and attempt to make an impression on members of the opposite sex.

A movie may also allow adolescents to understand themselves better by testing out their own emotions—discovering what makes them laugh, what saddens them, what fills them with terror. Perhaps the popularity of the "slasher" genre of films is not an indication of adolescent indifference to human suffering, as adults fear, but is an indication of adolescents' need to test their limits. Sitting through *A Nightmare on Elm Street* is admittedly a safe risk, but it may be for many U.S. adolescents a rare opportunity to test themselves in a world that is ordinarily risk free.

Adolescents also come to a greater understanding of themselves by identifying with the characters whose lives they are observing in a film. They often find themselves wondering, "What would I do in that situation? What would I have said? How would I react?" The answers may not be obvious, of course, but a degree of self-awareness can be attained simply by pondering the question. And, of course, an adolescent may be inspired by the life of a character in a movie or by that of the actor or actress who plays the role. Many adults report that they made important decisions about establishing their life direction after seeing an inspiring film or play or reading a book that captured their imagination.

Finally, the intellectual appeal of an interesting film is that it allows the viewer the opportunity to see the world not as it is, but as it might be or as it might have been. As mentioned earlier in the chapter, adolescents are likely to engage in a considerable amount of speculation about a hypothetical world. In everyday life, it is often difficult to do this because one must live in the real world even as one fantasizes about the imaginary one, and adolescents are often accused of being dreamers whose feet are 10 feet off the ground. In a darkened theater, however, the moviegoer may give free rein to his or her idealistic imagination and is allowed, even encouraged, to engage in the type of hypothetical, contrary-to-fact reasoning that is so typical of the adolescent.

Other Than Movies

We chose moviegoing as an illustration of the many needs that adolescent play fulfills: the need for communication, the need for identity, the need for abstract conceptualization. Other play activities serve the same functions, of course. Like a film, a television program, novel, or play can provide opportunities for self-testing, for identification with characters or life-styles, or for exploring the limits of hypothetical thinking. Hanging around with friends offers adolescents an opportunity to test and refine their social skills; after all, how does a person learn how to flirt, to notice the subtle nonverbal cues displayed by others, or to make small talk if not by trial-and-error? Social interaction also helps teen-agers understand themselves by seeing their own reflections in their peers' reactions to them or, even more directly, by actually hearing the assessments, flattering or painful, that are made by other people. Talking to close friends is perhaps the perfect antidote to adolescent egocentrism as teen-agers discover that they are not really so different from others and that their peers have also experienced many of even their most personal thoughts and feelings. Such a realization can bring disillusionment as adolescents come to realize that they are not so special after all, but it can also bring considerable relief in knowing that they are not so strange or unusual either.

Summary

There are three general characteristics that capture the essence of the period of middle childhood, corresponding to trends in the areas of intellectual, social, and personality development. From an intellectual standpoint, the major development is that children's thinking becomes more orderly, structured, and logical. As a result, their play will reflect a developing need for order. The major social change in middle childhood is that the peer group provides support that formerly was offered only within the family. Acceptance by one's peers is of great importance to children in this age group, and their play reflects a sometimes overwhelming need to belong. Finally, in the realm of personality development, a major challenge to the emerging self-concepts of school-age children is to demonstrate to themselves and others that they have talents, skills, and abilities that they can be proud of. In their play, there is reflected this need for industry.

Adolescence is also characterized by major transitions in the areas of intellectual, social, and personality development. In terms of intellectual development the adolescent is experiencing a transition from the concrete form of reasoning that typifies the middle childhood years to a reasoning that is abstract and hypothetical. The intellectual need of the adolescent is a need for abstract conceptualization. In social terms the adolescent needs more than simply to belong within the peer group: Now there is a need to single out particular individuals with whom one can have an intimate relationship; the overwhelming need is for communication. Finally, the adolescent is engaged in a struggle to create a stable and permanent sense of self, and play often forms the context within which this need for identity can be met.

Middle childhood brings with it a decline in make-believe play, perhaps because (1) children no longer need make-believe to serve their ego needs, (2) symbolic play naturally evolves into games that have rules, and (3) as children develop, they make greater efforts to adapt to reality, rather than distorting reality as in make-believe play.

Young elementary school children take pride in a variety of motor and intellectual skills, which both enhance their sense of industry and are likely to promote acceptance by the peer group. Collecting becomes a passion for many children of this age and allows them to gain a sense of accomplishment, as well as being an educational pastime. The organization of thought at this age leads to rule-oriented play, such as solitary rituals and games-with-rules, including organized sports.

Organized sports for children can be highly enjoyable, promote a sense of accomplishment, and provide an opportunity for social acceptance. Nevertheless, there is little evidence in support of the beliefs that sports are necessary for physical fitness, participation in sports will automatically enhance a child's self-esteem, or sports build moral character in any meaningful sense.

By the age of 12—and into the adolescent years—the most popular recreational activities include many that reflect a need for self-awareness, heterosexual socialization, and intimate communication. For example, adolescents like to attend movies, watch television, read, go to dances and parties, and listen to music or watch music videos. They also like simply to "hang around" with friends, and much adolescent play is of this unstructured variety.

Key Terms

Concrete Operations

Form Operations

Games-with-Rules

Graphic Collections

Hypothetico-Deductive Reasoning

Identity

Imaginary Audience

Industry

Personal Fable

CHAPTER SIX

Gender Differences in Play

When he was three, Jonathan found in the attic a doll that his mother had kept since her own early childhood. It was an old-fashioned rubber doll; it didn't walk or talk, it didn't roller skate, nor did it acquire a "tan" from exposure to the sun; it didn't grow hair, and in fact, it had no hair at all! It didn't eat or wet or develop diaper rash. Its wardrobe was decidedly unfashionable—a torn yellow dress that, like the doll itself, was more than two decades old.

Jonathan enjoyed playing with the doll but was somewhat confused by its appearance. He claimed it was a "boy" doll and therefore should not be clad in a dress. No, he was told, the doll is a little girl. He insisted, however, that it was a boy and, when asked why he was so certain, remarked that it had "boy hair." What did that mean? "Boy hair goes this way," he said, waving his hand back and forth in the air, "and girl hair goes this way," turning his hand in circles. When his mother finally succeeded in convincing him that the doll was intended to be a baby girl and that it was the dress and not the hair that indicated its gender, Jonathan reacted by saying that he didn't want to play with it any more!

Where did Jonathan get his ideas about the physical characteristics of gender? From his parents? His peers? From television? More importantly, why did he lose interest in the doll when he finally came to accept it as a girl? He wouldn't say. Perhaps he actually didn't know.

We begin this chapter with a discussion of the two major theoretical views on how the concept of gender is acquired. Then the research on gender differences in children's play will be discussed, and this has been concentrated in four areas: (1) toy selection, (2) fantasy play, (3) rough-and-tumble play, and (4) games-with-rules.

The Concept of Gender

No one knows for certain why even the youngest of children in the United States make clear distinctions among play materials and activities suitable for girls and those appropriate for boys. However, there are two major theoretical interpretations of gender typing. The viewpoint of *learning theory* is that children learn by the mechanisms of imitation and reinforcement to behave in "gender-appropriate" ways, such as by playing with certain toys and not with others. The young child, who may have no understanding of gender at all, will shape his or her behaviors in response to environmental experiences.

The process of imitation is illustrated by a two-year-old who acquires his preference for rough-and-tumble play simply by watching the activities of older boys and using them as models. Direct reinforcement occurs when a boy is praised for showing interest in owning a football, and a girl for wanting a baby doll. Conversely, a boy who chooses to play with a tea set may be discouraged and even ridiculed by parents and peers; a girl who enjoys playing with trucks and tanks may quickly sense the disapproval of those around her and change her toy preferences accordingly.

The basic premise of the *cognitive-developmental theory* is that children only gradually develop an awareness of the concept of gender and that they engage in gender-appropriate activities because such activities are consistent with their emerging gender concept. Illustrating this point of view is the work of Kohlberg (1966), who maintained that children pass through three developmental stages in their understanding of gender. In the stage of **gender identity,** the preschool child recognizes that males and females are different on the basis of their physical characteristics. **Gender stability** is the realization that gender will always remain the same and that boys and girls will grow up to become either men or women. Finally, at about the age of six or seven, **gender constancy** appears, the recognition that gender always remains the same regardless of surface physical changes in appearance.

Once they have begun to understand the concept of gender, children can then make an effort—often a conscious and deliberate one—to imitate the characteristics of their prescribed role. Engaging in gender-appropriate behaviors, such as playing with supposedly appropriate toys, becomes satisfying and rewarding because it affirms the correctness of the child's schema of categorization. As Kohlberg (1966) noted, the child concludes: "I am a boy (or girl), and therefore I want to do boy (or girl) things; therefore, the opportunity to do boy (or girl) things is rewarding" (p. 89). Such a statement is almost a reverse of the learning perspective, in which a child's conclusion might be that "I do boy (or girl) things, and therefore I am a boy (or girl)."

Toy Selection

The sensitivity of three-year-old Jonathan, whose story opened this chapter, to the subtleties of gender in his mother's doll was not unusual. In fact, children typically display an awareness of gender differences—and a preference for gender-typed toys—at some time between the ages of two and three. And just as Jonathan did, three-years-olds will go so far as to avoid playing with what they perceive as opposite-sex toys, even when no other toys are available to them! Some children even show preferences for gender-appropriate toys as early as 18–24 months of age (Caldera, Huston, & O'Brien, 1989; Fagot, 1978; Huston, 1983; O'Brien & Huston, 1985; Perry, White, & Perry, 1984), and in one study (Roopnarine, 1986) it was found that infant girls preferred dolls over other playthings at 10 months of age, although boys of the same age showed no such preference!

The Gender Appropriateness of Toys
What exactly are "boy" toys and "girl" toys? In this chapter there will be frequent reference to *gender-appropriate toys* and *gender-inappropriate toys,* so it is important to recognize how we define these terms. The assignment of toys to a particular gender category is usually done in response to (1) actual play preferences of children and/or (2) ratings of gender appropriateness made by adults. In other words, there is nothing inherently masculine or feminine about any particular plaything. A toy is seen as gender appropriate if children of one sex typically choose to play with it while children of the other sex do not or if adults are in general agreement that it is more suitable for children of one sex than for those of the other. The application of these criteria results in a classification of toys according to gender, as illustrated in Table 6.1.

The Influence of Culture on Toy Selection
As will be indicated later on, biological factors are often suggested as influences on the *ways* in which children play and on the *games* they choose to engage in. It would be

TABLE 6.1   Toys Designated as Gender Appropriate Based on
Actual Play Preferences of Children or on
Independent Ratings by Adults

Boy Toys	Girl Toys
Road racing sets	Fashion dolls
Trains	Fashion doll accessories
Toy guns and gun sets	Mother and baby dolls
Sports-oriented games	Doll carriages and strollers
Blocks	Doll houses
Cars and trucks	Housekeeping/cooking toys
Electronic toys	Beauty kits
Construction toys	Doll furniture
Model kits	Stuffed dolls
Sports equipment	Feminine clothing
Workbenches and tools	Beads
Walkie-talkies	Crayons, art materials

The data are from "Home Environments and Toy Preferences of Extremely Precocious Students" by C. P. Benbow, 1986. Paper presented at the meeting of the American Educational Research Association, San Francisco. "Behaviorally Based Masculine and Feminine Activity— Reference Scales for Preschoolers: Correlates with Other Classroom Behaviors and Cognitive Tests" by J. M. Connor and L. A. Serbin, 1977. *Child Development, 48,* pp. 1411–1416. "Sex-typed toy choices: What do they signify?" by N. Eiserberg. In *Social and Cognitive Skills: Sex Roles and Children's Play* (pp. 45–70) edited by M. B. Liss, 1983. New York: Academic Press. "Young Children's Use of Toys in Home Environments" by M. Giddings and C. F. Halverson, 1981. *Family Relations, 30,* 69–74. "Sex Stereotyping in Children's Toy Advertisements" by L. A. Schwartz and W. T. Markham, 1985. *Sex Roles, 12,* pp. 157–170. "Toys, Spatial Ability, and Science and Mathematics Achievement: Are They Related?" by D. M. Tracy, 1987. *Sex Roles, 17,* pp. 115–138.

difficult, however, to implicate biological factors in gender differences in toy selection unless it were argued that toys are selected for children in reaction to their biological predispositions. The more widely accepted explanations of male–female differences in toy preference center on cultural factors and particularly on the socializing influences of adults, peers, and the mass media.

Adult Interaction with Gender-Labeled Infants
To what extent are adult interactions with an infant determined by the child's gender? Ordinarily it would be extremely difficult to answer this question, because gender is an inseparable component of the self, and adults typically *know* whether the child they are cuddling or bouncing on their knee is a boy or a girl. What might happen, however, if the adults' knowledge about the child's gender was based solely on a designated label and the same baby were identified as a boy to some adults and as a girl to others? Would adults respond differently to the same child based on their *perceptions* of its maleness

or femaleness? Would they handle the baby differently? Would they use different words to describe its behaviors? Would they offer it different types of toys? Apparently the answer to all three questions is yes.

In a variety of different studies, adult strangers have been introduced to the identical baby labeled either as a boy or as a girl, depending on the experimental condition. Both gender-typed and neutral toys were made available, but the adults were not told how they should be used. The typical finding was that adults of both sexes more often offered supposedly female toys, such as dolls, to what they believed were baby girls; when the same baby was believed to be a boy, conventionally male toys, such as footballs and hammers, were more likely to be offered, although the effect with the presumed male babies was less consistently observed (Etaugh, 1983; Huston, 1983; Sidorowicz & Lunney, 1980; Smith & Lloyd, 1978; Will, Self, & Datan, 1976).

Implications of the findings from research on adult interaction with infants presumed to be male or female are far-reaching. It is obvious that the children were not providing specific behavioral cues about toy preferences, since the identical baby was thought of as either male or female depending on the introduction provided by the experimenter. Gender-related behavior, like beauty, seems to be in the eye of the beholder. Adults in the Will, Self, and Datan (1976) study, for example, remarked that Baby "Beth" was obviously a girl because her features were so soft and sweet, while Baby "Adam" was definitely a boy because his features were so strong and his body so muscular, but in fact, "Beth" and "Adam" were the same baby!

The Parent's Role in Gender Typing

Do parents, like the adult strangers in the studies mentioned above, choose gender-typed toys for their very young children? Most researchers find that they do. Psychologist Nancy Eisenberg and her associates (1985) asked parents to let them observe their normal patterns of interactions in the home with their one- and two-year-old children. Two 20- to 25-minute interaction sessions were videotaped, with the parent and child in a room with some of the child's own toys that the parent had selected for use in the observations. It was found that parents picked gender-typed toys for their children, particularly when the children were male.

Differences were not observed by Eisenberg et al. (1985) in parents' reactions to their children's play with gender-appropriate and gender-inappropriate toys. That is, the parents did not seem actively to reinforce their children for playing with gender-appropriate toys or to discourage them for playing with those that were inappropriate. It should be pointed out, however, that differential reactions by parents to young children's toy selections has been observed in other studies (Caldera, Huston, & O'Brien, 1989; Langlois & Downs, 1980; Snow, Jacklin, & Maccoby, 1983). For example, Caldera, Huston, and O'Brien (1989) noticed subtle parental reactions to the gender appropriateness of toys. While they didn't openly encourage the use of one type of toy or another, parents appeared to be more excited when they discovered that gender-appropriate toys were available, and they were more likely to become involved in their children's play.

In the Langlois and Downs (1980) study, parental influences on their children's play with sex-appropriate and sex-inappropriate toys were not quite so subtle. Children aged three to five years were brought into a room and given either "girl" toys (a dollhouse with furniture, pots and pans, female clothing) or "boy" toys (toy soldiers, a gas station with cars, cowboy gear). Some children were given gender-appropriate toys while others were not, and as the children played, either their mother, their father, or a same-sex friend entered the room. The researchers were interested in the visitors' reactions to children's play with gender-appropriate and -inappropriate materials.

It was found that when boys were playing with conventionally masculine toys, they were ignored by their peers, received mild approval from their mothers, and were strongly encouraged and rewarded by their fathers. When boys played with conventionally feminine toys, however, they were encouraged by their mothers but strongly discouraged both by fathers and by peers, who openly made fun of them, interfered with their play, or encouraged them to find other toys to play with.

By way of contrast, mothers, fathers, and same-sex peers all expressed their approval of girls' playing with gender-appropriate toys, and all expressed disapproval of girls' play with "boy" toys. Thus it appeared that girls were treated more consistently than boys, that, in general, fathers and peers responded more strongly than mothers, and that of all the visitors to the playroom, fathers seemed to exert the greatest amount of influence on the preschoolers (Langlois & Downs, 1980).

The Contents of Children's Rooms

One of the most frequently cited studies of the toys made available to young children is an analysis by psychologists Harriet Rheingold and Kaye Cook (1975) of the contents of children's bedrooms. The researchers obtained permission to enter the homes of 96 children ranging in age from 12 to 72 months, all of whom slept in their own rooms, and to take inventory of the toys and furnishings that the rooms contained. Thirteen classes of categories were identified, listed alphabetically in Table 6.2.

The researchers discovered that the contents of a child's room depended to some extent on the child's age. The average one-year-old had 28 different toys; this number increased to 96 by the time the child approached the age of six, a figure that may seem high to a person without children but would probably not surprise a parent who constantly fights the losing battle of keeping a preschooler's room tidy. The number of animal furnishings decreased with age, as did the number of floral furnishings. Increasing age brought increases in the number of books and dolls and in the size of the child's supply of educational and art materials.

Perhaps the most striking results of the Rheingold and Cook (1975) study, however, were those pertaining to gender differences in bedroom contents. Boys' rooms contained more animal furnishings, more educational/art materials, more spatiotemporal toys, more sports equipment, more toy animals, and more vehicles. The only content categories in girls' rooms that surpassed those found in boys' were dolls, floral furnishings, and ruffles. Finally, no gender differences were found in the number of books, musical objects, and stuffed animals or in the amount of furniture.

Looking not at the specific toys themselves, but at general patterns of gender differences, we see a most revealing contrast. First, although neither sex had more actual toys than the other, boys had a larger *variety* of toys; the range of toys for girls was considerably more restricted. Second, boys had more toys that were *educationally*

TABLE 6.2 Contents of the Bedrooms of 96 Children Ranging in Age from 12 to 72 Months

1. *Animal furnishings* (furniture, bedspreads, pictures, posters mobiles, rugs and pillows that contained animal characters)

2. *Books*

3. *Dolls* (baby and figures, toy soldiers, cowboys and Indians, and so forth)

4. *Educational/art materials* (charts with letters or numbers, materials for drawing, painting, coloring, or sculpting)

5. *Floral furnishings* (bedspreads, pictures, wallpaper, sheets, pillows, and rugs that depicted plants and/or flowers)

6. *Furniture*

7. *Musical items* (toy or real musical instruments, radios and record players)

8. *Ruffles* (bedspreads and curtains decorated with fringes or lace)

9. *Spatiotemporal objects* (materials, such as magnets, clocks, maps, and outer-space toys, designed to teach children about space, time, energy, and other aspects of the physical world)

10. *Sports equipment*

11. *Stuffed animals*

12. *Toy animals* (including housing, such as barns or zoos)

13. *Vehicles*

The data are from "The contents of boys' and girls' rooms as an index of parents' behavior" by H. L. Rheingold and K. V. Cook, 1975. *Child Development, 46,* pp. 459–463.

oriented. Third, boys' toys seemed to have an "away from the home" emphasis, as in the case of vehicles, military toys, machinery, and sports equipment, while girls' toys, such as baby and mother dolls and miniature household equipment, were more domestic. Rheingold and Cook (1975) wondered whether there was a message here. Do we communicate to our sons that their futures lie beyond the home but suggest to our daughters that maintaining a household and caring for children are their appropriate future roles?

Toy Preference as a Two-Directional Process

In discussing the gender-typed toys provided by parents to their children, we must remember that toy purchases usually reflect more than just the parent's preferences and values. Parents are not likely to force unwanted toys on their children, and a child will begin to make requests for specific toys as early as the age of two and possibly even before. After that point it becomes extremely difficult to know how active parents are in promoting the use of gender-appropriate as opposed to gender-inappropriate toys by their preschoolers. If accused of perpetuating gender stereotypes by providing their five-year-old daughter with a junior makeup kit instead of a dump truck, parents might justifiably respond that she *wanted* a makeup kit and wouldn't even consider a dump truck as a birthday gift.

There is evidence, in fact, to suggest that children themselves are *more* gender typed than their parents in their toy preferences. Robinson and Morris (1986) examined the Christmas toy requests of 86 children aged two-and-a-half to five-and-a-half and then looked at the characteristics of the nonrequested toys that their parents also bought for them. A panel of six child development professionals estimated the gender appropriateness of the various toys as "toys for boys," "toys for girls," and "toys for both."

The researchers found that most of the toys (63%) actually requested by children of all ages combined were gender-typed ones; approximately 75% of toys requested by boys aged three, four, and five were "toys for boys." The remainder of the boys' requests were gender neutral, and only one boy in the entire sample asked for a cross-sex toy. The pattern of girls' toy requests was somewhat different, however. In the first place, it seemed that boys developed gender-typed toy interests at a younger age than girls did. Only one-third of the toys requested by three-year-old girls were designated "toys for girls," although this percentage rose to 51% at age four and to 73% at age five. In addition, girls differed from boys in that several of them asked for such "toys for boys" as vehicles or weapons, a finding consistent with earlier research indicating that boys tend actively to dislike "girl" toys more than girls dislike "boy" toys (Eisenberg, Murray, & Hite, 1982).

Boys of all ages showed a strong preference for conventionally masculine toys like cars, trucks, weapons, and action figures and were, in fact, more likely to receive these than were girls. By the time they were five, girls typically requested conventionally feminine toys like baby dolls, cradles and tea sets and were more likely than boys to receive dolls, doll accessories, and domestic toys (e.g., play food, toy ovens, pots and pans). In fact, boys never asked for and never received such items.

Approximately 60% of the nonrequested toys, on the other hand, were categorized as gender neutral. These included art supplies (paints, felt-tip pens, crayons), musical toys (radios, musical instruments), and educational toys (books, puzzles, microscopes, magnetic letters and numbers, computers). It would seem, therefore, that children themselves are more attentive than their parents to gender appropriateness in toys. At least parents appear to make efforts to balance out their children's toy collections by providing gender-neutral play materials.

Are parents likely to go even further by offering cross-sex toys to their children? To some extent they are, but only to their daughters. One of every three girls in the Robinson and Morris (1986) study received an nonrequested toy in the category of "toys for boys"; not a single boy received a nonrequested toy from the "toys for girls" category. This finding is consistent with a pattern typically observed in research on gender roles in the United States: Males feel a greater pressure than females do to behave in gender-appropriate ways (Maccoby & Jacklin, 1974).

Messages from Toy Advertising

Parents often complain that toy manufacturers make life difficult for them by stimulating their children to want the latest and the newest toy, which seems to appear almost on a weekly basis. There is little doubt that toys are heavily advertised and that much of the advertising is aimed directly at children, rather than at their parents. There also appears to be little doubt that the gender typing of toys that we have been describing is clearly evident in the various forms of advertising.

Let us look first at television, which has been described as the most often used entertainment and information source in U.S. society (Comstock, Chaffee, Katzman, McCombs, & Roberts, 1978). An extensive analysis of commercials for children's toys during two consecutive Christmas seasons led Feldstein and Feldstein (1986) to conclude that certain toys are intended only for girls and others only for boys. The gender appropriateness of a toy is rarely directly stated, of course, but it seems an obvious conclusion that if members of one sex exclusively are shown playing with a toy in a commercial, the toy is being suggested specifically for children of that sex. Indeed, the researchers noted that it was typical for commercials to include children of only one sex. Boys *never* appeared in commercials for female dolls, doll accessories, or household items (e.g., stoves, pots and pans), while girls were *never* seen in commercials for male dolls, weapons, construction toys, or sports equipment.

Results similar to those of Feldstein and Feldstein (1986) have been found when other forms of advertising are analyzed. Schwartz and Markham (1985) presented a list of 48 categories of toys to several student groups to rate according to the degree to which "most people" see them as gender stereotyped. Of the 48 toys, 20 were seen as moderately or strongly gender-typed; guns, trains, and racing cars were seen as male toys, for example, while dolls, housekeeping toys, and beauty kits were seen as female.

The researchers then examined advertising for the various toys in 12 mail-order catalogues (a total of 392 pictures) and on the packages of as many of the toys that could be found in four different types of retail stores (538 pictures). Similar to the findings pertaining to television commercials, it was found that catalogue and package advertising often depicts children of only one sex playing with a toy, and it almost always does so when the toy in question is even moderately gender typed.

Schwartz and Markham (1985) also pointed out that other subtle cues to gender typing were found in the advertising. In the first place, girls' and boys' toys were often shown separately in different sections of catalogues, for example. In addition, even gender-neutral toys often contained references to gender appropriateness. Plastic tricycles for girls came in pastel colors and contained floral designs, while the same toys for boys came in dark colors, and had seemingly heavy-duty tires and a rugged-sounding name. Costumes for girls were typically those of brides, ballerinas, nurses, or cheerleaders, while boys' costumes were those of traditionally masculine roles, such as soldier, astronaut, or police officer. Finally, gender roles were often suggested in the advertising: A girl shown on a magic kit was a boy magician's assistant; a girl in a racing car advertisement watched from the background as two boys played; a girl in a play kitchen was serving a meal to a boy seated at the table.

Messages about gender appropriateness as indicated by the sex of the model seen playing with toys appear constantly in toy advertising (Tracy, 1987). What is not known, of course, is whether toy manufacturers actually shape children's interests or merely respond to them. Is the message of the advertiser that children *should* play with supposedly gender-appropriate toys, or is it simply that they do? If advertisers are shaping children's opinions about the gender appropriateness of their toys, we might expect that children exposed to the greatest amount of advertising would hold the most rigid gender stereotypes. At least as far as the medium of television is concerned, however, such a relationship has not been found consistently: A connection between the amount of television (and presumably television advertising) that is watched and the tendency to engage in gender typing of toys has been observed in some studies but not in others (Repetti, 1984; Tracy, 1987). Thus it seems that, again, as in the question of the influence of parents on children's toy preferences, we are faced with a complex interaction, a sort of chicken-and-egg question in which it is difficult to separate out causes and effects.

Can any definite conclusions be drawn about gender differences in the toy preferences of U.S. preschool children? Perhaps there are a few. It seems clear, first of all, that parental attitudes play at least some role in toy selection, since adults are likely to offer gender-typed toys even to infants too young to express a preference. It is clear also that by the age of three, and possibly earlier, children express definite preferences for gender-typed toys; these preferences appear sooner and are considerably more emphatic in boys than in girls. What is not clear is the extent to which cultural conditioning accounts for the toy preferences of *older* children; it becomes increasingly difficult as children develop to separate out the specific factors that influence their choice of play materials. Unfortunately, the children themselves are usually unable to give reasons for their preferences.

As a final comment on gender differences in toy preference, let us look at the ways in which boys and girls play with *identical* toys. Grinder and Liben (1989) observed 40 preschool children at play with toys that were stereotypically masculine (e.g., a workbench and tools) and stereotypically feminine (e.g., a tea set). They found that when children played with gender-appropriate toys, they were likely to engage in "typical toy play," meaning that they played with the toy according to its intended use, such as hammering nails at a workbench or pouring tea with a tea set. When they initially played with cross-sex toys, however, children were not as likely to use them as intended. The authors concluded that simply providing boys and girls with the same play materials will not guarantee that they will play with them in identical ways. Perhaps the reason is that they lack the experience to do so!

Correlates of Gender-Typed Toy Preference

Although the actual reasons for gender-typed toy preferences are not fully known, there is a growing body of research that examines the correlates of such preferences. It has typically been found, for example, that a preference for masculine, feminine, or neutral toys among preschoolers is related to the extent to which children assume traditionally masculine or feminine gender roles; toy choice is therefore thought to indicate the degree of a child's traditional gender role adoption (Cameron, Eisenberg, & Tryon, 1985; Eisenberg, 1983; Eisenberg, Tryon, & Cameron, 1984). Perhaps it is not surprising that gender-typed toy choice among children is related also to the extent to which the child's parents assume traditional or nontraditional gender roles (Repetti, 1984).

The sex of one's playmate is also related to the tendency to select gender-appropriate or -inappropriate toys. When children play with same-sex peers, they are more likely to make use of gender-appropriate toys (Connor & Serbin, 1977; Eisenberg, Tryon, & Cameron, 1984; Lloyd & Smith, 1985); in fact, a tendency to choose same-sex rather than opposite-sex playmates is correlated with a tendency to prefer gender-appropriate toys (Eisenberg, Boothby, & Matson, 1979).

Finally, there is a relationship between the tendency to play with gender-stereotyped toys and certain aspects of children's intellectual functioning. Specifically, it has been shown that school-age boys who indicate the strongest preference for masculine-stereotyped toys demonstrate superior performance on tasks requiring spatial skills and score higher on mathematics and science achievement tests; girls who are the most likely to play with feminine-stereotyped toys are the most likely to give evidence of superior verbal skills. In other words, highly gender-stereotyped toy play is related to traditional patterns of male spatial superiority and female verbal superiority (Serbin & Connor, 1979; Tracy, 1987).

How can the relationship between the use of gender-appropriate toys and the appearance of various intellectual skills be explained? It has been suggested that "boy" toys (e.g., Legos, Lincoln Logs, vehicles, Erector Sets) are more likely than "girl" toys to require construction, the manipulation of objects and patterns, and movement through space; "girl" toys (e.g., dolls and doll equipment, board games, art supplies) facilitate verbal interaction (Tracy, 1987). Nevertheless, it has yet to be demonstrated that the use of certain play materials actually *cause* gender differences in verbal and spatial skills. Perhaps it is the superiority in spatial or verbal skills that lead boys and girls respectively to seek out gender-appropriate toys.

Fantasy Play

Before discussing gender differences in fantasy play, we should point out that make-believe is influenced by a variety of factors in addition to the sex of the player. As indicated in Chapter Three, the child's developmental level is an important predictor of the amount and the quality of fantasy play, with older preschoolers engaging in this activity to a considerably greater extent and more imaginatively than younger ones. Factors of physical location, spatial density, and toy availability must also be considered; fantasy play is more likely to occur indoors than outdoors, in smaller, enclosed spaces than in wide open areas, and when suggestive props are available to stimulate the imagination (Connolly, Doyle, & Ceschin, 1983; Mann, 1984; Peck & Goldman, 1978).

There are, however, a number of fairly well-established differences in fantasy play that are related to sex of the player. Specifically, while most studies reveal no differences between boys and girls in the actual *amount* of fantasy play observed (Connolly, Doyle, & Ceschin, 1983), gender differences do appear in (1) the props used, (2) the roles assumed, and (3) the themes played out.

Props for Fantasy Play

The *props* for fantasy play are the materials that stimulate a child's imagination. As indicated in Chapter Four, such materials vary considerably in their degrees of realism; for example, a child playing out a kitchen scene may be equipped with a toy stove or only with a stack of blocks on top of which eggs are fried and water is boiled. We pointed out in Chapter Four that children differ in their need for realistic props to stimulate their creative play and that these differences depend primarily on the familiarity of the play materials. However, there is some evidence that boys and girls differ in their need for realistic props; during the preschool years, when most fantasy play occurs, girls seem to be slightly ahead of boys in their ability to initiate fantasy play without the benefit of realistic props, although this difference has been found only in play settings that have been somewhat structured by adults; in free-play situations, gender differences have rarely been observed (Fein, Johnson, Kosson, Stork, & Wasserman, 1975; Johnson & Roopnarine, 1983; Matthews, 1977; McLoyd, 1980).

Fantasy Play Roles

Gender differences in fantasy play *roles* have been clearly established in the literature on children's play. Girls are much more likely than boys to choose domestic and family roles, such as mother and baby, while boys prefer roles that are more adventurous, more action oriented, more fictitious than real, and further removed from the domestic environment. Boys often choose superhero and supervillain roles, for example, while girls are not likely to do so (Connolly, 1980; Greif, 1976; Johnson & Roopnarine, 1983; McLoyd, 1980; Sutton-Smith, 1979).

Children of both sexes typically assume roles of same-sex characters, although girls· are more willing than boys to play opposite-sex roles. Boys are extremely reluctant to assume the role of a female character (e.g., Mother in a game of house) or even to assume a functional role that is typically regarded as female (e.g., the person who makes and serves the food) (Garvey & Berndt, 1977).

Themes of Fantasy Play

Finally, gender differences have been observed in the *themes* of preschoolers' fantasy play. High drama, adventure, and danger characterize the make-believe play themes of boys, and vehicles and weapons of various sorts are likely to be incorporated into the action. Girls more often play out scenes pertaining to family relationships, use dolls as characters in their play, and rely more on verbal interaction and less on physical activity than do boys (Connolly, Doyle, & Ceschin, 1983). A typical girl's theme might involve a family interaction, for example, in which there is extensive conversation among the characters, while a group of boys might pretend to be pilots, astronauts, or the crew of a submarine dealing with the many adventures and dangers such roles entail.

Rough-and-Tumble Play

Eight-year-old Jerry and his six-year-old brother Nick got along reasonably well most of the time; occasionally, however, they would engage in the kind of rough-housing that invariably resulted in one of them, usually Nick, getting hurt and complaining to their parents. Mr. and Mrs. Schneider repeatedly tried to discourage their sons' play fighting, not only because it often resulted in bumps and bruises for Nick, but also

Rough-and-tumble physical play is more typical of males than females in all human cultures and in many lower animal species as well.

because it was such loud, raucous, and irritating play. The Schneiders worried too that this rough-and-tumble play might prepare their sons to become even more aggressive during adolescence and adulthood or, worse, that it might alienate the boys from one another as they grew up.

Rough-and-tumble play is an activity that many adults find difficult to tolerate in children. As Mrs. Schneider often remarked, "Why are they always *hitting* each other?" Parents and teachers might be comforted to know, however, that such play is extremely common, particularly among boys. In fact, rough-and-tumble play occurs not only in human beings, but also in other primates, such as monkeys and apes, and it is an activity quite different from serious aggression, as pointed out in Chapter Two.

What Is Rough-and-Tumble Play?

Rough-and-tumble play is characterized by play fighting, including hitting and wrestling, and chasing with the intent of fighting. However, there are many differences between such play and genuine acts of aggression (Smith, 1989). First, aggression is often triggered by children's competition for resources, such as space or equipment; rough-and-tumble play involves no such competition. Second, during acts of aggression, the participants behave seriously (staring at each other, frowning, crying), while in rough-and-tumble play there is much smiling and laughter. Third, in cases of real fighting, rarely are more than two children involved, while many children at a time may engage in play fighting. Fourth, play fighting draws and keeps the players together rather than driving them apart, as would be the outcome of genuine aggression. Finally, children engaging in rough-and-tumble play usually do not use their strength to the maximum; they restrain themselves lest another child be injured. In a sense, then, rough-and-tumble play is *mock* aggression (DePietro, 1981; Humphreys & Smith, 1984; Smith, 1989).

Rough-and-tumble play must also be distinguished from what has been referred to as **vigorous activity play** (Humphreys & Smith, 1984). Running, swinging, climbing, jumping, and pushing and pulling large objects are certainly vigorous physical activities, yet they differ from rough-and-tumble play in two important ways. First, such energetic motor play can be either a solitary or a social activity, while rough-and-tumble play is *always* of a social nature. Second, as noted, rough-and tumble-play always contains components of mock aggression, but vigorous activity play does not.

Functions of Rough-and-Tumble Play

Reasons for the occurrence of rough-and-tumble play in human beings are difficult to establish. For example, it seems clear that such play provides children with an opportunity for physical exercise. However, since it constitutes only about 15% of all of their vigorous physical play, it is unlikely that play fighting is engaged in primarily for exercise. Vigorous physical play seems more likely to serve that exercise function (Fagen & George, 1977; Humphreys & Smith, 1984).

Is rough-and-tumble play an opportunity to practice skills that will be useful in adulthood? Again, it seems unlikely: How often is an adult required to pursue and wrestle with other people? Perhaps the practice explanation makes sense, however, if viewed in evolutionary terms. Children do engage in rough-and-tumble play more often with peers who are close to them in strength than with considerably stronger or weaker peers (Humphreys, 1983), lending *some* support to the notion that an element of practice is involved. After all, people are considerably more likely to improve their motor skills when they test them against opponents who are closely matched in ability.

Does rough-and-tumble play provide children with opportunities for determining their status within the social hierarchy? As shown in Chapter Two, other primates often use play to establish their social rankings, and there is little doubt that children's peer groups are hierarchically divided in terms of popularity and social desirability. However, children's social hierarchies are apparently based on criteria other than proficiency at rough-and-tumble play. Quite often, the most popular and admired children, the natural group leaders, never engage in play fighting of any sort (Humphreys & Smith, 1984). In other words, children are not expected to fight their way, in a literal sense, to the top.

While the specific reasons for its occurrence and the benefits that it offers are not always clear, adults might be comforted to know that rough-and-tumble play does not apparently *cause* greater aggression at later points in life (Humphreys & Smith, 1984). Perhaps the wisest course of action for harried parents and teachers is to accept such play as normal and to try to prevent it from turning into real aggression, as it often does.

Gender Differences in Rough-and-Tumble Play

One of the most consistently observed gender differences in children's play is that males engage in considerably more play fighting than do females (Pellegrini, 1985; Rubin, Fein, & Vandenberg, 1983); the gender difference is particularly clear in the area of wrestling for superiority, although less so in the area of chasing (Aldis, 1975). This male–female difference is found among children of all ages but is especially noticeable among elementary school-age children (Humphreys & Smith, 1984). Furthermore, the difference has been observed in a variety of cultures throughout the world, including that of the United States (Whiting & Edwards, 1973; DePietro, 1981), England (Blurton-Jones 1967; Blurton-Jones and Konner, 1973; Brindley, Clarke, Hutt, Robinson, & Wehtli, 1973; Heaton, 1983; Smith & Connolly, 1972, 1980), Mexico, the Philippines, Okinawa, and India (Whiting & Edwards, 1973). And finally, gender differences in rough-and-tumble play have been observed consistently in animal research: Among every species of ape and monkey that has been studied to date, as well as in other animals, such as rats, play fighting is significantly more likely to occur among males than among females (Humphreys & Smith, 1984; Meaney, 1988).

Explanations for Gender Differences

As might be expected, two lines of argument have been set forth in attempting to explain gender differences in rough-and-tumble play. The first stresses the influence of culture and attributes the observed gender differences to differential reinforcement by parents—and others—of play fighting in young children. The second argument is based not on environmental factors but on internal biological mechanisms, and specifically on the influence of sex hormones, in predisposing young males to take pleasure in rough-and-tumble play.

Differential Reinforcement?

Infants do not initiate rough-and-tumble play activities as we have defined them; they are not socially mature enough to do so. However, it is possible that children in the first year of life may already be learning that play fighting is intended as a male activity. In ways they do not realize, adults may be communicating subtle messages about the gender appropriateness of certain behaviors.

In order to examine the subtle messages that infants often receive, Fagot, Hagan, Leinsbach, and Kronsberg (1985) observed 34 babies, aged 13 to 14 months, at play in a child research laboratory. Among the types of infant and toddler activity the researchers were interested in documenting was physically assertive or aggressive behavior, for example, grabbing for an object, hitting, pushing, or kicking another child. Interestingly enough, boy and girl babies engaged in roughly the same amounts of aggressive behavior. However, adult reaction to aggressive behavior appeared to depend on the sex of the baby. Aggression in 13-month-old boys was likely to draw a reaction from an adult; teachers would respond by picking the child up, offering him a new toy, or physically removing him from the situation. Aggression in female babies was typically ignored.

The researchers suggested that adults may expect boys to be more aggressive than girls and so may monitor aggressive behaviors more closely when a boy displays them. The net result is that male babies learn that behaving aggressively pays off. It earns attention from adults, and it brings about a change of one sort or another in the play situation. For female babies, on the other hand, assertive or aggressive acts, being followed by no consequences of any sort, are less likely to be continued.

There are other lines of research that support a differential reinforcement explanation of gender differences in rough-and-tumble play. As discussed in Chapter Three, fathers are more likely than mothers to engage in rough-and-tumble play with children, both during infancy and during the toddler years (Lamb, 1977; McDonald & Parke, 1986; Parke & Tinsley, 1987; Stevenson, Leavitt, Thompson, & Roach, 1988). Fathers are also more likely to initiate such play with their sons than with their daughters (Lamb, 1981) and so may be teaching their children, both by direct reinforcement and by serving as models, that such play is masculine behavior.

By the time their children are two years of age, most U.S. parents already hold stereotypes of rough-and-tumble play as an appropriate activity for boys but not for girls (Fagot, 1978; Smith & Daglish, 1977), and children realize, even before they are three years old, that certain forms of play are more appropriate for and with males than for and with females. Fagot (1984) found, for example, that a toddler is more likely to engage a male adult than a female in a game of throwing a ball back and forth but is more likely to seek various forms of help from a woman than from a man. Those who support a differential reinforcement position maintain that such stereotypes result from a cultural conditioning that is subtle but pervasive and begins in the early weeks of an infant's life, if not before.

A Biological Predisposition?

Exposure to higher levels of male hormone during pregnancy has an effect on the developing brains of a variety of animal species, including monkeys and rats, that apparently predisposes them to enjoy rough-and-tumble play (Meaney, 1988; Symons, 1978). Could the same be true of human beings? The genitals sexually differentiate in a fetus as a result of the presence of an XX (female) or an XY (male) chromosome combination. At about the sixth week after conception, the testes begin to develop and the ovaries are formed at approximately the third month. For the remainder of the pregnancy, sexual differentiation occurs because the infant secretes sex hormones from its own sex glands, and there is in the bloodstream of the male fetus and of the male infant at birth a considerably higher concentration of male sex hormones, or androgens, than is found in the female. It is thought that these male hormones may affect the developing brain tissue in the male fetus, predisposing it to certain supposedly male interests and activities at later points in development.

Animal research indicates that if a female fetus is exposed to abnormally high levels of male sex hormones that have been injected into her mother, she will resemble a male in terms of genital appearance at birth yet retain the XX chromosome combination. More relevant to our discussion here, she will later engage in amounts of rough-and-tumble play that are atypical for females, although still not at the high levels observed in males (Goy, 1975; Hoyenga & Hoyenga, 1979). Similarly, males whose bodies are insensitive in utero to the presence of male sex hormones later display more stereotypically feminine varieties of play (Meaney, 1988).

Ethical considerations preclude the use of experimental research of this sort with human beings, of course. However, prenatal developmental abnormalities can occur accidentally in humans, as when the adrenal glands produce excessively high levels of androgens in a female fetus, a condition known as the **adrenogenital syndrome.** And what effect does this condition have on the child's play at a later point? In a classic study that compared 25 girls who had been exposed to abnormally high male hormone levels during pregnancy with 25 normal girls, Money and Ehrhardt (1972) found that the former group was more tomboyish; that is, they seemed to be more interested in rough-and-tumble play than did the girls whose prenatal environment was completely normal (Ehrhardt & Meyer-Bahlburg, 1981).

It would be difficult to argue that research on the adrenogenital syndrome offers conclusive proof that biological predispositions account for gender differences in rough-and-tumble play, however. In the first place, there is no way to ascertain that cultural as well as hormonal factors are not involved. Those who reject biological explanations argue that childrearing practices must also be considered as influences on the supposedly masculine play patterns of girls experiencing the adrenogenital syndrome. They suggest that, since girls with the adrenogenital syndrome began life with rudimentary male genitalia, the parents may have unconsciously encouraged more masculine play in their initially masculine-appearing daughters. Ehrhardt and Meyer-Bahlburg (1981) replied that the opposite parental reaction was actually more likely: Parents would try harder to feminize daughters who displayed physical signs of masculinization at birth.

A more compelling reason for caution in interpreting the evidence for biological predispositions in rough-and-tumble play centers on the research design itself. As was mentioned above, genuine experimental research on the effects of sex hormones on human brain tissue is not possible; that is, ethical constraints prevent researchers from experimentally manipulating the amount of sex hormone that is secreted in utero in order to observe the results on later childhood play. Therefore, research on the effects of hormonal abnormalities in humans is correlational by nature; it is limited to examining relationships among variables. A relationship between hormone secretion during pregnancy and characteristics of later childhood play does not prove that the influence of hormone levels on the fetal brain actually *caused* certain forms of play to occur later on. And since conditions such as the adrenogenital syndrome in females and androgen insensitivity in males are quite rare, there are very few cases on which to base conclusions.

Games-with-Rules

In Chapter Five, games-with-rules were describe as forms of play that emerge when children begin to apply the structure of logic to their thinking; this happens when the child reaches the age of five or six and begins to use what Piaget referred to as concrete operations. It will be remembered that games-with-rules require the involvement of two or more children in a competitive activity, the rules of which are agreed upon in advance.

Evidence of Gender Differences

In describing the games-with-rules that he observed in children, Piaget pointed out that such activities were engaged in primarily by boys. After extensive analysis of the marble games of elementary school children, Piaget (1965) remarked: "We did not succeed in finding a single collective game played by girls in which there were as many rules and, above all, as fine and consistent organization and codification of these rules as in the games of marbles [played by boys]" (p. 77).

Consistent with Piaget's analysis, it has often been observed that traditional girls' games (e.g., hopscotch, skipping rope) are simpler in their rule structure than the games of boys (Parker, 1984). Usually there are no teams with specialized roles, no umpires, no referees. Furthermore, boys' games are played in larger groups (Waldrop & Halverson, 1975), and boys' games are more competitive and longer lasting and seem to require a greater amount of skill than do the games of girls (Lever, 1976).

In fact, the greater rule orientation that typifies the play of male children may be found in other areas of life as well.

The organized games of girls are simpler in their rule structures than are the games of boys and require a lesser amount of physical skill.

For example, psychologist Carol Gilligan (1982) suggested that in the area of moral reasoning, males are more likely to base decisions on abstract moral principles, without reference to the specific social context in which a decision is made, while females put greater emphasis on the interpersonal relationships and on the feelings of the persons involved. Gilligan (1982) did not mean to imply that females are any less moral than males in their decision making, but only that they may arrive at moral decisions by different routes. The male emphasizes general rules, whereas the female is more attentive to situational variables.

Cultural Explanations of Gender Differences

Cultural explanations typically focus on the anthropological significance of play, on the role of games in preparing children for their positions and functions in adult life (Parker, 1984). An emphasis on rules, in play and in other areas of life as well, is thought to provide a basis for the ranking of male dominance hierarchies in a safe, nonthreatening way. In organized games children are grouped according to ability; they quickly learn their positions within the hierarchy from observing the significance of their positions on the team or from their assignments as first-stringers, second-stringers, or benchwarmers.

Not only do children learn their status rankings from their games, but as a result of the grouping process, they have opportunities to develop their skills to the fullest by competing with peers who are similar to them in ability. This early status ranking and opportunity to refine competitive skills may prepare children to assume the status roles in which they can compete most effectively as adults for scarce resources; such preparation may have been, at some point in the process of human evolution, a reason for the emergence of games-with-rules.

Anthropologists point out that many of the children's games-with-rules that are commonly seen in our society bear a resemblance to certain forms of adult competition for scarce resources (Parker, 1984): Soccer, basketball, and football offer practice in territorial invasion, baseball prepares one for territorial raiding, checkers and chess practice invasion and the capture of one's enemies, snakes-and-ladders gives practice in overcoming a series of obstacles in order to achieve one's goals, and card games like Old Maid offer practice in bluffing and in calculating the odds. *All* games offer practice in rule manipulation, memory, quantification, and strategic coalition.

The Possible Role of Biology

Biological explanations of gender differences in games-with-rules typically emphasize the effects of male sex hormones on the fetal brain, which, as in the case of rough-and-tumble play, are thought to predispose males to engage in competition via games-with-rules (Parker, 1984). As a matter of fact, girls experiencing the adrenogenital syndrome have been found to be more active and to show a greater preference for playing outdoor sports and games (as well as for playing with cars, trucks, and blocks) than do other girls (Ehrhardt & Baker, 1974). Again it should be pointed out, however, that research of this type is correlational and is based on a very small number of cases.

It seems fair, at least at this point in time, to conclude that cultural explanations of gender differences in games-with-rules are more compelling than biological ones, particularly in light of the ethical constraints on biological research with human beings. Whether or not biological predispositions exist, cultural influences cannot be ignored. The impact of culture on children's games in general has certainly long been recognized (see Chapter Two). What is more, the cultural argument is supported by an examination of recent trends, both in the play of U.S. children and in their adult roles. Perhaps it is not surprising that as women in the United States today are increasingly likely to find themselves competing along with men to earn their livelihoods, girls of all ages are increasingly likely to engage in traditional male games-with-rules, such as organized sports (Parker, 1984).

Summary

The vast majority of the research on gender differences in children's play has been concentrated in four areas: (1) toy selection, (2) fantasy play, (3) rough-and-tumble play, and (4) games-with-rules. No one is certain why differences are found in any of the four areas, but there are two major theoretical viewpoints on the origins of gender stereotyping. According to *learning theory,* children learn by imitation and reinforcement to behave in gender-appropriate ways, even before they understand the concept of gender. The basic premise of *cognitive-developmental theory* is that children engage in gender-appropriate activities because such activities are consistent with their gradually emerging gender concept.

Gender differences in toy selection are usually attributed to cultural factors, in particular to the socializing influences of adults, peers, and the mass media. Adults are likely, for example, to offer gender-appropriate toys to very young children and to reinforce children, in often very subtle ways, for playing with gender appropriate toys. Research on the contents of preschool children's bedrooms indicates that boys and girls have decidedly different play materials and that boys' toys are characterized by greater variety, a greater educational focus, and an "away from the home" rather than a domestic emphasis.

Gender differences in fantasy play appear in (1) the props that are used, (2) the roles that are assumed, and (3) the themes that are played out. During the preschool years, when most fantasy play occurs, girls may be slightly ahead of boys in their ability to initiate fantasy play without realistic props. Girls are much more likely than boys to choose domestic and family roles, while boys prefer roles that are more adventurous, more action-oriented, more fictitious than real, and further removed from the domestic environment. Finally, high drama, adventure, and danger characterize the make-believe play themes of boys, while girls more often play out scenes pertaining to family relationships.

Gender differences in rough-and-tumble play have been observed consistently in human and animal research, with males engaging in this activity much more frequently than females. Explanations for the gender difference focus either on differential patterns of reinforcement or on biological predispositions related to the effects of male sex hormones on the developing fetal brain.

Finally, games-with-rules are characterized by gender differences, with boys' games occurring more frequently than girls' and being more complex, more competitive, and longer lasting. Cultural explanations of such gender differences emphasize the role of games in preparing children for competition in adult life and the greater need for the male to compete, at least in traditional societies. Biological explanations again focus on the influence on hormones on the fetal brain, but research on gender differences in fetal hormone production is by nature correlational and is based on a very small number of cases.

Key Terms

Adrenogenital Syndrome
Gender Constancy
Gender Identity

Gender Stability
Rough-and-Tumble Play
Vigorous Activity Play

CHAPTER SEVEN

Play in
Special
Populations

The Sandersons were pleased when their seven-year-old son Todd announced that he had been invited to a classmate's birthday party. Their pleasure changed to apprehension, however, when they discovered that the party was in honor of a child who was both mentally and physically handicapped. Roger, who had been admitted to Todd's class as a result of the school's new mainstreaming policy, was judged to be moderately mentally retarded and was confined to a wheelchair as well.

Mr. and Mrs. Sanderson had no negative feelings about handicapped children. In fact, they were strong advocates of the mainstreaming concept. Nevertheless, they now found themselves wondering whether they should prepare Todd in some way for the experience of attending Roger's party. What would the party be like, they wondered. Would the children play games? Would Roger be able to participate in games at all, or would he be only a spectator? What kind of gift should Todd bring? What kind of toy would a child like Roger play with? Do children like Roger play at all?

The Sandersons realized that they had never before considered the question of whether handicapped children play the way normal children do. They had imagined that the lives of children with special needs were dominated by learning to cope with life's everyday challenges, participation in various sorts of remedial programs, and just sitting around doing nothing! They never imagined such children at play, even though they could not imagine the lives of their own two "normal" children *without* a continuing element of play.

The Sandersons' confusion about an appropriate birthday gift for Roger should not be surprising. Little is known, even by child development professionals, about the play of handicapped children, the scarcity of information attributable to the shortage of carefully designed studies of the subject (Rubin, Fein, & Vandenberg, 1983). Furthermore, even the findings from well-constructed studies tell us little about the *reasons* for observed play differences. Too often it has been assumed that handicapped children have inherent play deficits when, in fact, differences in play might be more easily explained by environmental variables. Children like Roger differ from the norm by virtue of their handicaps, but they also grow up in a different sociocultural environment from that of the average child.

Before discussing what is known about the play of physically, emotionally, and intellectually handicapped children, let us turn to two central questions that should be kept in mind as the evidence is examined. First, why are the research findings in this area so often difficult to interpret? Second, what do the findings tell us about the origins of differences in play between children who are handicapped and children who are not?

Why Are the Findings Difficult to Interpret?

There are several related reasons for the hit-and-miss quality of the research on the play of handicapped children (Quinn & Rubin, 1984). First, the concept of *play* has not been defined consistently; for example, most research on the play of mentally retarded children is comprised only of observations of these children as they play individually with toys; social play has been virtually ignored.

Second, research on the play of exceptional children has taken several different philosophical directions, depending on the nature of the handicap in question (Quinn & Rubin, 1984), and it is difficult, therefore, to draw overall conclusions. Those who study physical disabilities come primarily from the professions of medicine and recreational/occupational therapy, and they have emphasized the uses of play in physical therapy; professionals interested in intellectual impairments have looked at play as a tool for educational and intellectual enrichment; specialists in emotional disorders, psychiatrists and clinical psychologists, have examined the uses of play in clinical diagnosis and psychotherapy, an emphasis that will be discussed in greater detail in the final chapter of this book.

Third, because of vast differences in the goals, methods, and professional backgrounds of the researchers, developmental theory has often been ignored in the formulation of research questions. Many of those who studied play among handicapped children displayed little knowledge of the role of play in the development of the nonhandicapped child—or even about normal child development in general.

Fourth, the research findings are often difficult to make sense of because the handicaps under investigation are not mutually exclusive. Children frequently have multiple handicaps. For example, a child who is mentally retarded may also have emotional problems, or a child who is hearing impaired may exhibit delayed speech as well. While multiply handicapped children were the subjects of much of the research, rarely were efforts made to identify *which* handicap was responsible for observed play differences.

Finally, it is not unusual to find studies comparing the play of normal and handicapped children in which the term "handicapped" refers to a wide variety of disabling conditions. As an example, in one recent study of social interaction patterns, the handicapped group consisted of 4 mentally retarded children, 4 with orthopedic handicaps, 18 with emotional or behavior disorders, including attentional deficits and extremes of social withdrawal, 4 with learning disorders, and 10 with language difficulties. And the results were not analyzed separately by handicapping condition (Quay & Jarret, 1986).

Where Do the Differences Come From?

As will become evident throughout this chapter, it is extremely important to differentiate between children's actual play behavior and their potential for play. Many times a child will display immature play patterns in one setting and will play quite normally in another. In the case of children with handicaps, this distinction is critical because the physical and/or social environments they find themselves in are often not conducive to the optimum display of their abilities.

Physical environments, such as classrooms and playgrounds, are often designed with little or no attention to the special needs of children with various handicaps (Frost & Klein, 1979). What is seen by a normal child as an inviting atmosphere to play in may be seen by a handicapped child as restrictive, hostile, and forbidding. In terms of the social environment, adults often believe that handicapped children are unable to play, and therefore they neglect to plan for and encourage the play of handicapped children as they would that of the nonhandicapped. Adults may also allow handicapped children to associate only with children who have similar handicaps, despite the fact that many researchers have found that the play of so-called

Playgrounds are inviting places for most children but are often designated with little or no attention to the special needs of the handicapped child.

special children is richer, more varied, and more sophisticated in an integrated social setting than in a segregated one (Esposito & Koorland, 1989; Kohl & Beckman, 1984). The most sophisticted play observed in handicapped children occurs when their playmates are not handicapped, are younger in chronological age, and are identical in developmental age (Bednersh & Peck, 1986).

The lack of appropriate physical surroundings to play in, the failure of adult supervisors to help them plan and carry out their play routines, and the unavailability of suitable playmates all conspire to foster an impression that handicapped children suffer from basic play deficits. In fact, this impression may be completely false: The observed play differences may be environmental in origin.

The Physically Handicapped Child

Studies of play among children with physical handicaps have been concentrated in the three areas of visual impairment, hearing impairment, and language disorder.

Children with Visual Impairments

Even after eight years of teaching, Jim Baldwin had never encountered a blind child in his classes. Now he was challenged by the presence of four-year-old Jordan, blind since birth, whose parents wanted him exposed to the same nursery school experiences as sighted children. Jim was happy to have Jordan in his class, yet he was apprehensive about what he could expect from the child, and more importantly, he was uncertain of his ability to integrate Jordan completely into the day-to-day life of the classroom. How could his classroom activities be adapted for use by a blind child? Would Jordan be able to play with the other children? Would Jim have to make special efforts to make the boy feel accepted?

Jim might have been interested in the conclusions of a number of studies of the play of children with visual impairments (e.g., Fraiberg, 1978; Singer & Streiner, 1966; Tait, 1973; Wills, 1972). First, like all children, blind children do play. There is *no* evidence that a visual impairment leads to a basic inability to play. Second, although the similarities outweigh the differences, the play of blind children differs in some ways from the play of sighted children. Blind children are less imaginative than sighted children in fantasy play. For example, Singer and Streiner (1966) found that blind elementary school children played in a manner that was more concrete, less varied, and less flexible than what ordinarily occurs among sighted children. Tait (1973) noticed that blind children ranging in age from four to nine were more likely simply to manipulate objects in their play and less likely to let their imaginations take flight into the world of make-believe.

It is important to notice that the differences in play between groups of blind and sighted children are of a quantitative rather than a qualitative nature. That is, the differences are primarily differences in *amount,* rather than differences in quality. A visual impairment does not imply that there is a basic play deficit; the capacity for make-believe is present in blind children, but they tend to demonstrate that capacity less often.

Is it surprising that blind children play less imaginatively than sighted children and engage less frequently in vivid imaginative play? After all, blind children's interaction with the world is greatly restricted, and visual impairment can make it difficult for them to orient themselves to space and time and to separate reality from nonreality (Frost & Klein, 1979). What is more, blind children often face as an additional handicap the unfortunate stereotype that they are unable, or simply do not want, to play as other children do.

What can adults do to encourage blind children to play to their fullest potential? A number of suggestions have been offered by Frost and Klein (1979). First, it is important for the adult to help orient visually impaired children by *planning for play.* Before a free play session, the supervising adult should discuss with the children all the options available in terms of play materials, equipment, activities, and playmates. The children should be encouraged to identify their favorite activities and to tell how they plan to use the upcoming play time.

Second, the adult should try to provide a *sensory-rich play environment.* This means that the play setting should contain a variety of sensory cues to guide the visually impaired child. Materials that vary in texture might be used; tactile maps might be placed in strategic locations throughout the environment, as might audio cassette recorders with taped directions. Areas of the room or outdoor playground might be made distinctive through the use of distinctive texturing, such as sand or wood chips on the ground or different styles of carpeting or linoleum on the floor.

Third, the supervising adult should *rehearse the uses of play materials* with the children. When children are given practice in the uses of play materials, they come to encode the activities motorically, in what has been described as **enactive representation** (Bruner, 1973). In much the same way that the skill of riding a bicycle or tying a knot in a necktie is stored in one's physical memory, so too can the play activities of the visually impaired child be encoded.

Fourth, the adult supervisor should use *liberal amounts of reinforcement* to encourage blind children in their play.

And finally, when the play session has ended, the supervisor and the child should reflect on the experience, to provide *feedback and evaluation.* Frost and Klein (1979) suggested that this feedback session should be used to encourage blind children to follow through on their play plans, as well as to offer additional support for their play.

Children with Delayed Language

Human language and symbolic, or make-believe, play both require the ability to use symbols: to let one thing stand for, or represent, something else (McCune, 1986). Some child development experts, most notably Piaget, have gone so far as to see language as an aspect of symbolic functioning that can be assessed through observation of the child's make-believe play (Piaget, 1962). Other psychologists suggest that, while there is little doubt that language and make-believe play are related, the relationship is not as simple as implied by Piaget's view of symbolic play as "inner speech"; language and make-believe may share common intellectual prerequisites, but each seems to rely on a variety of additional abilities (McCune, 1986).

Because of the relationship between the two, it should not be surprising that language and symbolic play assume parallel courses of development. As was pointed out in Chapter Three, both initially appear at the same time, early in the child's second year, and the shift in symbolic play from an uncoordinated collection of activities to one that is coordinated and schematic parallels the transition at the end of the second year from one-word utterances to original two-word combinations in speech (Fenson, 1986). What is more, individual differences among children in their rates of language development seem to mirror individual differences in the development of symbolic play (Gould, 1986; Shimada, Sano, & Peng, 1979).

The language–symbolic play relationship raises interesting questions about the make-believe play of linguistically impaired children. Would children delayed in their language, even though free of other intellectual impairments, show symbolic play deficits as well? In fact, a number of researchers throughout the years have discovered a relationship between language deficits and deficits in symbolic play (Lombardino & Sproul, 1984; Lombardino, Stein, Kricos, & Wolf, 1986; Lovell, Hoyle, & Siddall, 1968;

Terrell, Schwartz, Prelock, & Messick, 1984; Williams, 1980). But what do these findings mean? Do speech-delayed children exhibit basic deficits in overall symbolic functioning?

Some psychologists (Quinn & Rubin, 1984; Rubin, Fein, & Vandenberg, 1983) argue that the research fails to demonstrate the existence of a broad symbolic deficit among speech-delayed children because in many of these studies the children actually *did* engage in make-believe play, although less often than language-normal children and displaying a less mature variety of such play. Since the ability to engage in acts of make-believe was present, there seems no justification for concluding that speech-delayed children experience an underlying symbolic deficit.

How, then, can the quantitative differences in symbolic play that are found among speech-delayed children be explained? Again, it appears that the explanation may be environmental in nature. Clearly the relationship between language and symbolic play goes beyond a reliance on similar underlying mental abilities. Language can make it easier for children to engage in social varieties of make-believe, as in the case of complex forms of sociodramatic play (McCune, 1986; Quinn & Rubin, 1984). Perhaps speech-delayed children simply find dramatic play more difficult to sustain than do normal children, and thus retreat more readily into the less demanding world of solitary play.

Children with Hearing Difficulties

As noted in the previous section, children whose speech is delayed often exhibit less mature forms of play during the early childhood years, particularly as regards their interest in social forms of make-believe. A similar—and related—finding is that young children with hearing difficulties engage in lesser amounts of cooperative make-believe play and are less likely to make symbolic use of objects than are children of normal hearing ability (Darbyshire, 1977; Esposito & Koorland, 1989; Higginbotham & Baker, 1981; Mann, 1984). Again, however, it has not been demonstrated that such children have specific play deficits. It seems more likely that the play differences observed in comparisons of normal and hearing-impaired children are differences in performance rather than potential. And depending on their surroundings and on cultural expectations, children do not always display the behaviors of which they are truly capable.

Esposito and Koorland (1989) discovered, for example, that the play of the *same* children in settings that were integrated (i.e., with children of normal hearing ability) or segregated (i.e., with other hearing-impaired children) was substantially different. Three-year-old Michael and five-year-old Vicki, both diagnosed as having severe hearing losses, were observed at play in their self-contained class for hearing-impaired children and in the regular day-care centers they also attended. The number of children in the play groups and the specific roles of the adults were the same in both environments.

The play of both children in the integrated settings was judged by observers to be more socially sophisticated. Parallel play was more often seen in the class for hearing-impaired children, while associative play was more typical in the day-care centers. It will be remembered from Chapter Four that parallel play is thought to be less socially mature than associative play and more typical of the very young preschooler.

The Mentally Handicapped Child

Up until the later years of the 1960s, there existed, even among professionals, a serious misconception about the play of mentally handicapped children. This was the assumption that mentally handicapped children do not play, either because they do not want to or because they do not need to (McConkey, 1985). Fortunately, this belief has been changing gradually over the past 20 years.

Why, when it has become increasingly clear to modern child development professionals that play is an essential ingredient in the lives of children, has the play of the mentally impaired child been ignored? In part, it is because the emphasis of those professionals who work with mentally handicapped children has been on intellectual and educational enrichment; their efforts have been characterized by a decidedly remedial focus rather than an appreciation of basic patterns of child development displayed by children in this special population (McConkey, 1985; Quinn & Rubin, 1984).

The capacity of mentally impaired children for play has also been underestimated because much of the research on the subject has emphasized *differences* between normal and subnormal populations. In highlighting the ways in which normal and mentally impaired children differed in their play, researchers often failed to emphasize the fact that, the differences notwithstanding, mentally handicapped children do indeed play.

Object Play

Throughout the years there have appeared surprisingly few studies of the uses of toys in free play by mentally handicapped children. The findings from these studies are that (1) intellectually impaired children seem to prefer what might be thought of as structured materials, such as puzzles and jacks, while nonretarded children of the same mental age prefer open-ended materials (e.g., art supplies) that allow them to be creative and imaginative (Horne & Philleo, 1942), and (2) mentally handicapped children are less likely than normal children to combine objects appropriately in play (Tilton & Ottinger, 1964; Weiner & Weiner, 1974). Tilton and Ottinger (1964) discovered, for example, that normal children will bring objects together in play, as when they build with blocks, combine cups with saucers, or screw nuts into bolts. Mentally retarded children are less likely to do so, and instead engage in much nonspecific touching of their toys.

How can one interpret the observed differences in the object play of normal and intellectually impaired children? It is difficult to do so, both because there are so few studies and because such studies typically contain methodological flaws. Accurate measures of group differences were difficult to obtain in all three studies because in none were there attempts to distinguish between exploratory behavior and play (Quinn & Rubin, 1984). Since the children were observed only in their first session with the toys, the greater amount of nonspecific touching by the retarded group may have indicated only that they were less familiar than the normal children with the materials. It is possible too that retarded children need more time than normal children to learn how to play and how to use toys; after the novelty of the toys had worn off, both groups might have played with them in similar ways. This cannot be known, of course, since later play sessions were not observed. Interestingly enough, in another study, in which children were observed across extended play periods, object play differences between groups of retarded and nonretarded children failed to appear at all (Hulme & Lunzer, 1966).

Symbolic Play

Symbolic, or make-believe, play emerges during the second year of life as children acquire the ability to represent the world mentally to themselves. As discussed in Chapter Three, the normal pattern is of a gradual developmental progression into the world of make-believe. But what can be said about the make-believe play of intellectually impaired children? Three main conclusions can be drawn.

First, symbolic play has been observed consistently in mentally retarded children; there is no evidence that intellectual impairment prevents children from engaging in imaginative acts of make-believe (Casby & Ruder, 1983; Cunningham, Glenn, Wilkinson, & Sloper, 1985; Hill & McCune-Nicolich, 1981; Jeffree & McConkey, 1976; Li, 1985; Wing, Gould, Yeates, & Brierly, 1977).

Second, mental age is a better predictor of the onset of symbolic play than is chronological age; thus, symbolic play typically appears later in intellectually impaired children than in those whose intellectual development is normal. For example, Wing, Gould, Yeates, and Brierly (1977) examined the symbolic play of 108 severely mentally retarded children who ranged in age from 5 to 14 years. Symbolic play was found, but it did not occur before the children had attained a *mental age* of 20 months. As indicated in Chapter Three, this mental age is approximately the same as the age at which normal children begin to become involved in make-believe.

The third conclusion pertains to the fact that symbolic play does not appear suddenly; its onset is gradual, and there seems to be a series of stages through which children progress (Cunningham, Glenn, Wilkinson, & Sloper, 1985; Hill & McCune-Nicolich, 1981; Jeffree & McConkey, 1985). While the stage progression seems to be identical in children at all levels of intellectual ability, retarded children lag behind normal children and are less likely to reach the most sophisticated levels.

As an illustration of evidence in support of this third conclusion, Li (1985) compared the play of 25 mildly mentally·retarded children, aged five to seven years, with a matched group of normal children. All were given a sand tray and a variety of miniature life toys, such as people, animals, houses, vehicles, signs, trees, and fences, and told to "build something and tell a story about it." After five minutes, if a child had not yet begun to build, he or she would be asked, "What are you making?"

Four levels of make-believe play were identified, with each representing refinements of, and elaborations upon, the preceding ones. The simplest was *object-related symbolic play,* in which children played out one pretend action sequence, either alone or with a particular toy (e.g., "The soldier's shooting" or "It goes choo-choo"). Next came the level of *play with a scene:* the child decides in advance on an idea for the play and creates a scene around that idea (e.g., "This is a farm"). There followed the level of *play with a theme,* in which the play was characterized by a central preplanned theme or action sequence; one child's theme was "making a city in winter," for example, and all of the play materials were then integrated into this theme. Finally, there was *play with a story,* which consisted of (1) imaginative play with (2) a sustained theme throughout, and (3) verbalization about the story.

Li (1985) discovered that, not unexpectedly, almost all of the mentally retarded children engaged in some forms of symbolic play, but differences appeared in the levels at which the normal and the intellectually impaired children were found. For example, approximately half of the nonhandicapped five-year-olds were at the highest levels (themes and stories), but none of the mentally retarded five-year-olds played at those levels. By contrast, only 15% of the normal five-year-olds played at the first level, while 55% of the handicapped children engaged in object-related symbolic play.

In conclusion, it seems that children of all intellectual levels involve themselves in functional play with objects, and children at all levels engage in make-believe play. While the research tends to emphasize group differences, the overwhelming impression is one of similarity. That is, it appears that normal and mentally impaired children are not qualitatively different in their attitudes toward, and their approaches to, play. The handicapped group is simply delayed, but the handicapped can play as normal children do if groups are equated in terms of mental rather than chronological age.

The Emotionally Disturbed Child

Emotional disturbance in children is referred to by many names, including autism, childhood schizophrenia, and psychosis. By whatever name it is called, emotional disturbance refers to *distortions* in development: The timing, rate, and sequence of basic psychological functioning are distorted. In contrast, for intellectually impaired children, the issue is primarily one of delay (Quinn & Rubin, 1984).

Childhood autism, an emotional disorder that affects 4 in every 10,000 children, is characterized by significant impairments in communication, of both a verbal and a nonverbal type (American Psychiatric Association, 1980). Autistic children may also be diagnosed as mentally retarded, although many of them are of average or above-average intelligence. The common characteristic shared by all of them, however, regardless of intelligence, is a basic communication difficulty, a profound inability to understand and function within the normal social environment; the autistic child apparently fails to differentiate between the self and the external world (Atlas & Lapidus, 1987; Attwood, 1984; Baron-Cohen, Leslie, & Frith, 1985; Kanner, 1971; Lord, 1984; Rutter, 1983).

Toy and Object Play

Information about the play of autistic children is scarce, but a number of patterns have appeared in the literature. First, in toy and object play, autistic children are more likely than normal children to engage in repetitive, stereotyped manipulation and less likely to use objects symbolically in make-believe (DeMyer, Mann, Tilton, & Loew, 1967; Tilton & Ottinger, 1964; Wing, Gould, Yeates, & Brierly, 1977; Wulff, 1985). Compared to nonautistic children, autistic children as a group are less likely to engage in complex toy play and less likely to use toys appropriately. It should be pointed out, however, that group comparisons do not tell the whole story; many individual autistic children do *not* engage in stereotyped, repetitive behaviors with toys, and so it would be unfair to conclude that such behaviors are inevitable characteristic symptoms of autism (Quinn & Rubin, 1984).

Symbolic Play

The second, and more extensive, area of research on the play of autistic children concerns the use of symbolic play. The general finding is that autistic children rarely engage in symbolic play (Atlas & Lapidus, 1987; Baron-Cohen, 1987; Baron-Cohen, Leslie, & Frith, 1985; Churchill, 1978; Gould, 1986; Mundy, Sigman, Ungerer, & Sherman, 1987; Rutter, 1978). Even highly intelligent autistic children are unlikely to engage in symbolic play, whereas, as pointed out in the previous section, severely mentally retarded children will do so (Hill & McCune-Nicolich, 1981).

How can the scarcity of symbolic play among autistic children be explained? Two types of explanations have been offered. The first attributes the lack of make-believe to a basic symbolic deficit, which is also responsible for the linguistic and social impairments of these children. The second explanation focuses on motivational variables, and takes the position that autistic children *can* play symbolically if encouraged but, for reasons of their own, choose not to.

The Symbol Deficit Hypothesis

According to what might be called a **symbol deficit hypothesis,** autistic children lack representational skills—a deficit that explains both the social impairment of autism and the failure to engage in symbolic play. Both symbolic play and social interaction require an ability to impute mental states to oneself and to other people, an ability described as a theory of mind (Baron-Cohen, 1987; Baron-Cohen, Leslie, & Frith, 1985; Leslie & Frith, 1988; Perner, Frith, Leslie, & Leekam, 1989; Premack & Woodruff, 1978; Wulff, 1985). Consider the ways in which symbolic play requires children to represent to themselves the mental states of dolls, puppets, or characters whose roles they are playing.

In an interesting study of the ability to represent mental states of others to oneself, Baron-Cohen, Leslie, and Frith (1985) studied the behavior of three groups of preschool children, one normal, one diagnosed as autistic, and one diagnosed as having Down's syndrome. The children were seated at a table and shown two dolls, "Sally" and "Anne," as well as a basket for Sally and a box for Anne. Sally placed a marble in her basket, and then departed. Anne removed the marble from Sally's basket and placed it in her box. Then the children were asked three questions. First, "Where is the marble really?" The answer to this would indicate the child's understanding of reality. Second, "Where was the marble at the beginning?" This was designed to test their memory. Finally, "Where will Sally look for her marble?" This question was designed to determine if the children realize that Sally has a belief system independent of their own.

All three groups of children—normal, autistic, and mentally retarded—answered the first two questions correctly; all apparently had the same sense of reality and the same ability to remember the placement of the marble. However, the responses to the third question were quite revealing. Neither the normal nor the retarded children had difficulty realizing that Sally would *think* the marble was still in her basket, even though they knew that it was not. Four out of five of the autistic children failed the belief question, however; they indicated that Sally would look for the marble in the box, apparently failing to differentiate between their knowledge of the situation and that of the doll.

The Conative Hypothesis

The belief that both the social impairments *and* the make-believe play deficits of autistic children are the result of the same underlying failure to establish a theory of mind is certainly an interesting perspective, although it is premature to draw firm conclusions at this point. Even while some continue to argue in favor of a symbol deficit in autistic children (e.g., Baron-Cohen, 1987; Frith, 1984; Leslie, 1984), others hold an opposing view. Some psychologists prefer a **conative hypothesis** to explain the lack of make-believe among autistic children. They see the issue as primarily one of motivation: Autistic children may simply not want to engage in symbolic play to the extent that normal children do.

The conative hypothesis is supported by the observation that autistic children often perform well when specific intellectual abilities are tested, even though they will not display these abilities spontaneously in natural settings. For example, autistic children who score as well on formal language tests as children with specific language disorders are still less likely to use language spontaneously in unstructured social situations (Bartak, Rutter, & Cox, 1975). Autistic children who score well on formal reading tests still display no spontaneous interest in reading for pleasure (Gould, 1986). And finally, when symbolic play abilities are assessed by means of a standardized test like the one developed by Lowe and Costello (1976), autistic children give evidence of a greater capacity for make-believe than they ordinarily display in the classroom.

The argument that motivational factors account for the play deficits of autistic children is illustrated by a study by Lewis and Boucher (1988). The researchers examined the play of normal, autistic, and mentally retarded children under three conditions. In the *spontaneous* condition, a variety of toys (e.g., cars, trucks, a gas pump, blocks, dolls, doll accessories, toy animals) were set out on the floor, and the children were invited individually to play as they wished while the tester "did some writing." In the *elicited* condition, children were handed toys, such as a car and a gasoline pump, and asked, "What can these do? Show me what you can do with these." Finally, in the *instructed* condition, children were given directions, such as "Show me how the car goes under a bridge" or "Show me how the doll washes her (or his) hands."

On the basis of what other researchers have found, it was expected that autistic children would engage in less symbolic play than the other two groups in the spontaneous condition. However, spontaneous play differences were not found by Lewis and Boucher (1988), because none of the children in any group demonstrated spontaneous symbolic play. Support for the conative hypothesis was suggested, nevertheless, by the discovery of no group differences in either the elicited or the instructed conditions. When questions were asked or instructions given by the adult, all three groups of children engaged in equal amounts of make-believe play, with equal degrees of imagination.

The Child under Stress: Play in the Hospital

When he was just four-and-a-half years old, Joshua was hospitalized for six days, the result of an automobile accident that left him with a broken leg and three fractured ribs. Neither Joshua nor his parents were prepared for the psychological consequences of his hospitalization, an experience that can be one of the most trying ordeals of the childhood years (Wilson, 1986).

Although secure in the knowledge that his parents were not about to abandon him, Joshua was grief stricken by the separation from his family—and from his playmates—that the hospital stay required. In addition, he was terrified of the imagined harm that could be done to his body. He feared that he would be cut into and then sewn up. He feared that he might die as a result of having blood drawn from his body. Even the painless experience of having his blood pressure taken was frightening because Joshua thought that the pressure on his arm would suffocate him—hardly a logical interpretation, but young children are not known for their powers of logical reasoning. A good illustration of their logical confusion is that Joshua saw his hospitalization as a form of punishment for his naughty behaviors; he pleaded with his parents to let him come home, not realizing that it was beyond their power to make such a decision.

The Stress of Hospitalization

Hospitalization is often so stressful an experience for young children like Joshua that it can result in emotional withdrawal, various regressive behaviors, prolonged crying, disrupted sleep patterns, and forms of destructiveness as children lash out in anger at the indignities being forced upon them (Bolig, 1984; Wilson, 1986). In fact, the effects of hospitalization can last well beyond the time of the actual hospital stay; anxious and antisocial behavior in later childhood has been related to the number of times a child was admitted to a hospital before the age of five (Haslum, 1988).

The stress of hospitalization results from the fact that a stay in a hospital represents a radical departure from everything that is comfortable, safe, and familiar in a child's world. There is a temporary loss not only of family and friends but also of the many rituals that structure a child's life, ranging from eating and sleeping patterns to favorite television programs. And what is more normal in the everyday life of a child—and more alien to the routine of the hospital environment—than play?

To reduce the stresses of hospitalization for children, it is important to bring into the hospital ward as many as possible of the elements that are familiar in the child's outside world. These elements include familiar people, articles of clothing, stuffed animals, favorite toys (if it seems reasonable to do so), and opportunities for play with other children. Let us look now at some of the research on the ways in which play has been incorporated into the hospital routine and the subsequent benefits for the hospitalized child.

Hospital Play Programs

Because play is a natural component of every child's life and because this fact is usually recognized by adults, play seems to occur wherever children are found. When children are hospitalized, there is play in the hospital. It was not until the twentieth century, however, that formally organized programs of play were seen in U.S. hospitals. Some of the earliest programs were developed during the 1920s and 1930s, but the greatest period of expansion occurred fairly recently, during the 1960s and 1970s (Wilson, 1986).

What is involved in a hospital play program? Actually this is a difficult question to answer, since programs vary considerably in their emphases, methods, and particular goals (Bolig, 1984). The type of program that exists depends on many factors, the first of which is the *degree of institutional support* that the program receives. Do the hospital administrators view play as an necessary component of a child's life? Are they willing to staff a play program with regular employees, provide adequate space, and purchase the necessary play materials?

A second influence on the hospital play program is the *educational background of the staff*. Are the staff members familiar with basic principles of child development? More specifically, are they knowledgeable about the physical, intellectual, social, and emotional benefits of play? Do they know how to foster and support play, or is their training almost completely in the area of medical procedure?

Third, programs vary in emphasis depending on who is seen as the *primary intended beneficiary*. It may appear obvious that play programs are designed to benefit hospitalized children. However, an inquisitive parent might discover that play is often used less to promote the optimal development of the child than it is to make life easier for the staff. There is no reason, of course why *both* patient and staff should not benefit from a play program, but programs that exist primarily for the convenience of staff are often based on a limited understanding of the needs of children and often treat play merely as a convenient way to distract a young patient while necessary hospital procedures are carried out.

The broad spectrum of play programs in U.S. hospitals has been conceptualized in terms of a continuum, with simple diversionary programs on one end and comprehensive "child life" programs on the other (Bolig, 1984). The basis of assignment to position within the range is the degree to which a program (1) recognizes the particular developmental needs of children and (2) strives to promote children's optimal psychological development through the use of play. We turn now to an examination of the types of programs that fit into the various categories.

Diversionary Programs

On one extreme of the continuum of hospital play programs are those that use play merely as a diversion, an activity that will keep children occupied, entertained, and relaxed during a hospital stay. Children are typically given toys or encouraged into product-oriented activities, such as drawing pictures, that are in no way related to the experience of hospitalization. In addition, children are often put into passive roles as they are entertained, by films, clowns, or puppet shows, for example, that have distraction as their primary goal.

In **diversionary play programs,** there is rarely any recognition of developmental differences among children; all receive the same types of toys or attend the same types of performances. Furthermore, there is an implicit assumption that children are better off if they do not directly confront the stressful experience of hospitalization. The goal of the play program is to encourage them *not* to think about being in a hospital.

It should be pointed out that, fortunately, diversionary hospital play programs are the exception. They tend to be found in hospitals having no professionals trained to meet children's psychological needs, no consistent adult supervision of the play space, and limited access to a special area in which to play (Bolig, 1984).

Activity/Recreation Programs

A second type of program identified by Bolig (1984) is based on the belief that active children are happy children. The emphasis of such **activity/recreation play programs** is on *doing* things, on work with arts-and-crafts projects so that the child can gain the sense of accomplishment that comes from being busy and productive. The purpose of the activity is not simply to distract the child but to enhance the patient's sense of well-being.

Activities in such programs will vary considerably, of course. They might include drawing, painting, woodworking, stringing beads, reading, playing cards, playing a musical instrument, or making paper sculptures. Quite often the activities that are planned are intended for adult patients as well as for children, and adults and children may even engage in them together (Bolig, 1984).

Therapeutic Programs

Based primarily on psychoanalytic interpretations of children's play (see Chapter One), many hospital play programs use play as a form of therapy for their young patients. The underlying assumption is that children are better adjusted if they can release their feelings freely. Only by confronting those feelings can children overcome the anxieties that are triggered by the various elements of a hospital stay.

Children in **therapeutic play programs** are given materials designed to encourage the expression of feelings—for example, dolls, puppets, miniature hospital equipment, and creative art supplies. With these materials, children can confront and "work through" their fears and hostilities.

Consider as an example of this therapeutic approach the case of eight-year-old Brian, who was confined to his bed for a lengthy hospital stay. Brian was grieving for his normal life. As one component of that grief, he was furious at his parents for putting him in the hospital and at the doctors and nurses for keeping him there. He became rude and sarcastic each time his parents came to see him, and his father reacted by saying, "You have no reason to be mad at *us*. We couldn't help it." Brian's mother remarked that if her son was going to be unpleasant when she came to visit, perhaps she should visit less often!

The hospital play therapist realized that Brian's angry response to hospitalization was quite normal but felt that the boy would do better to release his anger in more constructive ways. She told Brian that exercise was an important element in his recovery, and so she had a punching bag suspended from a wire above his bed. Brian was free to use it whenever he wanted to, and he did so with great enthusiasm— channeling his angry feelings into a form of expression that was safe and, in doing so, perhaps coming to understand the feelings a little better.

Child Development Programs

A number of hospital play programs in recent years have based their philosophical orientation on general principles and theories of child development. They tend to focus on the whole child, on his or her intellectual, social, physical, and emotional development, and they see the role of the adult supervisor of hospital play as both counselor and nondirective educator.

Typical **child development play programs** include curricula that are found in preschool or elementary school classrooms. Children may listen to stories, draw, paint, sculpture, assemble puzzles, build with blocks, and learn a variety of quantitative, scientific, and verbal skills. In that sense, life in the hospital comes to resemble life in the outside world, and because it appears relatively normal to the child, the hospitalization experience seems to be less threatening.

Comprehensive Child Life Programs

During the 1960s there emerged a type of hospital play program that was referred to as "child life." Stimulated by the work of The Association for the Care of Children's Health, the focus of the **comprehensive child life play program** is on *all* aspects of the hospitalized child's development, seen in both an individual and a social context. The objective of such programs is to reduce children's anxiety, as well as that of their families, and help them maintain their self-esteem throughout the hospital experience. Working toward that goal is a health care team that includes a child life specialist, an experienced counselor well trained in a field like education, psychology, or child development.

The child life specialist works with entire families, rather than only with children. He or she educates them about the child's illness and about hospital procedures, helps them to communicate with one another during their stressful ordeal, and encourages parents to maintain their positions of influence over their children's lives.

It is clear that in comprehensive programs of this type, play is not the only emphasis. Nevertheless, play retains a central position within the child life model. Children, and their parents, are encouraged to play in order that they can continue to grow intellectually, socially, and emotionally while in the hospital *and* in order that they can communicate their feelings and, in doing so, come to understand them better. In that sense, the comprehensive child life program represents a blend of both the child development and the release-oriented models (Bolig, 1984).

Providing the Conditions Necessary for Play

The diversity of hospital play programs is overwhelming. Are there any conclusions that can be drawn about their relative usefulness? Perhaps there are. When the various programs are compared, it appears that the Comprehensive model is the one most likely to meet the multiple needs of the child under stress, as well as those of the child's family (Bolig, 1984). What is more, the proliferation of such programs in recent years tells us much about the importance of play in a child's life; it is significant that the most effective hospital programs, by whatever names they are called, are those that most adequately provide the conditions necessary for play to occur. We turn now to a discussion of those essential conditions.

In order for play to occur in a hospital setting, the following three conditions must be present (Chance, 1979). First, there must be a *child-oriented atmosphere*. Second, there must be available a supply of *appropriate play materials*. Finally, an essential component is the guidance of a *supportive adult supervisor*.

A Child-Oriented Atmosphere

Unlike most other areas of the hospital, the children's ward should be a warm and inviting place, decorated with colorful mobiles, pictures, and wall paintings and containing a variety of toys and play materials. Perhaps the sense of being invited into a special place might first be conveyed when the patient is greeted by the medical staff upon arrival.

If possible, a separate playroom should be made available, a place to which children will want to come, one that they will see as a point halfway between the hospital and the home. The playroom should be a sanctuary for children in that no medical procedures can be performed there, and it should be accessible to *all* children, even those who are not ambulatory. In the playroom, the child should have the opportunity to demonstrate the kind of independent behaviors that may not be tolerated elsewhere in the hospital, to express all their feelings freely and openly, and to engage in social play with other young patients (Bolig, 1984).

Appropriate Play Materials

Play materials in the hospital should be familiar to the child so that the psychological distance between home and hospital is minimized. In addition, they should be characterized by a high degree of diversity in order to be suitable for children who vary in their developmental levels and their interests. Included might be art supplies, crafts, books, games, musical instruments, and electronic equipment, such as films, tape recorders, radios, record players, television sets, and video games. If such activities are possible, the hospitalized child might also benefit from the use of outdoor play equipment.

Hospital play materials should certainly include toys that are medically oriented: stethoscopes, syringes, bandages, blood pressure kits, nurse and doctor costumes, toy ambulances, and an assortment of dolls and puppets that can be assigned the various roles in a hospital drama. By rehearsing the medical procedures they expect to go through, children can come to understand them better and fear them less. In these rehearsals, children often reveal to adult observers some frightening misconceptions about hospital care.

Claire, a well-adjusted five-year-old, was terrified of having her broken leg put in a cast. The evening before the procedure, the child played doctor with several of the dolls in the playroom; she took them one after another and wrapped them completely, head to foot, in bandages. The staff nurse, who was playing the role of a medical assistant, asked her why the bandages had to cover the dolls' entire bodies, and Claire replied that she was putting casts, and not just bandages, on the children. What did that mean? Claire pointed out that a cast is hard, and not soft like a bandage, and a cast covers your whole body for long periods of time. The nurse then tried to clear up Claire's misconception about casts, and as they spoke, the child mentioned seeing a television program recently in which a man lay in a hospital bed with his entire body in a cast. "He just had a hole where his mouth was," she said. Claire mistakenly believed that the same fate awaited her the following morning.

In addition to educating children and helping them to cope with their fears, dramatic play with a medical theme can give them a sense of control that is usually lacking during their hospital stay. The child can reverse roles in playing with dolls, and can become the powerful doctor instead of the helpless patient. This temporary illusion of power can help build self-confidence and can make the hospital experience a less threatening one.

Finally, when children, medical staff, and parents are involved together in a dramatic play experience, a sense of community is formed—a sense that the child is not undergoing treatment alone. In fact, parents who participate in such play, as is desirable in the case of a preschool child, become more comfortable in the hospital setting and transmit to their children an increased sense of well-being about the hospital experience. The children tend to recover faster, as indicated by physiological measures like heart rate, temperature, and blood pressure, and the parent is enlisted as a partner in the healing process, rather than being simply a supportive bystander (Skipper & Leonard, 1968; Wilson, 1986).

A Warm, Accepting Supervisor

The hospital playroom should be directed by an adult who is warm, accepting, permissive, and consistent. In the absence of an adult supervisor, young children may simply not be able to play; even older children usually need caring adult support until they are ready to develop relationships with their hospitalized peers (Bolig, 1984).

Because separation from the family is largely responsible for a child's negative reaction to a hospital stay, it is important that the play supervisor be a consistent figure, not just one of many. Such consistency promotes the development of attachment between caretaker and child and thereby reduces the childs sense of separation from parents. In fact, for this very reason, it is increasingly common to have young patients cared for by fewer nurses assigned to them on a case basis, rather than by many nurses assigned on the basis of task (Bolig, 1984).

Summary

Relatively little is known about the play of handicapped children, primarily because of numerous methodological problems that characterize much of the research on the topic. In addition, it has not been easy to determine the origins of differences between normal and handicapped children that have been observed. Handicapped children experience physical, mental, and/or emotional difficulties, but they also grow up in environments that are different from those of normal children. For example, they may lack appropriate physical surroundings to play in, adult supervisors to help them plan and carry out their play routines, and suitable playmates. These elements may conspire to foster an impression that handicapped children experience basic play deficits. In fact, this impression may be completely false since the observed play differences could be environmental in origin.

Children with visual impairments play less imaginatively than sighted children and engage less often in games of make-believe. Nevertheless, they do enjoy play, and their play can be enhanced if adults encourage them by helping them plan for play and providing them with sensory-rich play environments. Speech-delayed children and those who are hearing impaired engage less often than normal children in symbolic play, but the differences are quantitative rather than qualitative; there is no evidence of a far-reaching symbolic deficit in those with hearing difficulties or whose language is delayed.

In terms of their play with objects, intellectually impaired children seem to prefer what might be thought of as structured materials, such as puzzles and jacks, while nonretarded children of the same mental age prefer open-ended materials (e.g., art supplies) that allow them to be creative and imaginative. In addition, mentally handicapped children are less likely than normal children to combine objects appropriately in play. Symbolic, or make-believe, play has been observed consistently in mentally retarded children; there is no evidence that intellectual impairment prevents children from engaging in imaginative acts of make-believe. It should be noted, however, that mental age is a better than chronological age as a predictor of the onset of symbolic play; thus, symbolic play typically appears later in intellectually impaired children than in those whose intellectual development is normal.

Autistic children show evidence of a basic communication difficulty, a profound inability to understand and function within the normal social environment; the autistic child apparently fails to differentiate between the self and the external world. In toy and object play, autistic children are likely to engage in repetitive, stereotyped manipulation and less likely than normal children to use objects symbolically in make-believe. They are also less likely to engage in complex toy play and to use toys appropriately.

Autistic children rarely engage in symbolic play. The reasons for this pattern are not fully understood. There are alternative prevailing opinions on the subject: (1) Such children experience a symbolic deficit in that they are unable to impute mental states to others; (2) they simply are not interested enough to try to engage in make-believe.

Play can be very beneficial for normal children undergoing temporary stresses, such as that involved in the experience of hospitalization. In recognition of this fact, there has emerged a broad range of hospital play programs, particularly within the past 20 years. Some merely attempt to distract the child so that hospital routines can be more efficiently carried out. Others are firmly rooted in child development principles and work to maintain the emotional, social, and intellectual well-being of hospitalized children and their families as well.

It seems clear that play is unlikely to occur in a hospital setting, however, unless certain conditions are present. There must be a child-oriented atmosphere, a supply of appropriate play materials, and the guidance of a supportive and continuing adult supervisor.

Key Terms

Activity/Recreation Play Programs
Child Development Play Programs
Comprehensive Child Life Play
   Programs
Conative Hypothesis

Diversionary Play Programs
Enactive Representation
Symbol Deficit Hypothesis
Therapeutic Play Programs

CHAPTER EIGHT

Play and
Intellectual
Development

In large red letters, the magazine advertisement described the computer game as not only fun for children, but helpful in teaching them the basic mathematical concepts most necessary for success in life. On another page of the same magazine was an ad boasting that infants who played with the manufacturer's brand of toys would develop "handling skills" and "tracking abilities" and would also come to master "eye focusing." The advertisement went on to say that "even though these are playthings for your baby, they're also the most advanced learning instruments to be called toys." A third advertisement suggested that children should be enrolled in a read-aloud book club because child development experts agree that an early love of reading builds a love of learning, which leads to "future success." Indeed, it is striking how often the word *success* appears in advertisements for children's toys. Is the reader to assume that children deprived of these particular toys will grow up deficient in quantitative skills, will never develop proper eye-focusing or handling skills, or even worse, will be generally unsuccessful in life?

What exactly is known about the influence of play on children's intellectual development? This question is a challenging one, and the answers are certainly not as easy to arrive at as some toy manufacturers would suggest. In the first place, there has been virtually no genuine *experimental* research on the effects of specific types of play on later cognitive development. Most of the research is correlational, with the result that the direction of cause and effect is unclear. For example, it is known that infants who have a wide variety of play materials available score higher on some intellectual measures, but it has *not* been proven that the play materials actually caused any intellectual advancement. Instead, it may be the case that children who are brighter initially may seek out and receive from their parents a wider variety of toys (Bradley, 1986).

A second reason for the difficulty in arriving at simple answers about play and intellectual growth is that any child's environment is highly complex, with multiple simultaneous directions of influence. One must realize that the environment of play is both physical and social, and that a child's intellectual growth can be affected by the physical environment (e.g., amount and variety of stimulus material, noise level, crowdedness), the social environment (e.g., quality of interaction with parents and peers), and some complicated interaction of the two. The physical environment has often been neglected in the research, however, since the social influences on childhood cognition have typically been seen as the more meaningful (Wachs, 1986).

Despite the fact that easy and unequivocal answers may not be forthcoming, the question of the role of play in children's intellectual development is an important one, and it is to that question that this chapter is devoted. We begin with a discussion of the physical environment of play, emphasizing the effects of play materials on both general and specific cognitive development. Although it may be ridiculous to believe that providing the right toys will prepare children for admission to an Ivy League university, nevertheless it seems that the availability of stimulating play materials in infancy and very early childhood is definitely related to later intellectual development.

In terms of the social environment, the quality of the parent–child and peer relationships appears to be related to children's general intellectual functioning. In addition, a number of investigators have examined the influence of social play on specific areas, such as language ability, problem solving, and creativity.

Play Materials

Infancy

An examination of all the environmental variables in an infant's life reveals that the two most powerful predictors of intellectual development are parental involvement, discussed in Chapter Three, and the *availability of play materials* (Barnard, Bee, & Hammond, 1984; Bradley, 1986; Bradley & Caldwell, 1984; Gottfried, 1986; Gottfried & Gottfried, 1984; Johnson, Breckenridge, & McGowan, 1984; Siegel, 1984). Specifically, it seems that infants who have a variety of toys available for their use—and who choose to use them—perform better on various intellectual measures at the time, as well as later in life, than do infants who lack such materials.

The play materials, toys or nontoys, that are related to infant intellectual development are not necessarily the latest so-called educational innovations. In fact, psychologists rarely recommend specific toys by name but speak instead of those that serve particular functions. Of special value are play materials that facilitate the development of eye–hand coordination, pull and push toys, toys that allow children to fit things together and pull them apart, building toys like blocks, reading materials, musical toys, and for the child in the second year, toys that stimulate make-believe play (Siegel, 1984).

Let us turn now to a discussion of some of the specific findings. Based on repeated in-home observations of 36 infants and their mothers, Clarke-Stewart (1973) noted that by the time the children were one-and-a-half years old, they spent about 50% of their time exploring and playing with objects. She also discovered a significant relationship between the variety of toys available to infants and their performance on various intellectual measures, as well as a relationship between the same measures and the infants' actual use of their toys.

Wachs (1979) reported that the availability of books and audiovisually responsive toys during the first two years of life is correlated with IQ at 30 months of age, while other researchers have found correlations at even later points in children's development. For example, in a major study of 163 working- and middle-class families in Seattle, Barnard, Bee, and Hammond (1984) kept records of play materials available to children at 4, 8, 12, and 24 months of age. They also assessed the children's mental and physical progress at one and two years, using the Bayley Scales of Infant Development, and their intelligence at the age of four, as indicated by performance on a Stanford-Binet Intelligence Scale. Modest but significant correlations were discovered between availability of play materials during the first two years of life and performance on both the Bayley Scales and the Stanford-Binet.

In summarizing the research on play materials and intellectual development, Bradley (1986) offered several tentative conclusions. First, infants and toddlers are definitely interested in play materials and spend a good deal of time with them. Second, a modest relationship exists between the availability of play materials early in life and later intellectual development, and this relationship cannot be completely explained by differences in quality of the parent–child interaction. In other words, the physical environment really does seem to be important in intellectual growth, independent of the effects of the social environment. Third, play materials are beneficial in that they serve as an incentive for social interaction, as well as offering opportunities for skill development and the mastery of tools. Finally, in an older infant, toys can serve as a stimulus for imaginative play, which in itself can lead to advances in intellectual development.

The Preschool Years

Little is known about the intellectual significance of toys for infants; even less is known about the influence of play materials for children beyond the age of two (Bradley, 1986). Nevertheless, some psychologists, and particularly educators, have addressed the issue of the relationship of specific toys to specific areas of intellectual development in older children.

Wolfgang and Stakenas (1985) divided commonly found preschool children's toys into several categories and correlated their uses with performance on subsections of the McCarthy Scales of Intellectual Development, a well-known intelligence test for children. They found that toys with different functions contributed in different ways to children's overall cognitive growth.

Fluid construction toys are those with a fluid quality, such as paints and clay, that can be used to create an unspecified product. It was found that these contribute mostly to perceptual performance (drawing, block building, puzzle forming, right–left orientation). *Structured construction* toys (e.g., blocks, Legos, puzzles) are those that retain their structure as they are used to make something; these contribute most to children's verbal, perceptual, quantitative, and memory development. *Microsymbolic* toys are miniature life toys, such as cars and trucks, dolls, and toy buildings; these were found to enhance children's memory. Finally, *macrosymbolic* toys include child-size play equipment, such as props for dramatic play. These were found to influence memory, perceptual performance, and quantitative skills (Wolfgang & Stakenas, 1985).

Psychologists who study children's intellectual development report that a wide variety of underlying cognitive skills are enhanced during play, particularly during the course of symbolic play. These skills include measurement, equivalency, balance, spatial concepts, conservation, decentration, reversibility, and logical classification (Copple, Cocking, & Matthews, 1984; Elder & Pederson, 1978; Fein, 1975; Jackowitz & Watson, 1980; Piaget, 1962; Rubin, 1980; Rubin, Fein, & Vandenberg, 1983; Rubin & Pepler, 1982; Ungerer, Zelazo, Kearsley, & O'Leary, 1981; Vygotsky, 1967). Rather than attempting to explain these cognitive skills out of context by referring to relevant examples from children's play, we shall look at some of the play materials and activities commonly found in preschool classrooms and attempt to describe them in terms of specific intellectual benefits, with particular reference to the skills mentioned above.

We are not suggesting, of course, that the materials and activities discussed below—blocks, clay, water, and creative movement—are the only ones that can influence children's cognitive growth; they are simply among the most widely available to young children and the most frequently evaluated. It should be kept in mind, however, that the extent of their influence may depend on the specific ways in which they are used, and the availability of adult encouragement and support.

*Putting a puzzle together is a structured activity
that can enhance a child's verbal, perceptual,
quantitative, and memory skills.*

Blocks

Blocks are among the most appealing of all toys for young children. They are safe,
clean, sturdy, and familiar, and so they will not threaten any child. What is more, blocks
are astonishingly versatile in terms of their age appropriateness. From the one-and-a-
half-year-old who simply stacks small cubes or drags floor blocks around the room to
the five-year-old who plans and executes sophisticated building projects with wooden
blocks of various shapes to the twelve-year-old who plays with Legos containing
hundreds of tiny parts that can be made into elaborate and intricate designs, children of
all ages enjoy block play. Perhaps adults continue to do so as well.

   Not only are blocks appealing, but they have the potential to teach a variety of
quantitative and spatial concepts to the child. In the first place, blocks teach about
measurement. In order to measure correctly, one must understand the concepts of *unit
iteration* and *subdivision* (Piaget, 1962). Unit iteration is the ability to realize that a
number of individual parts can be put together to make a whole, as when one realizes

that 12 units of distance called inches can be put together to make a unit known as a foot. Subdivision is the ability to separate distances mentally into smaller segments; one can estimate, for example, the number of individual yards into which a playing field can be subdivided.

Children playing with blocks can acquire an understanding of measurement principles. They can regularly perform acts of unit iteration and subdivision, *without* direct instruction on the part of an adult. For example, five-year-old Katie wants to build a road that extends from one end of the block corner to the other, but how many blocks will she need to do the job? She asks her teacher, who wisely responds that Katie should try to figure it out for herself. The child examines the length of one rectangular block, observes the distance she wants to span, mentally subdividing it into block lengths, and then selects six blocks to build her road. As it turns out, Katie's estimate is low; six blocks take her only half way across the space, so now she must determine how many are needed to fill the remaining space. Katie's measurement error and her self-correcting behavior provide a valuable learning experience for the child.

Related to measurement is the mathematical concept of equivalency, another important learning concept that can result from block play. **Equivalency** is the recognition that space can be divided into different-size units and that a certain number of units of one size correspond to a different number of units of another. For example, Brian is building a "raft," in the process using all the 24-inch rectangular blocks in the block corner. Todd wants to make an identical raft but must rely on blocks of different shapes. But how many 6-inch rectangles correspond to the long blocks that make up a side of Brian's raft? How many blocks arranged in a lengthwise fashion will correspond to one of Brian's blocks laid widthwise? This is for Todd a problem requiring an understanding of equivalency.

Blocks teach children about the concept of balance: When stacking objects on top of one another, it is necessary to place the largest and heaviest objects at the bottom and the smallest and lightest at the top. If a child fails to do so, the structure will not stand. Children often choose to build upward into space with blocks of various sizes and shapes, creating structures that are top-heavy and crash to the floor. With each such experience, children learn something about principles of balance, and in fact, they may delight in testing their limits, intentionally placing a block at the top of a structure that is likely to cause it to collapse.

Children at play with blocks learn much about *spatial concepts*. A mature understanding of space is what Piaget and Inhelder (1956) called a **Euclidean spatial concept**; that is, space is thought of as an overall network, independent of the number or the arrangement of elements within it. The amount of space in a room, for example, remains the same regardless of the arrangement of furniture within it. A mature spatial concept allows people to imagine their own positions within the context of an overall spatial grid and to measure space on three dimensions. A college student might be able to envision an aerial view of the campus and to estimate with a fair degree of accuracy his or her current location. The same student might be able to estimate his or her distance from particular buildings and, using the imaginary spatial overlay, determine which building he or she is closest to and farthest from at a given time.

The ability to look at space from a broader perspective is not usually found in children until the age of seven or eight (Piaget & Inhelder, 1956). As a result, preschoolers experience confusion on spatial tasks. Hide a toy at a certain spot in a nursery school classroom and provide children with a detailed map indicating the various objects in the room, with an *X* marking the location of the hidden toy, and the children will still have difficulty finding it. Why? Because they are unable to form an overall image of the room and then to measure the space on two dimensions at once (e.g., from left to right, from the front to the back of the room). As a result, they attend primarily to the specific objects within the space rather than to the overall space itself. If on the map the hidden toy is "near the round table," they may search in that general vicinity, but they are just as likely to look on one side of the table as the other. They are unable, in a sense, to see the "big picture."

Playing blocks, children come to understand space better because they are constantly building up and out in all directions. They also spontaneously form both horizontal and vertical grid patterns with floor blocks (see Figure 8.1), they enclose space horizontally and vertically, they divide enclosed spaces into smaller spaces (see Figure 8.2), and more significantly, they are able to stand back from, and above, their block creations and acquire experience at getting the lay of the land.

Even the experience of putting one's blocks away after playing with them can offer opportunities for intellectual growth. Blocks are typically organized according to size and shape in the block area, and many classrooms have templates indicating where the various blocks should be placed. When children return them to their proper places, they are learning to attend to the sometimes small differences among them, and they are also learning to sort them according to their logically defining properties, a skill that is referred to as **logical classification.**

In order to classify objects, children must be able, first, to perceive the logical similarity among them and then to sort them according to their common features. Preschool children often fail to use logic when they classify and instead rely only on

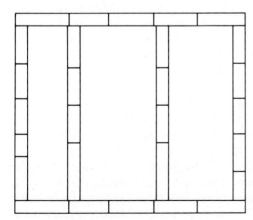

FIGURE 8.1   Grid Patterns Made with Floor Blocks

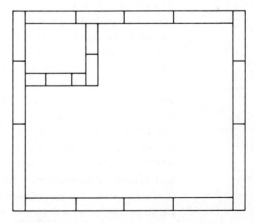

FIGURE 8.2   The Use of Blocks to Divide Enclosed Space into Smaller Spaces

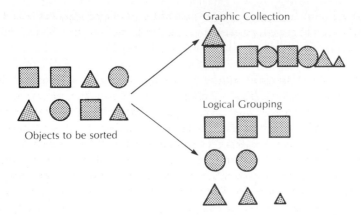

FIGURE 8.3   Graphic Collections: Pleasing arrangements of figures produced by preschool children when asked to group objects.

perception. That is, they sort objects not in relation to one another, but in relation to an overall pattern of which each object forms a part. Inhelder and Piaget (1964) referred to this immature type of sorting as **graphic collections,** which are pleasing or interesting arrangements of the figures (see Figure 8.3). Give a preschooler a group of different-size blocks in the shapes of squares, rectangles, and circles, and the child may line them up and say "I made a train," or arrange them in a circle to make a "necklace." An older child, in contrast, would sort them according to size and/or shape.

Experience can certainly improve children's classification skills. It has been found that if adults demonstrate for preschoolers exactly how objects are to be sorted and then give them the opportunity to practice what they have been shown, classification ability improves considerably (Smiley & Brown, 1979). The experience of putting one's blocks back in their appropriate locations after playing with them can certainly encourage children to be responsible. It may also teach them something about the skill of logical classification.

We mentioned earlier that the availability of various play materials does not guarantee that they will be of intellectual benefit to a particular child: Much depends on the ways that materials are used and the attitudes of the adults in the child's surroundings. Block play provides many examples of the importance of the appropriate adult attitude. How likely is it that a child would learn to measure by playing with blocks if, when the child tried to estimate the number of blocks needed to span a given space, a supposedly helpful adult quickly made suggestions or, even worse, went to fetch the blocks for the child? What would the child learn about balance if an adult hovered about constantly, advising the child on which block should or should not be placed on the tower? Would a child learn as efficiently about spatial concepts if his or her block play was excessively restricted in terms of numbers of blocks or available play space? And finally, what opportunities for practicing logical classification skills would be lost if the children were not required to pick up after themselves?

Clay

Aaron is busily playing with a large lump of clay. He pounds it repeatedly against the table, then pulls off a large piece, breaks it into several smaller pieces and rolls them into balls. He soon grows tired of rolling, and so he flattens the balls into "pancakes," which he distributes to each of the other three children seated at his table. Later he collects his pancakes and stretches them into "hot dogs." Then he rolls them into balls again. Next he takes some of the balls, breaks them in half, and makes smaller balls of the broken pieces. Finally, when he begins to tire of the clay, he rolls the balls together in the following manner: First, he combines two small ones into a larger one; then he repeatedly adds another ball to the growing mass until he has a fairly large lump, which he proceeds to join to the original lump of clay that the teacher had given him.

In the process of playing with his clay, Aaron is learning a good deal about the concept of quantity, or amount. Such learning is important in the acquisition of what Piaget (1983) described as **conservation,** a skill that emerges as children move from a stage of intuitive, prelogical thinking that characterizes the preschool years to a stage of logical thinking that is typical of grade school children.

A true understanding of quantity, which clay and other play materials and experiences can help a child to acquire (Rubin, Fein, & Vandenberg, 1983), involves an awareness that, regardless of changes in physical appearance, the amount of a substance remains the same if no material is added or subtracted. A simple in-home experiment can illustrate developmental differences in the ability to conserve. Break a cookie in half and ask a child if there is still as much cookie as there was before. A preschool child often decides that now there is more than there was before because two pieces *look* like more than one piece. An older child will realize, of course, that no matter how the pieces of the cookie are arranged, in halves, quarters, or even if the cookie is reduced to crumbs, the amount remains exactly the same. Unlike the younger child, the older child is said to conserve quantity, to recognize that the amount does not change simply because of a change in the physical appearance of the material. It is for this reason that Piaget referred to this ability as conservation.

Let us now return to Aaron's experience at the clay table to see how his understanding of quantity can be influenced by his play. Aaron is constantly changing the appearance of the clay, even though he realizes he is working with a predetermined amount provided by his teacher. He changes the shape of the clay and later reverses the process; he divides it into smaller and smaller parts and puts it together again. In the process of changing shapes and reversing the changes, dividing and then combining again, Aaron is learning something about the fundamental nature of matter: that appearance changes do not mean quantity changes. In that sense, he is learning that appearances can be deceiving, and such learning can help to bring about the transition from what cognitive psychologists see as the perception-based thinking of early childhood to the logical thinking of older children and adults.

Water Play

When children play at a water table, or in a bathtub or sink for that matter, there is an opportunity for a considerable amount of learning to occur. For example, they can come to understand something about the principle of flotation as they analyze the properties of their play materials that float and compare them with those that do not. When bubbles are involved in the play, children often become sculptors, creating a variety of shapes, many of which will form a basis for sociodramatic play, and all of which contribute to the "ego building" that Hartley, Frank, and Goldenson (1951) described as a benefit inherent in bubble play.

One of the major intellectual contributions of water play is that children can enhance their ability to use principles of measurement, much as they can when they play with clay. When children play with water, they typically have available to them a variety of containers of different sizes and shapes, as well as tubes, funnels, strainers, egg beaters, plungers, and droppers. A part of their enjoyment is the constant pouring of the water back and forth from container to container and through the assorted props they have been provided with. As they do so, they measure the liquid. How many small jars of water will be needed to fill up the large one? Will the water from one jar overflow if poured through a funnel into a jar that differs in size?

In addition to measurement, the child at the water table can acquire a greater appreciation of what Piaget (1983) spoke of as *conservation of liquid,* an understanding of quantity in a fluid medium. Children who are successful on tests of conservation of liquid realize that, regardless of the size, shape, or number of containers used, the amount of liquid remains the same so long as none is added or taken away. Nonconservers, on the other hand, seem to believe that the actual amount may change when the container changes. Many a parent has experienced the frustration of trying to convince preschool children that they are receiving equal amounts of juice when the juice is offered in differently shaped glasses, one short and wide, for example, and another tall and thin. Even if the nonconserving child actually watches as the juice is poured from its bottle and carefully measured out, he or she may still insist that one glass (usually the taller one) has more because it looks bigger.

When children are engaged in water play, they often pour water from one container to another, and in doing so they learn that sometimes containers actually do hold the same amount of liquid even though they are different in appearance. A tall, thin beaker may hold exactly as much as a short, wide container. What sense do children make of this odd discovery? They come to realize that the height of a container is not the only dimension of relevance; the width must be considered at the same time. Indeed, it is characteristic of preschool children that they often focus, or *center,* on the most noticeable features of the environment and ignore others. The thinking of the more mature child, on the other hand, is characterized by **decentration,** the ability to attend simultaneously to two or more environmental features. Thus, play with water can facilitate the development of decentration, as can a variety of other forms of make-believe play among preschoolers (Rubin, Fein, & Vandenberg, 1983).

In addition to learning to decenter, children playing with water can also acquire **reversibility** in their thinking, a critical underlying element in logical reasoning. As an example of reversibility in water play, consider the actions of two five-year-old children, Jack and Helen. The children establish the goal of emptying a large plastic container that is filled with water, and they begin by pouring some into a plastic cup approximately one-fifth the size. Soon the cup is full, but a considerable amount of water still remains in the container. Jack and Helen pour some of it into a second cup. In a short while, another cup is needed, and a fourth, and a fifth, until the large container is finally empty. Their goal accomplished, Jack and Helen now decide to fill the plastic container again, using the water in the five cups. One by one, the cups are poured back until the large container is full again. The two children have learned that, if certain of their actions are reversed, the material they are working with can be returned to its original state.

Creative Movement

Typists occasionally have the experience of being asked to describe from memory the locations of the various keys on a keyboard, and discover that they are unable to do so correctly. Yet when that person sits down and begins to type, his or her fingers find the correct keys instantly. It seems that the information is encoded not in the mind but in the physical activity itself.

Many cognitive theorists, including Jean Piaget and Jerome Bruner, have suggested that physical activity is an essential component of knowledge acquisition. It was Piaget's (1983) contention, for example, that the earliest forms of thinking and problem solving are of a sensory and a physical nature and that the child's earliest concepts are consistent action patterns, which he referred to as **schemes.** As an example, infants might possess a sucking scheme, meaning that they would categorize, as it were, by their actions upon them, certain objects as things to be sucked on and others as things not to put in one's mouth.

Bruner (1974) spoke of the concept of **enactive representation,** by which he meant that information about the world can be encoded motorically instead of, or as well as, mentally. This concept is illustrated by the knowledge people have of riding a bicycle, typing, shifting the gears of an automobile, playing a piano, or tying a knot in a necktie. Typists might indeed have excellent working knowledge of the keyboard, but their knowledge might be primarily in their fingers. They might be unable to explain to others how they type so well, they might "forget" the keyboard layout until they sit down to type, and they might even confuse themselves if they think too much about what they are doing.

Considering the importance of motor activity in the acquisition of knowledge, it seems clear that creative movement as a form of play can be an enriching intellectual experience. The learning potential of creative movement was explored in great depth by Werner and Burton (1979), who offered numerous suggestions for incorporating playful movement activities into the curriculum. It was Werner and Burton's contention, in fact, that almost any academic subject can be taught through the medium of movement. They considered movement to be the oldest of all teaching methods because among the most primitive of human societies the major form of education consisted of learning how physically to survive.

Let us look at two of the intellectual concepts that Werner and Burton believed could be taught through movement and at the specific activities they recommended to facilitate the teaching. The subject is the geography of the British Isles, and the specific lesson is that the British Isles are divided into the countries of England, Ireland, Scotland, and Wales. The teacher has the children make with rope an outline map of the British Isles on the floor and place objects that represent each country (e.g., coal for Wales, linen for Ireland) in the designated areas.

The children are then divided into teams, and when the teacher calls out the name of a country, a child from each team has to run quickly to the map, take an appropriate object, and return to his or her teammates. After all the children have had a turn, the teacher reviews the locations of the countries and talks about the significance of the objects the children have retrieved in terms of the physical and economic characteristics of the country they come from.

A second example provided by Werner and Burton (1979) illustrates how principles of physics can be taught through creative movement. The specific topic is friction, and the teacher wants to demonstrate that friction is necessary to start and stop the motion of an object. The children are organized into two teams, each of which must run through an obstacle course in the gym, one wearing tennis shoes, and the other wearing only socks. The children in socks will slip and slide as they run the course, making the process slower for them, while friction will prevent the group wearing shoes from sliding. After the game, the teacher can discuss the results attributable to the characteristics of friction, which can be helpful when a person tries to start, stop, or change directions.

This exercise indicates that children can learn about the properties of physical matter by using their bodies in a most enjoyable way. Again, as in the geography lesson, it can be seen that the information is encoded motorically, as well as mentally, and will in all likelihood be easier to remember as a result. More importantly, the activity is pleasurable for the participants. The teacher's goal may be to transmit a body of academic subject matter, but for the children, the lesson may seem like nothing other than purely physical play, which, of course, it is!

Language Play and Language Development

In several sections of this book, most notably in our discussions of developmental play patterns in Chapter Three and play in language-delayed children in Chapter Seven, it was pointed out that there is a strong relationship between language and make-believe play. Both language and symbolic play involve the ability to represent the world mentally to oneself. It is not surprising, therefore, that the developmental patterns of language and play are parallel and that language impairment is related to deficits in symbolic play.

We now turn to an examination of the ways that play can facilitate children's language development. There is evidence to suggest that the very experience of playing can benefit children's language abilities in a number of ways. Before discussing language play, however, let us look briefly at some of the major components of the human language system.

Aspects of Human Language

Human language consists of several different aspects, each related to the formulation of rules pertaining to a different area of language production. These aspects are the phonological, the syntactic, the semantic, and the pragmatic. The **phonological aspects of language** are those that pertain to the production of sound. A knowledge of phonology allows a person to pronounce, put together, and properly stress the sound system of a language (Hughes, Noppe, & Noppe, 1988; Menyuk, 1982). For example, when English-speaking people ask a question, they proceed toward the end of the utterance with a steadily rising intonation, whereas this sound pattern would not occur in making a declarative statement. Even toddlers recognize this phonological rule, saying "Ball?" to mean "Is that a ball?" or "Where is the ball?" and at other times saying "Ball!" to mean perhaps "I want the ball."

The **syntactic aspects of language** concern the rules by which words are put together into sentences. For example, in English we typically place the adjective before the noun ("the red hat"), whereas in French the order is usually reversed (*"le chapeau rouge"*). Young children realize, for example, that the order of words in a sentence is changed in a systematic manner when a statement is transformed into a question. For example, "The hat is red" becomes "Is the hat red?"

The **semantic aspects of a language** are those that deal with the selection of words that appropriately convey the intended meaning (Menyuk, 1982). A young child may be able to produce words and to put them together correctly in a sentence, for example, but still be unable to convey intended meaning. Three-year-old Laura says, "How far is it to day care?" and her mother answers in terms of the distance from their home to the day-care center. Laura says, "No! How *far?*" and her mother tries again to describe the distance from one place to the other. The child is frustrated and continues to ask the question because she is not receiving a satisfactory answer. Gradually Laura's mother realizes that the child wants to know *when* she will be going to the day-care center again. "How far?" referred to time and not to distance. Semantic confusion of this type is a common feature of the conversations of preschool children.

Finally, the **pragmatic aspects of language** refer to the rules that govern the behaviors for engaging in effective communication (Menyuk, 1982). They involve the recognition that the meaning of language depends to some extent on the social context. For example, the facial expressions, gestures, and personality characteristics of the speaker must be taken into account when interpreting speech, as must the features of the social setting. The words "You look wonderful today" convey a very different meaning when spoken by an acquaintance whose opinion is highly valued but who rarely pays a compliment and when spoken by someone who *always* tells us we look wonderful.

Pragmatics also involves the recognition that effective speech must follow certain social conventions. We must take turns in conversation and must recognize when it is acceptable to interrupt another speaker and when we should not do so. We must tailor our speech to the needs of listeners; we speak differently to a child, for example, than we do to an adult, and we may alter our speech when interacting with a foreigner who has limited knowledge of our language.

Types of Language Play

Children play with all four aspects of the human language system (Kuczaj, 1982, 1985). In fact, Garvey (1977, 1984) suggested that there are four different types of language play, roughly corresponding to the different aspects of language discussed above. These are (1) play with sounds and noises, (2) play with linguistic systems, such as those involving word meanings or grammatical constructions, (3) play with rhymes and words, and (4) play with the conventions of speech.

Play with Sounds

As an example of play with sounds and noises, take the spontaneous babbling of the infant in the first year (Athey, 1984; Garvey, 1977); it is an intrinsically motivated and freely chosen activity that lacks external goals, and it appears, at least to an adult eye, to afford the child a good deal of pleasure.

How might the sound and noise play of infancy aid in the child's intellectual development? Such play seems to be an important element in the development of language. Even though psychologists no longer believe that adults train children to speak by the use of reinforcements, it is likely that social reinforcement does occur in response to infant babbles. Therefore, parents may unintentionally influence their child to make sounds appropriate to the language they speak. "Da-Da" is more likely to gain a favorable adult reaction than is "Ga-Ga." In that sense, the sound play of the infant may ultimately result in advances in sound production (Athey, 1984).

By the end of the first year, infants will produce a variety of playful sounds with their mouths—humming, smacking their lips, bubble blowing, and so forth. Indeed, play with the sounds of language occurs not only during the first two years but can also be found among older children. For example, children at about the age of three or four become fascinated with songs, chants, and rhymes and enjoy producing nonsensical rhyming patterns. And play of this type in older children is related to language development: The ability to rhyme is highly correlated with early reading achievement in children (Athey, 1984).

Certain words or sounds may strike preschoolers as being particularly amusing, and they may repeat them until eventually they lose their comic effect. Preschoolers also play with sound by "talking funny" (Garvey, 1977): They distort their voices, attempting to speak in a high-pitched squeak, in a throaty rasping sound, or in the flat monotone of a favorite robot character.

Play with Grammatical Constructions

During the second year of life, when the child is producing one-word utterances and, by 21 months of age, two-word phrases, there is even greater evidence of play with language (Athey, 1984). Toddlers continue to play with sounds and noises, but now they also experiment in their solitary play with the syntactic and semantic elements of language, such as word order and the uses of different parts of speech. For example, they repeat sentences, each time substituting a new word of the same grammatical category: A child might say, "Daddy go out," "Mommy go out," "Babby go out"; again, "Doggie fall down," "Kitty fall down," "Baby fall down" (Weir, 1962). They build up and break down sentences (e.g., "Give it to me," "Give the cup to me"), and in doing so they isolate sentence components and come to a better understanding of their functions (Garvey, 1977). They ask questions and then provide the answer themselves. They recite lists of words, numbers, or letters. They engage themselves in conversation. They comment on their own behaviors.

It has been suggested that solitary experimental play with the rules of word order may form the basis for the development of the grammatical structures of language (Bruner, 1974; Garvey, 1977, 1984; Ratner & Bruner, 1978). As Garvey (1977, 1984) noted, the private language of the solitary monologue gives children a perfect opportunity to experiment with the elements of speech; the language of social interaction, on the other hand, is goal directed and lacks the element of playfulness found in the solitary monologue. In language play, children can take apart and put together the building blocks of speech in ways that they will not be able to do consciously until the early years of elementary school.

Symbolic Play and Language Comprehension

Symbolic, or make-believe, play can also benefit a child linguistically. As an example, Terry, Jill, and Mark listen to a story being read to them by their kindergarten teacher. Then they are asked to assume the roles of the story characters and to enact the scenes they have just listened to. They do so with great enthusiasm under the gentle direction of their teacher. Later, the teacher asks the children a number of questions about the story, to see how well they understood it and how much they can remember.

Is it possible that the story was more understandable to the children and easier to remember because of their experience in acting out the roles? Some psychologists believe so, suggesting that the strength of the language–play connection in early childhood leads to a natural conclusion: Play can help children better understand the spoken word (Williamson & Silvern, 1984).

Research on the role of play in language comprehension typically takes the form described above: one group of children listens to a story and then plays out the scenes, while another group either engages in discussion of the story or becomes involved in unrelated activities. Later, the children's memory for details of the story is tested. The finding that emerges repeatedly in studies of this type is that the play group displays the greatest understanding of, and memory for, the story's details (Pellegrini & Galda, 1982; Saltz, Dixon, & Johnson, 1977; Silvern, Williamson, Taylor, Surbeck, & Kelly, 1982; Silvern, Williamson, & Waters, 1982; Williamson & Silvern, 1984).

The link between play and language comprehension is not a simple one, however. Children do not *have* to play out a specific story in order to understand it completely. Many stories are quite understandable to children without the necessity of playing them out dramatically. However, when children regularly engage in the enactment of scenes from the stories they listen to, they seem to improve over time in their ability to draw meaning from spoken language (Williamson & Silvern, 1984).

Play, Creativity, and Problem Solving

Within the past 20 years, there has been a considerable amount of research, conducted mostly on preschool children, on the relationship between play and problem solving. More specifically, researchers have looked at the impact of *either* object play or fantasy play on children's ability to solve *either* single-solution or multiple-solution problems. The typical research design has been to (1) allow children to engage in free play with materials that they would later use to solve single-solution problems or (2) examine the relationship between make-believe play and children's ability to deal with multiple-solution problems (Rubin, Fein, & Vandenberg, 1983).

Convergent Problem Solving

Single-solution problems require the ability to engage in what is known as **convergent problem solving** (Pepler, 1979; Pepler & Ross, 1981), the ability to bring a variety of isolated pieces of information together to come up with the one correct solution. As an example, consider the nature of the problem presented to a group of preschool children by Sylva (1977). The children were seated and told to attempt to obtain an object that was beyond their reach, without standing up or leaving their chairs. Two long sticks were provided, neither long enough to reach the desired object. However (and this was the only solution to the problem), if the sticks were clamped together, the children could attain their goal.

Sylva (1977) divided the preschoolers into three groups. The first were allowed to play freely with the problem-solving materials prior to engaging in the task. A second group watched as the experimenter solved the problem before they were asked to do it. Finally, a third group, the control, was given neither the play experience nor the opportunity to observe the problem being solved.

It was found that the children who either played with the materials in advance or watched an adult solve the problem became more successful problem solvers than those in the control group. More interesting was the finding that the play group appeared to be more highly motivated to solve the problem and worked at it more persistently than did the observation group, whose members either solved the problem immediately or simply gave up

Divergent Problem Solving

Multiple-solution problems require the use of **divergent problem-solving** skills, the ability to branch out from a starting point and consider a variety of possible solutions. A person might be asked, for example, to list all the possible uses for a paper clip, besides holding pieces of paper together, of course. A child in a classroom might be asked to discuss the feelings George Washington may have had as he crossed the Delaware River, as opposed to simply providing the one correct answer to a question like "Which major battle was he preparing to fight?

Divergent problem solving has often been linked to the processes involved in creativity, whereas convergent problem solving has been related to performance on conventional intelligence and classroom tests, on which there are usually single correct answers (Guilford, 1967). The distinction is not quite so simple, however. Although many studies have found correlations between divergent problem-solving ability and various measures of creativity, many others have not (Kogan, 1983; Wallach, 1985). What is more, convergent problem solving may also be involved in creativity, particularly in the area of the natural sciences; it seems fair to say that both types of problem solving are involved in varying degrees in the creative process (Barron & Harrington, 1981; Hudson, 1966).

It was noted earlier that studies linking play and single-solution, or convergent, problem solving typically examined the impact of prior play experience with the materials used in solving such problems. Research on divergent problem solving has also examined the role of prior play with objects, but more often it has investigated the impact on divergent problem solving of pretense, or fantasy, play.

Object Play

Is it possible to help children improve their divergent problem-solving skills by providing them with appropriate types of objects to play with? In fact, there does appear to be a relationship between divergent problem-solving ability and the characteristics of children's play materials (Pepler & Ross, 1981; Smith & Dutton, 1979; Sylva, Bruner, & Genova, 1976). Consider the findings of Pepler and Ross (1981), who gave 64 preschool children the opportunity to play repeatedly with convergent materials (e.g., puzzles with one correct solution) or divergent materials (e.g., blocks, which can be assembled in a variety of ways). Later, the children in the two groups were asked to solve a variety of problems, and their problem-solving approaches were examined.

The children who had engaged in divergent object play were found to be more flexible and more original in their problem-solving approaches. For example, they were quicker than those in the convergent play group to abandon ineffective approaches to solving problems and to come up with new approaches. The researchers concluded that the experience of working with puzzles or other toys that suggest a single correct way to play with them may teach children that there are correct answers and encourage them to seek them out. Playing with open-ended materials, on the other hand, may tell a child that numerous approaches can be taken to any problem and the possibilities for the use of one's creative imagination are limitless.

Similar results were found by Dansky and Silverman (1973, 1975), who assigned preschool children to one of three conditions (1) divergent play with novel materials, (2) imitative play, or (3) problem-solving experience, before testing all of them on a divergent problem-solving task. The researchers discovered that the children in the first condition performed better on the divergent problem-solving task, both when the same and different play materials were used.

Fantasy Play

Object play has clearly been related to divergent problem-solving ability in young children; so, too, has make-believe, or fantasy, play (Dansky, 1980; Hutt & Bhavnani, 1976; Johnson, 1976). For example, Dansky (1980) observed 96 preschool children in a free-play situation and categorized them as high or low in their pretend play ability. (As pointed out in Chapter Four, there is considerable variation among children in fantasy predisposition.) He then assigned them to one of three categories, similar to those used in the Dansky and Silverman (1973, 1975) studies described in the previous section, except that instead of a divergent play condition, he included a condition in which children were allowed to play as they wished.

Dansky (1980) found that the children in the free-play situation performed best on the divergent problem-solving task, but *only* if they were spontaneously high in their level of make-believe play. He concluded that it is not play in itself that predicts problem-solving skill, but the extent to which children become involved in make-believe when they are playing. This connection between level of fantasy predisposition and success at creative problem solving has been found in other studies as well (Johnson, 1976, Rubin, Fein, & Vandenberg, 1983), although it should be remembered that such a relationship does not prove that engaging in fantasy play actually *causes* children to become better creative problem solvers. Perhaps it is the case that fantasy play and divergent problem solving share a common intellectual prerequisite.

It has been suggested that the link between fantasy play and divergent thinking can be found in the concept of decentration (Rubin, Fein, & Vandenberg, 1983). Decentration, discussed earlier in this chapter, involves the ability to attend simultaneously to many features of one's environment, to transform objects and situations while at the same time understanding their original identities and states, to imagine at one and the same time things as they are and also as they were. For example, the child engaged in make-believe knows that the object he is sitting in is really a cardboard box, but he pretends it is a car; in a sense, it is both a box and a car at once, and perhaps it was a submarine ten minutes earlier! Make-believe play, therefore, provides evidence of a considerable amount of intellectual flexibility in the child, and flexibility is a key ingredient in the creative process.

Summary

There is little in the way of experimental research indicating that certain forms of play actually bring about advances in children's intellectual development. However, there is strong evidence in support of a relationship between the various types of play and intellectual growth.

The availability of play materials is one of the most powerful predictors of intellectual growth during infancy. Specifically, infants who have a variety of toys available to them—and who choose to play with them—perform better on various intellectual measures, both at the time and later in life, than do infants who do not have such materials. Books and audiovisually responsive toys have proven to be particularly useful for this purpose.

A number of play materials and/or activities have been identified as being highly likely to stimulate intellectual growth: blocks, clay, water, music, and creative movement. Blocks teach children about measurement, the mathematical concept of equivalency, balance, logical classification, and they help children to view space in a more mature way. Clay teaches children how to recognize that amount remains the same regardless of changes in the appearance of substances, a skill described as conservation. Play with water helps children learn about flotation, measurement, and the conservation of liquid. Creative movement stimulates children to encode information about the world physically, or motorically, as well as intellectually, and to realize that there are many ways of knowing.

Human language consists of several different aspects, each related to the formulation of rules pertaining to a different area of language production: the phonological, the syntactic, the semantic, and the pragmatic. The phonological aspects of language are those that pertain to the production of sound. The syntactic aspects of language concern the rules by which words are put together into sentences. Semantic aspects of a language are those that deal with the selection of words that appropriately convey the intended meaning. Finally, the pragmatic aspects of language refer to the rules that govern the behaviors for engaging in effective communication.

The four different types of language play are (1) play with sounds and noises, (2) play with linguistic systems, such as those involving word meanings or grammatical constructions, (3) play with rhymes and words, and (4) play with the conventions of speech. Sound play in infancy is important in that it leads to selective social reinforcement on the part of adults, which may bring about an increasing sophistication in the quality of infant sounds. Some forms of sound play in older children are correlated with early reading achievement.

Solitary experimental play with the rules of word order may form the basis for the development of the grammatical structures of language. The private language of the solitary monologue gives children an opportunity to experiment with the elements of speech; the language of social interaction, on the other hand, is goal directed and lacks the element of playfulness found in the solitary monologue. In language play children can take apart and put together the building blocks of speech in ways that they will not be able to do consciously until they are much older.

Playing out the themes of a story that has been read to them seems to make the story more understandable and to help the listeners remember it better. When children regularly engage in the enactment of scenes from the stories they listen to, they seem to improve over time in their ability to draw meaning from spoken language.

Many psychologists believe that the experience of play with appropriate materials helps children become better convergent problem solvers effectively using information to arrive at a single correct solution. Play with open-ended materials is thought to stimulate children to become more creative in general. Finally, a clear connection has been established between fantasy predisposition and ability to solve divergent, or multiple-solution, problems, and it is thought that the basis for the connection is the cognitive concept of decentration.

Key Terms

Conservation

Convergent Problem Solving

Decentration

Divergent Problem Solving

Enactive Representation

Equivalency

Euclidean Spatial Concept

Graphic Collections

Logical Classification

Phonological Aspects of Language

Pragmatic Aspects of Language

Reversibility

Schemes

Semantic Aspects of Language

Syntactic Aspects of Language

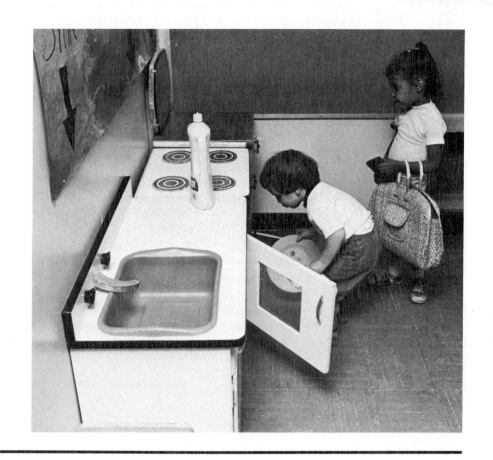

CHAPTER NINE

The Social Benefits
of Play

P aul is rolling around on the floor during free play, and Maura, his playmate, remarks that he looks like an alligator. "Yeah, I'm an alligator," says Paul, and he begins to crawl menacingly toward her. Maura shrieks, "Help! An alligator is after me," and runs to the other side of the room, with Paul slithering after her on his belly. Both children quickly realize, however, that Paul cannot move very quickly in his alligator role, so Maura suggests that he become a bear. Paul agrees, gets up on all fours, growls once or twice, and begins to crawl rapidly after Maura.

Paul and Maura's game continues through many variations. First, Maura simply runs and hides, and Paul seeks her out and chases her from her hiding place. Then Maura begins to stand her ground and hit the bear with a pillow, making him run away from her. Later, the game is varied again as Paul begins to snatch the pillow from Maura's hands with his sharp teeth, and so the outcome may be *either* the routing of the bear with a pillow or the removal of Maura's weapon, which forces Maura to flee in search of some other means of chasing Paul away.

Paul and Maura's game is an example of the social play that is so typical of the years of childhood. Indeed, we have been discussing social play, as well as the more solitary forms of play, throughout this book. In this chapter, however, we shall emphasize the specific ways in which play promotes the social development of the child, beginning with a brief discussion of the nature of social play and the underlying abilities it requires and then turning to an examination of its outcomes. We shall look at the ways in which social play facilitates parent–child attachment, social integration, group cooperation, role-taking ability, and altruism.

What Is Social Play?

Social play is characterized by engagement in nonliteral behaviors (an essential component of *all* forms of play) within the context of a social interaction; that is, the successive nonliteral behaviors of one child are contingent upon the nonliteral behaviors of a partner (Garvey, 1983).

As an illustration of this definition, Paul and Maura both know that they are only pretending when they play; this is indicated by their willingness to change Paul's role from alligator to bear in order to make the game more exciting. Moreover, what each child does depends on what the other has done immediately before. If we were to analyze the children's behaviors sequentially, the following pattern of interaction would emerge: (1) Paul runs after Maura, (2) Maura runs and hides, (3) Paul finds Maura, (4) Maura runs to seek a new hiding place, and (5) Paul looks for Maura again. Soon the game is varied: (3) Paul finds Maura, but then (4) Maura hits Paul with a pillow, and (5) Paul runs away. In other words, there is an element of taking turns in Paul and Maura's play, with each child accommodating his or her behaviors to those just displayed by the partner.

According to Catherine Garvey (1983), three abilities are essential for social play. First, the child must have a firm grasp on reality, because he or she must make a clear distinction between what is real and what is make-believe. Second, the child must be able to recognize the existence of and obey the rules for taking turns, even when these are not specifically laid out at the beginning of the game. For example, without prior discussion or agreement, Paul and Maura easily came to an understanding of the rules of their alligator-turned-bear game ("You chase me, and I'll respond by running and hiding," and so forth.). Third, the players must share their imaginations when developing the themes of a play episode. One child may initially suggest a theme, but the script varies as the play progresses, so that eventually all of the players collaborate to determine the direction of the activity. We can see this component of the definition in Paul and Maura's game: It is impossible to determine which of the two children actually created the game as it appeared in its final form. In a very real sense the game took on a life of its own as it proceeded, with each child introducing variations at different points along the way.

Benefits of Social Play

Social play has benefits in both a general sense and in many specific areas of socialization. In the most general sense, social play encourages children to focus on the rules that underlie the play episode and makes them aware that certain rules underlie *all* social interactions. The Soviet psychologist Lev Vygotsky (1896–1934) believed that for these reasons play was essential in the formation of the child's symbolic abilities.

In play, Vygotsky argued, all of a child's actions take on symbolic meaning, and play involves an emphasis on these meanings rather than on the specific actions that signify them. In Paul and Maura's game, for example, Maura knows that Paul does not really intend to hurt her when he catches her, nor does she intend to hurt him when she hits him with a pillow. The chasing, the hitting, and the biting are merely symbolic. Paul and Maura are acting out a ritual, the symbolic theme of which is the threat created by and the avoidance of a dangerous attacker. Their specific actions during the game—the location where Maura chooses to hide, her method of defending herself against the bear, the words the children speak to each other—are secondary in importance to the enactment of the symbolic danger theme.

As Garvey (1983) noted, the themes of social play are inherently social, with each player taking cues from the immediately preceding behaviors of a partner. This emphasis in social play on symbolic social themes not only encourages children to make up the rules to govern their own interactions, but also stimulates them to focus on the meaning behind *all* human social interaction. To understand the ways in which children at social play focus on the underlying themes of social interaction and come to understand such interaction better, consider the following example offered by Vygotsky. Two little sisters, aged five and seven, were asked to play a game in which they assumed the roles of sisters. When they did so, their behavior toward each other differed markedly from their usual interaction pattern. Now, in trying to act out the roles of sisters, they displayed ritualistic stereotyped behaviors illustrating what sisters were conventionally supposed to be. The learning component of this experience was that "In the game of sisters playing at sisters, they are both concerned with displaying their sisterhood; the fact that the two sisters decided to play sisters makes them both acquire *rules of behavior.* (I must always be a sister in relation to the other sister in the whole play situation.) Only actions which fit these rules are acceptable to the play situation" (Vygotsky, 1976/1933, pp. 541–542).

An awareness of the rules of social interaction is necessary for acceptance in any social situation. Consider the ways in which adults, like children at play, sense these rules and display behaviors contingent upon those emitted by their partners. Engaging in successful conversation requires the ability to listen, to take turns at speaking, and to make comments that are appropriate in that they are related to those just made by the person one is speaking to. Adult interaction also contains much in the way of symbolic meaning. If the person to whom one is speaking occasionally checks the time on his watch or makes eye contact with someone other than his partner in conversation, this may indicate, to a sensitive listener at least, a lack of interest in continuing the interaction.

The Facilitation of Attachment

If 100 people were asked to describe any person they currently knew or used to know, would there be one person they would most likely name? Apparently there is, according to developmental psychologist Lillian Troll (1972), who asked just such a question. The overwhelming majority of those responding, with an age range of 10 to 91, named one of their parents. It is fascinating to realize the extent of parental influence on children's lives, even years after the parents have died.

In Chapter Four we discussed the differences in play between toddlers who are securely attached to their parents and those who are not. There is another sense, however, in which attachment and play are related. Play not only provides clues to the strength of the bond between parent and preschool child but may also facilitate the attachment process itself during the first year of life. Let us now take a closer look at the role of play in the establishment of the parent-child relationship.

To understand the ways in which play facilitates attachment, one must bear in mind that, as briefly discussed in Chapter Four, attachment is not an all-or-nothing phenomenon. Instead, there are degrees of closeness between parents and their young children. In addition, there are parental characteristics that facilitate secure attachment and those that do not; a willingness to play with one's child is just one of these characteristics.

Degrees of Attachment

In an attempt to identify a range of variation in the quality of parent-infant attachment, psychologist Mary Ainsworth (1977; Ainsworth, Blehar, Waters, & Wall, 1978) developed a test known as the **Strange Situation**. The infant and its parents would be brought into a playroom that contained a variety of interesting toys, as well as an adult stranger. Shortly thereafter, the parent would leave the room and return and would do so again later in the session; at these points of departure and return, the infant's reaction would be recorded.

Babies who were the most securely attached to their parents would notice their parents' departure and would briefly seek physical and emotional contact with them when they returned but would soon resume their independent play activities. A second group of babies, identified as insecure-avoidant, would react with hostility and resistance when their parents returned to the room after leaving them briefly. Finally, a third group, referred to as insecure-ambivalent, would react with anger on their parents' return to the room but would also display a great need for contact with them.

Attachment and Parental Characteristics

Why do some parents have securely attached infants, while other parents have children who are anxious and insecure? Much depends on the personality characteristics of the parents themselves and on their parenting styles. Parents of closely attached infants have a high degree of self-esteem and a quiet confidence in their ability to be good parents. They are interested in their babies and make themselves available whenever possible. They handle them with love and affection and are skilled in feeding and taking care of them. They make frequent eye contact, smile at their babies a good deal, and are emotionally expressive with them. In marked contrast, parents of insecurely attached children tend to be irritable and anxious people who lack self-confidence and do not seem to enjoy parenthood. Often abrupt and mechanical in their parenting behaviors, they project a quality of general unavailability and insensitivity to their children's needs (Bretherton & Waters, 1985; Egeland & Farber, 1984; Main, 1981).

Attachment and Parental Playfulness

If parents vary in their attitudes toward themselves and their parenting roles, might they also vary in their approaches to play with their children? Indeed they do! There are noticeable parental differences in willingness to initiate social play with infants, and these differences are related to variations in the quality of attachment. As an illustration of this point, consider the findings of Blehar, Lieberman, and Ainsworth (1977), who visited 26 mother-infant pairs at home every three weeks during the first year of the child's life. After instructing the mothers to behave as they normally would if an observer were not present, the researchers proceeded to record a variety of maternal and infant behaviors. Later, at approximately the time of their first birthdays, all the children were observed in Ainsworth's (1977) Strange Situation procedure to obtain measures of the degree of attachment to their mothers.

The researchers discovered that maternal playfulness was correlated with the closeness of attachment at the end of the first year. Mothers who regularly involved their infants in play—and appeared to enjoy doing so—were the most likely to have securely attached one-year-olds. What does this relationship mean? Perhaps it is the case that parents who enjoy playing with their babies are simply more fun to be around, and as a result, the babies are more likely to form close attachments to them (Beckwith, 1986). Infants are certainly more responsive to playful than to nonplayful parents: they look and smile at them and gesture to them more often than do children of parents who rarely play (Crawley, et al., 1978; Tronick, 1982). Thus, the degree of positive affect, on the part of both parent and child, appears to be related to the ease with which the social bond is formed.

A parent's willingness to play may be one predictor of the closeness of attachment, but willingness alone seems not be enough. A second strong predictor of quality

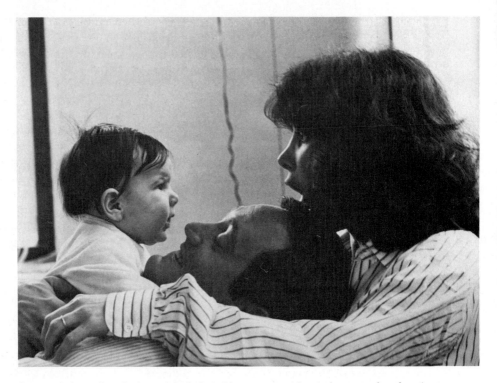

Parents who enjoy playing with their babies are more fun to be around and easier to form attachments to.

of attachment is the contingent pacing of social interaction by the mother: the extent to which she allows her infant's behavioral cues to influence her own behavior (Blehar, Lieberman, & Ainsworth, 1977). This contingent pacing is an indicator of maternal sensitivity.

The connections between playfulness, contingent pacing, and attachment suggest that parents are easier to bond to if (1) they like to play *and* (2) they are sensitive enough to their children's needs to pace their play activities accordingly. Such a parent is quick to sense, for example, that a child is bored and needs additional stimulation or that a child is overly excited and needs to be calmed down. They know when to offer a new toy, as well as when to let their child continue playing with the one he or she already has. They know when to initiate a play routine and when to end it. And they know when their child does not want to play at all.

If willingness to play and sensitivity to children's needs are typical of the parents of securely attached children, then what can be said of the play of the parents of children who are anxious and insecure? Such parents engage less often in social play, either because of an inability or an unwillingness to do so (Blehar, Lieberman, & Ainsworth, 1977). In fact, a common finding is that these parents seem to lack an attitude of playfulness in their demeanor. When they are interacting with their babies, they appear to be serious, silent, and unsmiling, displaying an amazing lack of facial expression (Ainsworth, 1979). What is more, on the occasions when these parents *do* play, they seem to be insensitive to their infants' interests and social cues. Apparently unable to keep their babies at an optimal level of arousal, they instead under- or overstimulate them; for example, they typically initiate games in which the infant is a passive object rather than an active participant, and their idea of play may be simply to tickle or tease the child for long periods of time (Beckwith, 1986).

In summary, it seems that social play between infants and their parents may facilitate attachment, in the sense that (1) playful parents display the greatest amount of positive affect (they are the most likable and the most fun to be with), (2) their warmth and likability seems to generate greater amounts of infant responsiveness and positive affect, and (3) the combination of parental likability and infant responsiveness increases the probability of a close bond between parent and child (Beckwith, 1986). This is not to say that it is play that actually *causes* attachment to occur, but only that the types of parents who are easiest to bond with are also the types of parents who see the value of infant social play.

Social Integration

When she arrived at the nursery school at the beginning of the school year, Theresa appeared nervous and clung to her mother's skirt. After a few sessions, however, she began to relax and did not protest when her mother left. Nevertheless, it was clear to the teachers that Theresa was not comfortable interacting with large groups of children at a time. The child's teachers did not push her, however. They knew that social play has the potential to draw children out of themselves effortlessly and painlessly, and they also knew that Theresa could become even more isolated if pressured into social interaction.

For the first several weeks, Theresa said nothing at all; she only sat and watched as her classmates played with various materials. She was particularly fascinated by fingerpaints, although she refused to try them herself. The teachers could not help noticing, however, that Theresa sat increasingly closer to the other children as they played and soon spontaneously pulled her chair up to the table at which the others were fingerpainting. It was not long after that that Theresa tentatively dipped a finger into a jar of paint and then quickly wiped it clean. Did she want to try a picture? She shook her head.

As the days passed Theresa grew increasingly attentive to the conversations around her as she sat at the painting table; she smiled and laughed when the others did. It finally happened. Theresa shyly commented to the girl next to her that she needed more blue in her picture. It was a first step and a small one, but it was followed by increasing bolder social overtures. Eventually, without pressure from the adults in the room, Theresa was talking expansively as she worked away on her art projects.

Theresa's story is not at all unusual, because one of the major benefits of play is its power to integrate socially withdrawn children into a group. Adult intervention can facilitate such social integration, in as much as adults can suggest appropriate activities, but it is play itself that often brings young children out of themselves. Although not the only play materials and activities to do so, blocks, clay, music, movement, and sociodramatic play are especially helpful in promoting social integration.

Blocks

Often considered to be among those play materials that contribute the most to the overall development of the preschool child, blocks have even been described as the most important material in the preschool or kindergarten classroom (Benish, 1978; Rogers, 1985). They are also a play material that has been found to enhance children's social development greatly.

How can block play facilitate social integration among children? Let us attempt to answer that question by looking at a child who is totally lacking in social skills and/or interests. Hartley, Frank, and Goldenson (1952) described the case of three-and-a-half-year-old Lonnie, a child unwanted by his parents and abandoned to the care of a succession of housemaids. When Lonnie arrived at nursery school in the morning, he would typically begin smashing any object he could get his hands on, smearing the walls with paint or food, and attacking other children. His outdoor play was so aggressive and antisocial that he typically spent that time in the director's office instead. He rarely spoke but would shriek and scream when he could not have his way, and, if told by a teacher that she liked him, he would answer, "No, you don't, damn you!"

Now let us observe Lonnie in the block corner, and we will see that, at least for those brief moments when he is under the spell of the blocks, this troubled little boy appears to be normal in his degree of socialization:

> The teacher walks to the block shelf. "Anyone care to build?" she asks, and places the blocks on the floor near the shelf. Lonnie relaxes, slides down from the window sill to the stove, and from the stove to the floor using the broom for support. [The teacher] says in an encouraging tone, "Lonnie is going to build something for us." Lonnie removes his thumb from his mouth. Charlie follows him, quickly gets down on his knees and pulls the long blocks from the bottom shelf to the floor. Lonnie's expression changes to one of anticipation and a happy smile lights up his pale little face. He squats down on the floor next to Charlie, picks up a long block and props it up on the floor, long end up. "Sit up, block," he says happily. He laughs loudly, and sings, "Happy Birthday to You" to the block. Charlie rests one side of the long block on the shelf and the other side on the floor, then adds others to build an incline. The block slips. Lonnie does not seem to mind. Charlie stands up, picks a small green car from the top of the shelf, stoops over and slides it down the incline. Both boys laugh loudly. "Do it again?" he asks Lonnie. Lonnie happily answers, "Yep." They send car after car down the ramp. Both boys are now laughing so loudly that they are bending over clasping their stomachs. (Hartley, Frank, & Goldenson, 1952, pp. 139–140)

For an ordinary three-year-old, the episode described above would be unremarkable. For Lonnie, who was usually unable to engage in *any* type of social play with peers, the degree of social integration displayed during the block episode was unusual indeed. But what is there about block play that can have a socializing influence even on a child who is ordinarily a social isolate? Hartley, Frank, and Goldenson (1952) suggested that blocks are an ideal first medium for children because (1) their appeal is universal, (2) they are sturdy and clean and are therefore seen as safe, and (3) they offer the possibility of a broad spectrum of social interaction.

Children at play with blocks can choose a level of social participation that is most appropriate for them (Rogers, 1985). They can play in total isolation, since blocks require no cooperative efforts. They can play in parallel, as when two or more young children share the block corner, aware of each other's presence but engaged in separate activities. And blocks, of course, allow for extensive forms of cooperation, as when children share responsibility for building towers, roads, entire cities, or ramps and racetracks like those assembled by Charlie and Lonnie.

Furthermore, it is not unusual in childhood for an activity that begins in total solitude to evolve gradually into one that is inherently social, and this transition may occur even without the realization of the children involved. In that sense block play not only allows timid or socially immature children to acquire needed social skills by watching the play of more sophisticated peers, but can also seduce them into increasingly higher levels of social integration (Rogers, 1985). It will be remembered that Lonnie approached the block corner by himself and only then was joined by Charlie. In addition, Lonnie's initial block play, propping up the long blocks and singing to them, was a solitary activity. Only later did the shared activity of rolling the cars down the ramps begin.

While it would be difficult to demonstrate that blocks actually *cause* an increase in prosocial behavior among young children, it has been found that children playing with blocks rarely engage in behavior that is truly antisocial: Rogers (1985) observed a group of kindergarten children in a block corner, and reported that behaviors like hitting, threatening, throwing blocks, or grabbing another child's blocks were rare. On the contrary, prosocial behaviors such as smiling, asking, helping, and taking turns appeared more often during block play than during other play times. Rogers (1985) also noticed that the degree of social integration depended to a certain extent on the types of blocks used. Unit blocks—small blocks in a variety of shapes—were more often used in solitary and parallel activities; the use of large hollow blocks, ideal for building, was correlated with a greater intensity of social interaction.

Clay

Psychologist Ruth Hartley, a legendary figure in the field of research on children's play, spoke of the "almost magical tongue-loosening quality of clay" (Hartley, Frank, & Goldenson, 1952, p. 192). By this she meant that even the most inhibited of children will often socialize freely when they play with clay. When using clay, children are allowed to be entirely alone, yet they are given the right to group membership without the pressure to socialize that might occur in the housekeeping corner. Thus clay can serve as a protective shield behind which children can hide and study their peer group until they are ready to enter the group on their own terms. However, the opportunity for shared activity, the freedom to talk, and the ease with which clay can be handled combine to invite the child into group activity. And when they do engage in social interaction while playing with clay, children often reveal their innermost thoughts and feelings as they chatter constantly to those around them.

As an illustration of the socially facilitating effects of play with clay, consider the record of four-year-old John, who begins by playing alone and soon draws other children into shared social activities:

> John had a large gob of clay in front of him. He thought for a moment and then said, "I guess I'll make a sidewalk today." Thereupon he pulled off several segments from the mound and proceeded to thoroughly flatten them into a creditable appearing sidewalk.
>
> [Later] he used [a tongue depressor] to cut thin grooves with little depth into his sidewalk. While thus engaged, Vi [another child at the clay table] handed the teacher a flattened oval hunk of clay and said, "Here's a birthday cake." In less than a second, John called out to the teacher, "Teach, here is my birthday cake." When the teacher came over, she asked what was the matter with his sidewalk. He answered, "My sidewalk is broken." Then he called over to Phil (who had brought a little cement mixer), "Cement mixer man, my sidewalk is broken." Phil came over and John watched him go through the motions of mixing the cement and repairing the sidewalk. Then he spoke up, "Teacher, look! I've got a fixed street. Cement mixer fixed it." Then he proceeded to cut another long thin groove and yelled out, "Cement mixer, my street is broken." Phil came over and went through his activity under the close scrutiny of John. As soon as Phil left, John hastened to cut some more grooves, and again called out, "My street is broken, cement mixer." (Hartley, Frank & Goldenson, 1952, p. 192)

In this brief record, under the tongue-loosening influence of the clay, John began with what was essentially a solitary activity, moved into parallel play as he accepted Vi's idea of making a birthday cake for the teacher, and ended in a cooperative shared activity with Phil, with both playing different but complementary roles. John's and Phil's activity typified the essence of Garvey's (1983) definition of social play as discussed at the beginning of this chapter. Each child's pretend activities were directly related to the pretend activities displayed immediately before by the play partner.

Music

Music is an integral part of the young child's life. Even by the age of three, children can recognize familiar tunes and can sing them with a fair degree of accuracy (Davidson, McKernon, & Gardner, 1981). The naturalness of music is evident in the fact that children at three or four will spontaneously sing while engaged in other forms of play (Day, 1988; Winner, 1982). Little wonder, then, that music so often is found in the educational experience of the preschool child.

There are four general types of musical experiences that are provided by preschool educators (Hartley, Frank, & Goldenson, 1952). The most common form of musical experience is called *rhythms,* in which a musical selection is played and the children are allowed to respond to it with their bodies, either with or without specific directions from an adult. Rhythms combines creative movement with music. A second type of musical experience is *listening to records or tapes,* during which children are typically expected to sit quietly and pay attention; they are not encouraged, and often not allowed, to move about. Third, there is *group singing.* Finally, children are often involved in the *playing of musical instruments* that vary in their level of sophistication.

Exposure to music undoubtedly benefits the young child in numerous ways, but Hartley, Frank, and Goldenson (1952) considered its major social benefit to be the integration into the peer group of children who for various reasons have experienced social rejection or neglect. Children who have difficulty gaining entrance to the world of their peers are of two types. They are sometimes aggressive and uncontrolled, with the result that other children try to avoid them. Alternatively, social isolates may be so timid that social overtures are painful to them, and so they voluntarily withdraw. Music has special benefits for children in each of the two groups.

Aggressive, extremely active children can be soothed by listening to or playing music. Their anxieties often temporarily disappear as they are drawn under the spell of a relaxing tune. They may become absorbed by the challenges of mastering a musical instrument or learning the words to a song. At rhythms they may throw themselves freely—and safely—around the room as they listen to a lively musical selection.

Illustrating the soothing qualities music offers to an overactive child is the case of three-and-a-half year old Bud, whose mother had placed him in his preschool group because she felt that she couldn't handle him. Bud was indeed a difficult child who fought constantly with the other children and regularly destroyed play materials in the classroom. Now observe this overly active, destructive little boy as he listens to music:

> The teacher has brought her accordion. Bud has not left the phonograph or made a sound during the entire half hour of listening. He is sitting on the table, swinging one leg as he watches the group almost going wild as they listen to various rhythms. . . . The teacher says, "I'll bet Bud would make a good horsie." Although he has apparently been dreaming, with a far-off gaze, he almost falls off the table in his eagerness, throwing himself on the floor on all fours, and progressing noisily and bumpily in a sort of strenuous hop. (Hartley, Frank, & Goldenson, 1952, p. 307)

It should be pointed out that Bud's immediate response to the teacher's suggestion represented an extremely rare form of cooperation for the boy. His usual behavior was decidedly uncooperative. Observe Bud again at a later point in the same session:

> Everyone . . . is tired, and someone suggests "Rock-a-Bye Baby." The teacher takes Jack's hands and swings his arms back and forth to the song. Watching them, Bud looks about eagerly for a partner. He goes to one boy and says "You want to rock?" and without waiting for an answer, he grabs him and says forcefully "Rock, play rockabye." He seems clumsy and h-

rhythm all his own, not related to the music, but enjoys himself in this quieting manner. (Hartley, Frank, & Goldenson, 1952, p. 307)

The other group of children who gain the most social benefit from the musical experience are those who are timid and withdrawn. Music for these children can make them feel more vigorous, more capable, and more powerful. It can make them feel as if they truly are a part of the group. At the age of five, Molly was timid, overly controlled, and adult oriented; her play was mostly of the solitary variety. In the following exercise, Molly was integrated into the group because the various children were assigned musical roles to play:

> Molly kneels on the floor and holds her ankles. The children are singing, and when they begin to sing loudly, she continues singing in the same tone. The teacher gets the toy instruments. Molly: "I'll play the bells." She puts the bells on her wrists and shakes them, smiling at Patsy. The teacher plays "Jingle Bells" on the piano as the children begin to sing. The teacher says, "Now, bells. . . . Good, Molly!" Molly swings her hands in and out, "Like this?" She shakes her wrists up and down vigorously. The teacher plays the piano once more and tells the children only to sing this time. Molly sings along. Teacher: "Now, jingle bells, play with me." Molly swings her arms out and in with lips slightly parted. She now slaps her hands on her knees to make the bells ring, then claps her hands, and shakes her wrists once more. (Hartley, Frank, & Goldenson, 1952, pp. 315–316).

Creative Movement

Play with music often involves movement as well, although it need not do so. Much of a child's play, whether musical or not, involves movement of one sort or another. In fact, it will be remembered that during infancy, before the ability to represent the world symbolically has developed, physical, or sensorimotor, play predominates, and play of a physical nature (e.g., rough-and-tumble) continues to constitute a large part of an older child's play activities.

More specifically, we are referring here to **personal movement**: that which allows children to express their inner moods, feelings, and perceptions of the world, using only their bodies (Day, 1988; Lynch-Fraser, 1982). Personal movement can be extremely beneficial in helping children understand themselves and realize what their bodies can and cannot do, but it can also be the kind of educational experience that promotes social integration. Effective communication is an essential prerequisite for social integration, and movement, like speaking, is a form of communication. Children involved in creative movement experiences can learn to be more sensitive to their own unspoken messages, as well as to those of others.

Recognizing the importance of movement as a form of communication, Werner and Burton (1979) suggested a number of activities to encourage children of all ages to become more sensitive communicators. The message of the following exercise is that body gestures and actions can be used to express feelings, moods, or emotions. The teacher speaks:

I'm going to say a feeling or mood word and I want you to show me a body shape or action that expresses this word. My first word is "surprise." First show me a surprised face. Then add your arms and whole body. Show me surprise with whatever word I say. With a jump. With a stretch. With a twist. With fast moves. With slow, sustained moves. Make up a sequence of movements that show your surprise.

Next show me how you laugh. With your head. With your whole body. Can you change your level while you laugh? Can you move about while you laugh? Can you laugh a little? Change, show me a big side-splitting belly laugh. Exaggerate your laugh with really big movements to show me how funny it is. (Werner & Burton, p. 52)

Another exercise recommended by Werner and Burton (1979) is somewhat more advanced, requiring children to use their entire bodies to express a theme or concept. For example, a child might be asked to act out nonverbally the role of a person trapped in a stalled elevator and beginning to panic, a creature from another planet arriving on Earth, or a person hanging out clothes to dry on a windy day. Such exercises represent quite a challenge to children instructed to be spontaneous and to avoid timid, restrained movements, but the social benefits are considerable. Activities of this sort teach that communication can be nonverbal as well as verbal and, if other children in the group are asked to guess the meaning of the pantomime, can become part of an enjoyable game that sensitizes youngsters to the unspoken messages of the body.

Sociodramatic Play

In Chapter Four we refer to the commonly made observation that sociodramatic play, in which children assume various roles while engaged in various action sequences, is the form of play that is the most social and has the greatest impact on the development of social awareness in children (Hartley, Frank, & Goldenson, 1952). Involvement in dramatic play seems to improve children's ability to cooperate in group settings, to participate in social activities, and to understand human relationships (Fink, 1976; Smith & Sydall, 1978; Smith, Dalgleish, & Herzmark, 1981).

There are two basic explanations for the social benefits of sociodramatic play. The first is that such play requires group cooperation. It is by definition a group activity and a cooperative one. A child can certainly engage in acts of make-believe that are not group oriented, but sociodramatic play is *organized make-believe* in a *social setting,* with a *set of rules* to ensure cooperation on the part of the players.

Not only do children behave cooperatively while actually engaged in sociodramatic play, but it appears that they may generalize this cooperative attitude to other areas of social interaction as well. This generalized cooperation was illustrated by the findings of Rosen (1974), who worked with kindergartners described as deficient in dramatic play skills. She provided them with toys, such as medical kits and firefighter's and police officer's hats, that were designed to simulate role playing. She actually joined the children in play, asking leading questions and offering suggestions whenever appropriate. For example, if she saw a child playing aimlessly with a truck, she would model truck driver behavior and encourage the child to join her in the activity.

Rosen (1974) found that children trained in sociodramatic play showed improvements in what she called "group productivity." This was defined by the ability to work with other children as a team to create specific objects out of interlocking blocks, a task that required planning, cooperation, and the ability to avoid disagreements and acts of aggression. In addition, members of the training group improved in their ability to assume the perspectives of other children and to predict the wants and preferences of others when those wants and preferences differed from their own.

The second socialization benefit of dramatic play is that it allows children to experiment with a variety of roles, to try on those roles, as it were, and determine their appropriateness, and to develop a better understanding of the roles of other people (Athey, 1984; Greif, 1976; Sachs, Goldman, & Chaille, 1982). It is unlikely that major changes in the ability to understand other people will result from a few dramatic play episodes, of course. A child who plays Mommy or Teacher will not come away from the game with a thorough understanding of a mother's or a teacher's role, just as a nonhandicapped adult will not develop a complete appreciation of the problems of the handicapped as a result of spending one day confined to a wheelchair. Nevertheless, children engaged in sociodramatic play may undergo very slight and very gradual changes in their ability to understand other people, and these changes make the play so valuable as a socialization experience.

Role-Taking Ability

If children are ever to be successful in social interactions, they must get beyond their self-centered perspectives and try to see the world through the eyes of other people. This ability to assume the roles, or viewpoints, of others is necessary for the establishment of close interpersonal communication (Harter, 1983) and, among older children, is related to altruistic, or helping, behavior (Cialdini, Baumann, & Kendrick, 1981; Froming, Allen, & Jensen, 1985). Role-taking skill is also related to the ease with which children establish intimate peer relationships (McGuire & Weisz, 1982), and perhaps not surprisingly, the most popular children in elementary school are also among the most sophisticated role takers (Kurdek & Krile, 1982).

Why are some children better role takers than others? Level of development is obviously an important variable. There is no point during childhood at which an appreciation of the viewpoints of others suddenly emerges. Instead, there is a gradual progression through a series of increasingly sophisticated stages of role-taking ability (Selman, 1980; Selman & Byrne, 1974; Selman & Jacquette, 1978).

Other variables responsible for individual differences in role-taking ability are intelligence, with children who score higher on IQ tests also displaying greater evidence of sensitivity to the views of others (Shantz, 1983), and childrearing practices. Parents of skillful role takers are likely to emphasize **induction** in their discipline: stressing the impact on other people of the child's undesirable behaviors (Bearison & Cassel, 1975): "It makes me happy to see you sharing your toys" or "Scott is very sad because you don't seem to want to play with him," rather than "Nice children always share their toys with their friends" or "You'll play with Scott because I *told* you to do so."

If a child is not a particularly sensitive role taker, can he or she be taught to improve in this area? Indeed, role-taking training has been found to be quite effective (Feshbach, 1979; Ianotti, 1978). For example, Ianotti (1978) read stories to kindergarten and third-grade boys and asked them to act out the parts of various story characters. He also asked them many questions about the feelings and motivations of the characters in order to encourage them to imagine themselves in the roles of other people. When role-taking skills were assessed after this training condition, it was found that the children had improved in sensitivity to the perspectives of others, compared to a control group who had been given no role-taking training.

Of course, a large percentage of a child's time is spent in play without adults to reinforce role-taking skills. Might the experience of play with peers in itself help children to become more sensitive role takers? Psychologists Susan Burns and Charles Brainerd (1979) attempted to answer this question. As a measure of affective perspective taking, they showed preschool children three pairs of pictures and read them a short story about each pair. Each set of pictures told a story about two children, one of whom clearly represented the child being tested; the events in the stories were such that they produced completely opposite emotional reactions in the two story characters.

A puppet play can provide opportunities for social development, as children speculate about the feelings and motivations of characters and even assume the characters' roles on occasion.

The preschoolers were then asked how the two characters, the one representing themselves and the one representing another child, were feeling. It was expected that children skilled at role taking would realize that the story characters had opposite feelings (e.g., one was happy and one was sad), while a less capable role taker would respond egocentrically that both characters shared the shared the feelings of the character representing the child being tested.

Burns and Brainerd then exposed some of the children to a constructive group play condition, others to a sociodramatic play condition, and the control group to no experimental treatment at all. In the constructive condition, cooperative play was encouraged; the children were told to work together to make something (e.g., a house, a wagon) out of materials provided, and to discuss their work plans as a group. In the dramatic play condition, a play theme was suggested by the researcher, and the children were asked to discuss how the theme would be enacted and which of them would play each of the various roles. Then they played out their make-believe scenes at length.

At the end of the treatment phase, the affective perspective-taking test was again administered to see if any changes in role-taking ability resulted from the play experiences. Burns and Brainerd found that children in both play groups, that emphasizing group cooperation in constructive play and that requiring the enactment of dramatic scenes, improved in their role-taking abilities; the children in the control group did not.

The findings of the Burns and Brainerd study, as well as those of other studies of this type, suggest that role-taking skills can be improved not only by direct adult intervention but also by gently supervised forms of social play (Athey 1984; Golomb & Cornelius, 1977; Greif, 1976; Rogers-Warren, Warren, & Baer, 1977; Rubin, Fein, & Vandenberg, 1983; Saltz, Dixon, & Johnson, 1977; Saltz & Johnson, 1974). Most of the research points to the necessity of an adult social director to stimulate children to play in a way that enriches perspective-taking ability, although some psychologists (e.g., Rubin & Maioni, 1975) suggest that role-taking ability *may* be enhanced by social play that is totally spontaneous and not at all influenced by adults.

In any case, it seems clear that play can serve as a vehicle by which young children can learn that other people see the world from perspectives different from their own. Considering the importance of perspective taking as a basis for successful social interaction, it is obvious again that play plays a central role in the social development of the child.

Play and Peer Group Acceptance

Even by the age of three, some children are already well liked by their peers, while others clearly are not. Well-liked preschoolers engage in a lot of cooperative play, and they are successful in social conversation, making relevant and appropriate comments to other children and offering constructive suggestions. Disliked children often make inappropriate statements in conversation (i.e., remarks not related to the immediately preceding statement made by another child) and negative comments about what others are doing, without offering constructive alternatives (Hazen & Black, 1989).

The most popular children in elementary school are friendly, intelligent, high in academic achievement, athletically skilled, and physically attractive (Hartup, 1983). In addition, popular children are higher in self-esteem than the average child and have more positive perceptions of themselves (Boivin & Begin, 1989).

Grade-schoolers are likely to be rejected if they are antisocial, hostile, physically unattractive, or low in achievement (Hartup, 1983). Rejected children are seen as poor leaders. While not all rejected children are overly aggressive, aggressive behaviors are more common among rejected than among nonrejected children (Coie, 1985). It seems that it is not the aggression itself that brings about social rejection, but aggression combined with a lack of social skills (French, 1988).

There is a third group, children who are neither liked nor actively rejected. Instead, they are virtually ignored by the peer group. This category of neglected, or socially isolated, children has received much attention in recent years (Gottman, 1977; Dodge, Coie, & Brakke, 1982; Asher, Hymel, & Renshaw, 1984). Neglected children are not viewed as hostile or aggressive and in fact are often thought of as shy. They are usually more physically attractive than children who are clearly rejected. What they share in common with rejected children, however, is that they lack social skills or social experiences.

As might be expected, differences in social acceptance are reflected in differences in children's play. In the first place, popular, well-liked children display signs of initiative and leadership in play, while rejected and neglected children do not.

Second, popular children know how to play cooperatively and to share their play materials with others (Dodge, 1983; Ladd, Price, & Hart, 1988). Rejected children, on the other hand, have difficulty sharing and often deliberately exclude other children from their play (Dodge, 1983; Dodge, Coie, & Brakke, 1982; Hartup, Glazer, & Charlesworth, 1967).

Third, like the popular preschool child, popular grade-school children are constructive in play, rather than negative. For example, a well-liked child who does not want to play a game that other children are involved in will express displeasure with the activity and *then* offer constructive alternatives; a less popular child may simply complain without suggesting any new directions for the play (Putallaz & Gottman, 1981).

Finally, if a group of children are already playing and a child arrives later and wishes to join them, there are differences in the ways popular and unpopular children gain entry to the group. The popular child seeks entry and then adapts his or her behavior to the group flow; the child who is likely to be rejected barges in and imposes him- or herself on the other children with little regard for what the others are already doing. The socially neglected child, however, is likely to stand back and watch from the sidelines (Dodge, Coie, & Brakke, 1982).

The recognition that the quality of children's play interactions is *related* to their overall acceptance by the peer group has led psychologists and educators to wonder if play might be used to actually facilitate such acceptance. In fact, there has been growing interest among professionals in helping unpopular children become better-liked by their peers. Rather than using the traditional method of pressuring the group to accept the child, newer approaches involve working directly with the isolated child, coaching

Play as a Measure of Social Success

Much of the research linking play and social interaction skill is correlational in nature. That is, psychologists have discovered connections between children's play and their degree of acceptance within the peer group, but it is difficult to determine the direction of cause and effect. Does social play actually cause children to be more succesful in their social interactions, or do successful socializers simply play differently than their less popular peers?

Despite the difficulty in making causal connections, the findings from research of this type are quite instructive, in the sense that children's play may offer clues to their degree of social acceptance. It has been found, for example, that children in the age range of four to six who engage in a large amount of solitary play in which they simply manipulate objects are also rated by teachers as socially incompetent and are disliked by peers (Rubin & Clark, 1983). By way of contrast, children of the same age who engage in a good deal of group activity that involves games-with-rules, the most socially advanced form of play, tend to be rated as the most popular, the most socially mature, and the most sophisticated in their social sensitivity (Rubin, 1986).

Psychologist Kenneth Rubin (1986) has developed the **Play Observation Scale,** which can be used to study children's behaviors when they are at play and, he believes, to identify children who may be at risk in terms of their social development. Various categories of play can be recorded on the Scale for an individual child, and drawing on the play-socialization relationship that is commonly found, clues might emerge about a child's social success. In that sense, play can be used as a diagnostic instrument.

If six-year-old Toni rarely interacted with other children during the play periods recorded, if she never engaged in games of any sort, and if she typically played alone, she would fit the profile of a child with social interaction problems. It is possible, of course, that Toni is a socially well-adjusted child who is having a difficult day. No firm conclusions can be drawn from one, or even a few, limited samples of behavior. Nevertheless, the behavior recorded on the Play Observation Scale might at least suggest that further questions should be asked about Toni's social development.

him or her in specific social skills necessary for group acceptance, and the vehicle used in such coaching has often been play.

Illustrating the approach of working directly with the isolated child, Oden and Asher (1977) identified third- and fourth-graders judged by their classmates to be socially undesirable and coached them individually for a month in techniques of cooperation, participation, and communication with their peers. The coaching seemed to work since, even within the first week after the sessions ended, the once unpopular children had gained considerably in social acceptance, and half of them were now ranked in the top halves of their classes in terms of popularity. More encouraging was the discovery that the gains in social acceptance were long-lasting: they were still in evidence when the researchers returned a year later to check on the progress of the children.

Since that time, many other researchers (e.g., Bierman, 1986; Bierman & Furman, 1984; Coie & Krehbiel, 1984; Gresham & Nagel, 1980; Ladd, 1981; Ladd, Price, & Hart, 1988) have also found evidence to support the view that coaching children in a variety of social skills (e.g., sharing, cooperating, initiating friendships, making conversation, playing games) can lead to advances in peer acceptance. It is encouraging to realize that social skills that are used in play can be taught to children deficient in them, and that increases in the sophistication of social play can lead to greater overall acceptance by the peer group.

Summary

Social play is characterized by engagement in nonliteral behaviors within the context of a social interaction; that is, the successive nonliteral behaviors of one child are contingent upon the nonliteral behaviors of a partner. According to Garvey (1983), three abilities are essential for social play. First, the child must have a firm grasp on reality, because he or she must make a clear distinction between what is real and what is make-believe. Second, the child must be able to recognize the existence of and obey the rules for taking turns, even when these are not specifically laid out at the beginning of the game. Third, the players must share their imagination when developing the themes of a play episode.

In the most general sense, social play encourages children to focus on the rules that underlie the play episode and makes them aware that certain rules underlie *all* social interactions. More specifically, social play has benefits in many particular areas of a child's life. In the first place, parent-infant play seems to be important in the attachment process, as indicated by the fact that maternal playfulness is correlated with the closeness of attachment at the end of the first year. Mothers who regularly involve their infants in play, enjoy doing so, and are sensitive enough to pace the play activity in response to the child's needs are the most likely to have securely attached one-year-olds.

Social play facilitates children's integration into their peer groups, a particular benefit for a child who is socially withdrawn. Certain types of play materials and activities—blocks, clay, music, creative movement, and sociodramatic play—have been found to be especially helpful in promoting social integration.

Social forms of play helps children to learn how to cooperate with one another and get beyond their self-centered perspectives to try to see the world through the eyes of other people. This ability to assume the roles, or viewpoints, of others is necessary for the establishment of close interpersonal communication and, among older children, is related to altruistic, or helping, behavior.

Key Terms

Induction	Play Observation Scale
Personal Movement	Strange Situation

CHAPTER TEN

The Uses of Play in Therapy

War is a phenomenon that stimulates the imagination of many young children, but it is confusing and frightening to them as well. It is particularly frightening when it has a direct personal impact on their lives. Let us look at the effects of war on a generally happy and socially outgoing little boy named Stewart, who is, in fact, the most popular child in his nursery school. Lately, however, he has been moody. He is troubled by the fact that two of his uncles are serving in the armed forces and the country has recently gone to war. Although obviously anxious about the safety of his uncles, he is unwilling and probably unable to talk about his fears with his parents or his nursery school teacher. Notice, however, how clearly Stewart communicates his feelings about war in this brief excerpt from a play session with psychotherapist Clark Moustakas (1959, pp. 70–71):

(*Stewart gathers the soldiers and lines them up in the sandbox. He plays silently for ten minutes.*)

S.: Junk.

T.: Junk?

S.: Yes, the war is junk. Where is that garbage truck? (*S. locates the truck and places soldiers in it.*) I'll put them in the junkyard. They will all burn up.

T.: You think that will stop the war to burn them all up?

S.: Yes. He's going in and he's going too. They all fight—even ladies and little girls fight.

T.: So you're taking them all to the junkyard to be burned.

S.: I'm going to put them in the sandbox. They are all getting burned. (*S. puts the truck in the sandbox and pours sand on the figures.*) They all get buried, see? (*S. takes the soldiers out of the truck and buries them in the sand.*) Every one will be buried and die.

T.: Is that how you feel about soldiers and war?

S.: Yeah. They're all getting buried. I'm putting more sand on and they're all going to get buried under this hill. (*Pause*) Can I get buried too?

T.: That's up to you.

S.: I'm almost all buried, but not quite. (*S. gets out of the sandbox.*) Here is a little girl, but I won't bury her.

T.: You bury all the soldiers but not the little girl.

S.: Yeah. If they're buried, they can't use their guns.

T.: You bury them so there will be no more killing with guns.

S.: This one I'm going to free. He'll work on a farm. This one too. None of them are buried. They aren't in a trap. They are all freed.

T.: You want them to go back to their own work on the farms and cities.

S.: Yeah. They all have to stand up and go back to their families.

The therapist observed (Moustakas, 1959) that in the very brief play sessions he shared with Stewart, the child struggled constantly with the implications of war and its effects on individuals and on families. He expressed the fear that men will not only kill one another but that ultimately women and children may be destroyed as well. It is a sign of Stewart's maturity that, although he entertained the possibility of putting an end to war by killing all the soldiers, he realized the futility of that solution and instead returned the soldiers to their homes in the cities and on the farms.

A theme frequently expressed throughout this book has been that play allows a child to communicate when no other forms of communication are possible. A related theme is that such communication is beneficial for children. After a few play sessions, for example, Stewart seemed to come to terms with his anxieties about war, and his behavior in the classroom reflected that resolution (Moustakas, 1959). The point is that play can be an extremely therapeutic activity for any child (or adult), and so, in this final chapter, we turn specifically to a discussion of the therapeutic benefits of play.

The Therapeutic Value of Play

As will be seen in a later section, a number of different approaches have been taken to the psychotherapy of children. Regardless of their particular orientation, however, virtually every school of psychotherapy shares one common belief: that the use of play or a play setting is an indispensable feature of the diagnosis and/or treatment of children who have problems (Guerney, 1984). Why is play so essential to the psycho-therapy of children? Throughout the years, a number of psychologists (e.g., Amster, 1943; Guerney, 1984; Gumauer, 1984; Nickerson, 1973; Schaefer, 1985; Thompson & Rudolph, 1988) have articulated the reasons:

1. Play allows children to communicate their feelings effectively and is a natural avenue for their doing so.
2. Play allows adults to enter the world of children and to show children that they are recognized and accepted. When an adult plays with a child, there is a temporary equalization of power, and the child is less likely than usual to feel threatened by the adult.
3. Observing children at play helps adults understand them better.
4. Since play is enjoyable for children, it encourages them to relax and thereby reduces their anxiety and defensiveness.
5. Play gives children opportunities to release feelings, such as anger and fear, that might be difficult to express otherwise; it allows them to take out their frustra-tions on play materials, without fear of censure from adults.
6. Play affords children the opportunity to develop social skills that might be useful in other situations.

7. Play gives children a chance to try out new roles and to experiment in a safe setting with a variety of problem-solving approaches.

Approaches to Play Therapy

Let us turn now to an examination of three general approaches to the uses of play in therapy. It should be noted that there are both similarities and differences among the three and that each subsumes a variety of specific approaches too numerous to mention here. The three general approaches that will be concentrated on are those outlined by Schaefer (1985): the *psychoanalytic approach,* the *structured approach,* and the *relationship approach.*

The Psychoanalytic Approach

To understand why psychoanalytic therapists felt the need to incorporate play into their therapy with children, we must first be aware of three conditions seen as essential to successful psychoanalysis. First, patients must be highly motivated to change. They must come into therapy with a clear recognition that they have a problem, a commitment to seeking a solution, and a belief that the therapist will be able to help them deal with their difficulties. Second, patients must be able to achieve **transference** with their therapists. That is, a patient must be open to the possibility of thinking of the therapist as a substitute for someone of great significance in his or her life—as a mother, father, husband, or wife figure, for example. Third, patients must be able to engage in the process of **free association.** They must be verbal enough to put into words, in the presence of their therapist, their innermost thoughts and feelings; they must be able to speak openly about anything on their minds at a given moment.

Each of the three essential characteristics of psychoanalysis is more difficult to achieve with a child patient than it is with an adult. According to Anna Freud (1968), the first difficulty in the analysis of children is that they often lack the necessary motivation to change. It is typically not they, but their parents, who make the decision that therapy is needed, and the therapist must often force from the child a recognition of a problem and a commitment to change. In the following passage Freud describes the challenge she faced in motivating one of her small patients:

> The little girl already knew two children who were being analyzed by me, and she came the first time to the appointment with her slightly older friend. I said nothing special to her and merely left her to gain a little confidence in her strange surroundings. The next time, when I had her alone, I made the first attack. I said that she knew quite well why her two friends came to me . . . and I wondered whether she too had been sent to me for some such reason. At that she said quite frankly, "I have a devil in me. Can it be taken out?"
> Certainly it could, I said, but it would be no light work [and] she would have to do a lot of things which she would not find at all agreeable. . . . She replied, "If you tell me that it is the only way to do it, then I shall do it that

way." Thereby of her own free will she bound herself by the essential rule of psychoanalysis. We ask nothing more of an adult patient at the outset." (pp. 6–7)

A second potential obstacle to the psychoanalysis of children is that transference is often difficult to achieve. Adults in therapy achieve transference more easily than children because the significant person whom the therapist represents is no longer actively involved in the role the therapist assumes. For example, an adult patient may readily allow a therapist to become a substitute father because her own father no longer fulfills that authoritative role in her life. Children, however, already have strong parent figures and are often reluctant to allow the therapist to assume a similar role.

As an illustration of the problem of achieving transference in the psychoanalysis of children, consider the following case of a patient of Freud's, who refused to transfer to the therapist the feelings she had toward her nanny; notice the effort required to persuade the child to transfer her feelings of dependency and trust from the nanny to her therapist:

I once analyzed an unusually gifted and sensitive child who cried too easily. She wanted to get over this tendency with the help of analysis. But the work with me always stuck at a certain stage. At that point there emerged as an obstruction a tender attachment to a nurse, who was not friendly towards analysis. The child indeed believed me as to what emerged from the analysis and what I said, but only up to a certain point—a stage to which she had allowed herself to go and where her loyalty to her nurse began.

Then I began a keen and sustained battle with the nurse for the child's affection, conducted on both sides with every possible expedient; in it I awakened her criticism, tried to shake her blind dependence, and turned to my account every one of the little conflicts which occur daily in the nursery. I knew that I had won when one day the little girl told me again the story of such an incident which had affected her at home, but this time she added "Do you think she's right?" (pp. 12–13)

Freud went on to say that it was only then, after she had succeeded in getting the child to transfer to her the feelings of attachment and trust that had been reserved for the nanny, that the therapy was able to progress.

Finally, children do not easily engage in free association, the third essential component in the therapy of adults. Children lack both the self-awareness and the verbal skills necessary to free associate as adults do, so other approaches to free association must be tried with children. How is it possible to encourage children to communicate freely to a psychotherapist their innermost thoughts, feelings, and needs? Is there another, nonverbal means of communication available to them? Indeed, there is, and that form of expression is their play.

It will be remembered from Chapter One that psychoanalytic theorists view play as an activity that helps children cope with objective and instinctual anxieties. Play allows children to repeat and work through specific life experiences that were too threatening, too overwhelming, too difficult to assimilate when they first occurred (Freud, 1968). It follows, then, that play can offer insights into the mental life, both conscious and unconscious, of the child. Play can offer clues about the problems children are coping with and the mechanisms they are using to cope.

The Play Analysis of Melanie Klein

The therapist Hermine Hug-Hellmuth is generally recognized as the first to incorporate play into psychoanalytic therapy with children. Nevertheless, it was Melanie Klein who, beginning in 1919, used play extensively to deeply explore the child's unconscious mind (Landreth, 1987; Schaefer, 1985). Play was for Klein the childhood equivalent of free association. In play, she felt, children divulge all of their secrets—their feelings about the important people in their lives, their likes and dislikes, their fears, their joys, and the causes of their hostilities.

One of the assumptions underlying what Klein referred to as her **play analysis** was that most of a child's play activities are symbolic expressions of sexual conflict or aggression that pertain to the relationship between the child and his or her parents. A child's feelings toward his or her parents often consist of many contradictions and confusions. There are combinations of love and hatred, hostility and resentment, dependency and frustration at being dependent. Such a complex array of feelings would be difficult enough for an adult to articulate; they are nearly impossible for a child to make sense of, let alone put into words. The child, however, can play out this tangle of feelings with dolls, puppets, toy trains, and trucks.

Since she believed play was the language in which children express themselves most easily, Klein equipped her therapy room with a large variety of toys and particularly those that encouraged self-expression; many of these toys (e.g., parent dolls, baby dolls, household furnishings) were suggestive of, or pertained in some way to, family interactions (Schaefer, 1985). When one of her little patients entered her office, Klein would unlock his or her private drawer, and take out a variety of playthings, including little wooden figures representing human beings and animals, houses, cars, balls, marbles, and various creative materials, such as paints, pencils, and clay.

As the child played, Klein would observe carefully to hear what he or she was *really* saying and would then translate into words the underlying symbolic messages of the play. If a little boy was playing with a family of dolls and regularly buried the father doll in the sand, Klein might remark that the boy felt anger toward his own father; if another child regularly caused the trucks she was playing with to collide, Klein might suggest that this action referred to the child's vision of a sexual union that was significant in her life. In short, every action took on some symbolic meaning.

It was the child's reaction to her interpretive comments that would tell Klein whether she was correct in her interpretation. For example, the validity of her comments might be indicated if the little boy burying figures in the sand looked knowingly at her or smiled in response to her comment about his hatred for his father, or if the little female patient responded with vehement denials to Klein's suggestion that her truck collisions had sexual implications. The therapist would assume that a sharp denial on the part of the child was evidence that she had struck a nerve.

*Psychoanalytic theorists believe there is much to be learned
about the psychological world of children from an analysis of
their play with dolls and other miniature life toys.*

The success of Klein's interpretive play analysis was predicated upon two
assumptions. The first was that children will have the insight to recognize the
meaning of their behaviors if the symbolism is clearly pointed out to them. Actually,
this assumption is controversial. On the one hand, many child analysts argue that
children's capacity for insight is even greater than that of adults. Critics of Klein's
approach suggest, on the other hand, that children are not capable of understanding
the hidden meaning of their play even when it is pointed out to them, and even if they
could have such understanding, insight alone is not adequate to solve their problems
(Schaefer, 1985).

Klein's second assumption was that, once her young patients better understood
their feelings and needs, they would begin to develop new adaptive behaviors more

effective than those that resulted in their seeking the help of a therapist in the first place.

Anna Freud's Use of Play in Therapy

Even among psychoanalytic therapists, there was a lack of total agreement on the value of Melanie Klein's interpretive approach to the play of children. Anna Freud (1968), for example, expressed serious reservations about that component of Klein's work. Freud contended that play lacks the element of purpose that is necessary in a therapeutic situation, since a child at play, whether at home or in a therapist's office, does not do so for external reasons. Children play because it is enjoyable to do so and not because they want to rid themselves of emotional problems. As was mentioned earlier, successful therapy requires that patients realize the purpose of the activity and want to be helped by their therapists.

Freud went on to say that, because play lacks the purposeful attitude of free association, there is no justification for treating the two as analogous. And if indeed they are not equivalent, then the interpretations offered by Klein might easily stray far from the mark (Schaefer, 1985). For example, a child who causes two trucks to crash might simply be playing out a scene she witnessed on the street the day before! The child who greets a female visitor to his home by opening the woman's purse might not be symbolically expressing curiosity about whether his own mother's womb conceals a new baby brother or sister; he might only be looking to see if the visitor has brought a present for him.

Despite her view that Klein's particular uses of play in therapy were somewhat inappropriate and her interpretations often excessive and extreme, Freud did not deny that play can contribute much to the psychoanalytic treatment of children. The major therapeutic value of children's play, she felt, was that it allowed the therapist to gather useful information about the child. By carefully watching a child at play, an adult can see in one stroke the whole of a child's psychological world in the limited space of the therapy room. The observation of children at play in a therapist's office can actually provide *more* information than can be gotten from observing them in their natural surroundings. Why? Because toys are controllable, and children can carry out actions with them that are possible only in fantasy in the large and uncontrollable everyday world.

Freud typically used play in the early stages of therapy with a child as an information-gathering technique that could be supplemented with material supplied by the parents during the course of interviews (Schaefer, 1985). She used interpretive feedback more sparingly than Klein and only at a much later point in the therapy, and she maintained that while children's play is sometimes imbued with meaningful symbolism, it is often symbolic of nothing at all.

During the 1930s, psychoanalytic play therapy was still in its infancy, but already there was a growing disagreement over the extent to which the patient's activities should be structured. Some psychologists advocated **passive play therapy,** in which toys were provided but the therapist did not specify which toys should be played with or how. In addition, the child at play was free to include or exclude the therapist; if included by the child, the therapist, in keeping with the psychoanalytic tradition, would feel free to offer interpretations and encouragement. Passive play therapy was later to shed its psychoanalytic emphases (e.g., the use of play as a basis for interpretation of dreams, fantasies, and past experiences), and would evolve in the 1940s and 1950s into what is known today as nondirective relationship therapy. The relationship approach will be examined in detail in the section following this one.

In opposition to those who advocated passive play therapy were many therapists who argued the need for **active play therapy,** in which the therapist decided in advance what the child's problem was and then tailored the therapy to the patient's specific needs (Gumauer, 1984). In marked contrast to the open-ended passive approach, the therapist would not offer the child the choice of any toy to play with but would present specific toys and make suggestions for play activities. As will be seen, active play therapy exists today in many forms, some of which will be discussed in the section dealing with structured approaches.

The Relationship Approach

Evolving from the passive play therapy of a decade earlier, the relationship approach to play therapy made its appearance during the 1940s. Inspired by the work of psychotherapist Carl Rogers, the relationship approach to psychotherapy with children puts great emphasis on the quality of the interaction between therapist and child. The therapist strives to create an atmosphere of total acceptance. The therapist does not criticize the child or attempt to force the therapy in any particular direction; instead, he or she is *nondirective* and attempts to communicate a feeling of warmth, openness, and respect. Respect for the client is essential because a general assumption of such therapy is that it is the child and not the therapist who will find the means of bringing his or her self-image "out of the shadow land and into the sun" (Axline, 1969, p. 13). When this has been done and the child is able to identify, express, and accept his or her own feelings, the child will be better able to integrate and make sense of those feelings. A major goal of relationship therapy, therefore, is the achievement of self-awareness and self-direction on the part of the child (Schaefer, 1985).

Why would a child need a therapist in the first place? The assumption of nondirective relationship therapy is that the climate of acceptance, or what Meador and Rogers (1984) referred to as "unconditional positive regard," is not available in the child's everyday life. Instead of accepting the child's feelings as genuine expressions of the self, parents or others rejected certain feelings and thereby rejected the child. Take as an example the case of three-year-old Paul, who came to resent the presence of his new baby sister in the home. Paul told his parents that he hated the baby and asked them to return her to the hospital. His parents responded that they couldn't believe that such a nice little boy could really hate the new baby; he might *think* that he hated her, but actually he loved her as much as they did. Now Paul became confused. The hatred he felt was genuine, but he was told by people he loved and respected that he was misreading his own feelings and, more significantly, that certain of his feelings were not acceptable. One can imagine Paul as the years go by, disguising his genuine anger and resentment toward his sister, as well as toward other people and situations in his life, until he himself no longer knows what he is feeling.

Many children—and adults—do not even recognize their feelings of anger, fear, or sadness because in the course of time they have lost contact with them.

Psychotherapist Virginia Axline (1950) described the heartbreaking case of a seven-year-old boy who was hospitalized for an operation, and, not surprisingly, was very frightened. The child transformed his inexpressible fears into anger, and became aggressive and hostile toward the hospital staff. His parents, who had never done much to help the boy express and cope with his feelings, were ashamed of their son's behavior and told him so; he was an embarrassment to them, and they hoped he would learn to "behave like a man." Then they bribed him with an offer of a new bicycle if he would stop behaving badly, assuring that, in any case, there was nothing to be afraid of. The child obeyed his parents and kept his feelings in check; he also developed a case of asthma as his body expressed the fear and sadness that he could not outwardly display.

According to Rogers, it is difficult to accept another human being fully, and rejection takes a number of forms. Rejection occurs when, as in the case of little Paul, who was adjusting to the presence of a new sibling, adults deny the child's feelings. Rejection also occurs when adults criticize children for what they feel, as opposed to criticizing them only for what they do. It is one thing to punish a child for fighting, but it is quite another matter when a child is punished for *feeling* angry enough to fight. Finally, rejection occurs when adults try to change or to reinterpret a child's feelings: "You say you hate your brother, but I think the problem is that you're nervous about the exam you will take in school tomorrow."

As might be expected, nondirective relationship therapists try to provide in their therapy sessions the ingredients that have been missing in other areas of the child's life. Let us now examine the therapeutic approach of one of the best known child psychotherapists, Virginia Axline, whose treatment of a little boy named Dibs has become familiar to millions of readers since the book of the same name appeared in 1946.

Virginia Axline's Nondirective Therapy

Axline, a psychotherapist and a professor at Ohio State University, has outlined eight basic principles of her relationship therapy.

First, the therapist must *establish a warm and friendly relationship* with the child, and the child must come to see the therapy room as a comfortable and inviting place to play. He or she might greet the child, or children in the case of group therapy, with a friendly smile or another expression of genuine interest. Axline points out, however, that rapport is not always easy to establish, since the child in therapy may be unaccustomed to following the established rules of social behavior. A friendly smile from the therapist may be repaid with a scowl from a child who resents having to be involved in therapy in the first place.

A second principle is that the therapist must *accept the child completely* for what he or she is, without praise and without criticism. Such total acceptance often requires a considerable amount of patience on the therapist's part, especially if the child and therapist are at cross purposes, as when the therapist wants to be of help but the child does not want any help. Axline describes such a circumstance with reference to the case of 12-year-old Jean, who responds to the therapist's friendly greeting with stony silence and reacts with indifference to suggestions that there are a lot of wonderful things to play with in the therapy room. Jean sits in silence. The therapist tries to be accepting of the child's attitude but, because of her own inexperience, is having difficulty doing so. Finally, she says, "You know, Jean, I'm here to help you. I want you to consider me your friend. I wish you would tell me what bothers you." Jean responds with a sigh, "Nothing bothers *me!*"—a perceptive remark in that she knows that it is the therapist who is upset. The therapist has not accepted Jean's feelings, and the therapy is blocked.

Axline's third principle is that the therapist must establish a *climate of permissiveness*. The materials in the room and the time are to be used as the child wants to use them. When the therapist remarks that their time together belongs to the child and may be used as the child sees fit, he or she must be totally sincere. There must be no attempt to force the child to use the materials in any particular way. For example, the therapist may realize that Paul has been stressed because of his parents' constant fighting in the home and may feel that the child might develop insights into his problems by playing with the family dolls, but she should not pressure him to do so.

Similarly, there must be no probing questions that pertain to the child's life experiences. Axline describes the consequences of such probing in the case of May, a five-year-old who is in therapy trying to deal with her reactions to a traumatic hospital experience. May is playing with a family of dolls, and the therapist, hoping to be of help, begins to push too hard. When May puts a little girl doll in a wagon and pushes her across the floor, the therapist asks, "Is the little girl going to the hospital?" May answers that she is. "Is she afraid?" the therapist asks. Again, May responds in the affirmative. "Then what happens?" asks the therapist. May simply gets up and goes over to window, where she stands with her back to the therapist, and asks, "How much longer?"

A fourth principle is that the therapist *recognizes the child's feelings and attempts to reflect them back* to the child. The reflection of children's feelings, as they are expressed in words or, gestures or in the symbolic meaning of the play, is intended to help them to gain insight into those feelings. Even when the feelings are expressed in words, the therapist must be careful to recognize exactly what the child is saying and to avoid reading into the child's statements more than was intended. Jack says, "I spit on my brother. I spit on my father. I spit right in their very faces. They wouldn't give me my toys. He broke my gun. I'll show them. I'll spit on them." The therapist responds, "You are very angry with your brother and your father. You would like to spit right in their faces because of the way they have treated you" (Axline, 1969, p. 101).

When feelings are expressed symbolically through play, the therapist must exercise even greater caution. Axline points out that the recognition and the interpretation of a feeling are two different processes, but in reacting to the patient's play, it is difficult to separate the two. In marked contrast to the interpretive approach often used by psychoanalytic therapists, Axline warns against the overuse of interpretation. Interpretation should be used very sparingly, she says, for two reasons. First, any particular interpretation can be in error, particularly if made by an inexperienced therapist. Second, even if an interpretation is on target, the therapist may be pushing the patient along faster than the patient wants to go. If, however, the interpretation is both accurate and timely, the child advances in the therapy, and the therapist can actually see the patient gaining insight into his or her problems.

The fifth play therapy principle expressed by Axline is that the therapist always maintains *respect for the child* and a recognition that the child is capable of solving his or her own problems. The responsibility for the success of the therapy rests with the child, and in that sense the therapy is centered in the child and not in the therapist. As children realize that the responsibility is theirs, they gain a measure of self-confidence and self-respect that would not be possible if they came to rely totally on the therapist to help them.

Sixth, the therapist recognizes that in therapy, the *child leads the way* and the therapist follows. As indicated earlier, nondirective therapy involves no probing questions, no directions, no suggestions, no prompting, no criticism, and no approval of the child's actions. Axline (1969) believes that approval, like criticism, is a form of manipulation and may result in children's behaving in certain ways simply to please the therapist rather than because the behaviors are right for them.

The seventh principle is that the *therapy must not be hurried*. Many times the progress of the therapy will not be obvious, particularly if the child sits and plays quietly in session after session, but if progress is not immediately evident, that does not mean it is not occurring. Hurrying the child in therapy violates many of the principles described thus far. It may damage the rapport that has been built up between therapist and child, it does not indicate a climate of permissiveness, it does not show respect for the child, and it hardly suggests that it is the child who leads the way.

Finally, an important principle of nondirective therapy is that *limits must be set*. No area of a child's life is totally free of limits, and this includes the therapy session. Limits anchor children in reality and help them realize that they have responsibilities to fulfill. Limits and structure also provide a sense of security.

The limits of nondirective therapy are generally of three kinds. First, the children are not allowed to harm themselves or the therapist. Second, they are not allowed to cause damage to the materials in the playroom. And third, while they may use their time with the therapist in any way they want to, the children must leave the room when the session is at an end. Observe the way in which nondirective therapist Clark Moustakas (1959, pp. 17–18) establishes, kindly but firmly, the time limit on his session with five-year-old Tim:

T.:   In a short while, we'll have to leave.

Tim: No. I'm going to stay.

T.:   I can see you're not ready to stop, but we have only so much time to be here, and when that time is up we must leave.

Tim: My mommy can play with me.

T.:   I know your mommy *can* play with you, but I must close the room.

Tim: I'm not going.

T.:   You are determined to stay, but I must ask you to leave soon.

Tim: I'm going to tell my mommy; she'll come and play with me.

T.:   I guess she would, but not here. When you walk out the door, I'm turning off the lights and closing the room.

It will be noticed that the therapist accepted Tim's feelings as valid, reflected the sentiments back to the child, and offered no criticism at all. Yet he made very clear to Tim that the rules of the playroom must be obeyed.

Structured Approaches

As we have seen, the early psychoanalytic approach to play therapy was somewhat directive in its willingness to offer interpretations, while the relationship approach was firmly rooted in the principle that it is the child, not the therapist, who takes the lead. The current trend in thinking about the uses of play in therapy, however, represents a sort of compromise between these two extremes of directiveness. This recent tendency to seek the middle ground in psychotherapy with children is exemplified by changes in the psychoanalytic approach since the time of Melanie Klein (Rutter, 1975; Thompson & Rudolph, 1988):

1. An emphasis on shorter treatments, with specific goals and strategies clearly outlined at the beginning of therapy
2. A focus on present realities rather than on unconscious mechanisms rooted in the past
3. An avoidance of the use of heavily symbolic interpretation
4. A stress on the importance of the relationship between therapist and child
5. A growing tendency to use the expressive arts, including music, literature, drama, puppetry, and free play.

Modern child psychotherapists of every philosophical orientation continue to use a variety of forms of play in their approaches to treatment. Dolls are used with younger children, as are puppets, miniature life toys, art materials, punching toys, and sandbox play; with older children there are also board games, construction materials, paper-and-pencil games, and even computer games. However, the ways that play materials and activities are currently used differs considerably from what was seen in the past. The tendency today is to avoid both the excessive interpretation that was characteristic of the early psychoanalytic therapists and the extremely permissive atmosphere favored by relationship therapists. In fact, instead of following a general set of theoretical principles, the modern therapist usually tailors the treatment to the needs of the individual child. The amount of structure provided by the therapist, including the extent of the limits, the particular toys made available, and the play activities suggested, depends on the child's level of development and personal characteristics, as well as on the specific goals of the therapy (Thompson & Rudolph, 1988).

As we now examine some of the more widely used structured approaches to play in therapy, notice that all contain as a common element the recognition that play allows a child to communicate even the most complicated and most painful feelings from a safe distance: The child at play speaks, as it were, from behind a curtain of make-believe.

Release Therapy

Although formulated over a half-century ago, **release therapy** (Levy, 1939) illustrates the modern emphasis on a more structured approach to child psychotherapy. The underlying premise of this therapy is that, if children are strong enough to tolerate significant emotional upheaval, they will benefit from releasing their pent-up emotions; only when these emotions are finally expressed can children cognitively assimilate significant life events and learn to master them (Schaefer, 1985). It is the role of the therapist, first, to identify the problem the child is struggling with and then to suggest the toys and play activities most likely to encourage the child to confront the problem directly.

Let us look at a fictitious illustration of release therapy. Five-year-old Alan had never been an aggressive child, but since the birth of his baby sister, he has been involved in numerous playground scuffles with his kindergarten classmates. Even more disturbing to his parents is Alan's growing tendency to disrupt his classroom and speak rudely to his teacher when he is reprimanded.

Dr. Page, the therapist called in to help Alan, decides that sibling rivalry is at the root of the problem. She brings Alan to the playroom with her but does *not* tell him that he may play with any of the toys however he wishes. Instead, after she and Alan have established a comfortable relationship, she offers the boy a baby doll, a mother doll, and a nursing bottle to play with, and as he plays, she asks him to tell her what the dolls are thinking and what they are saying. The first two times Alan plays this game, he has little to say that is meaningful or revealing; nevertheless, Dr. Page persists in suggesting the activity until finally Alan begins to release his pent-up hostility. At first he expresses only mild irritation toward the baby doll, but soon he displays the full strength of his rage; during the fourth session, for example, he roughly pulls the nursing bottle from the baby's mouth, inserts it in his own mouth, and throws the doll across the room! All the while Dr. Page makes comments, both verbal and nonverbal, that are reflections on, rather than symbolic interpretations of, Alan's play; sometimes she even assumes the role of one of the characters in the little drama. And gradually, by releasing his anger Alan learns to recognize its real target and to control it; the disruptive school behaviors soon come to an end, and Alan gets on with the business of adjusting, like so many children, to life as an older sibling.

Costume Play Therapy

We are often surprised to hear some actors describe themselves as shy and private people; appearing in character in front of thousands of spectators does not faze them, but appearing as themselves before an audience fills them with terror. The rationale for this apparent inconsistency is that when actors play their roles, it is not they but the characters they portray who stand in front of the audience. There is safety in the role;

there is safety in the costume. And this is the premise of **costume play therapy,** developed by Irwin Marcus (1966).

Most adults can remember the joy of dressing up in costume as children and engaging in unlimited flights of fantasy in their make-believe roles. Marcus (1966) suggested that children in costume are remarkably free to express themselves. A goal of psychotherapy is to allow troubled children to express themselves completely, so Marcus' clients dress in costume and act out imaginary conflicts; in doing so, the children may unintentionally reveal much about their own problems, and the therapist can interpret these play sequences in the context of the child's current or former relationships (Guerney, 1984).

Storytelling

People often find their troubles easier to talk about if, instead of referring directly to themselves, they can describe the problems of a hypothetical "friend." And sometimes while describing the problems of this surrogate, the narrator gains valuable insights into his or her own emotional difficulties. Such storytelling affords people the safety of distance from their own lives and allows them to develop objectivity about and perspective on the issues that are troubling them.

The safety of distance and the possibility of gaining insights into one's problems provide a rationale for using storytelling as a form of therapy. As an example of this approach, consider the case of Marcia, described by Thompson and Rudolph (1988), a bright and imaginative child who lied habitually to her parents, her peers, and even her counselor. In one session, the counselor related to Marcia the story of a girl named Mary, who resembled Marcia in age and in many other characteristics. Like Marcia, Mary lied constantly to friends and family in order to impress them. One day, however, Mary's lying caught up with her: She witnessed a robbery in progress in her neighborhood, but when she went for help no one would believe her. Marcia was then asked what she thought of Mary's predicament and how it could be resolved. As Marcia discussed Mary's situation, she soon began to speak of what "I" should do and how "I" should go about recovering the trust of my friends.

An interesting approach to the storytelling technique was developed by psychotherapist Richard Gardner (1971, 1972). Instead of simply telling a story to a child and asking for reactions, Gardner engaged in what he described as **mutual storytelling.** He would first ask the child to make up an unusual and exciting story and, as the child spoke, he would try to identify whom the story's characters were intended to represent and what was the symbolic significance of the setting and the theme. Then, on the assumption that an adult who speaks in the child's own language has the best chance of being heard, Gardner would retell the story but in a revised version in which any conflicts expressed in the original story were resolved in constructive ways. The child would then realize that there might be more effective ways of dealing with problems than those already being used.

Illustrative of Gardner's approach is his work with 12-year-old Frank, who suffered from anxiety, excessive guilt, and hypersensitivity to criticism (Gardner, 1972). Frank's parents were cold and inflexible people who tolerated no signs of weakness or insubordination in their son. Here is Frank's story:

This story is about a man who killed his wife for her money. This man was greedy and he got so greedy with his money that he thought he was the best guy going. He knew that he had a lot of money, so he went and bet on a lot of different things. One night he bet and he lost all his money because he was conceited and selfish, and now he's on a street corner begging for money.

The moral of the story is: don't brag about yourself because only something bad is going to happen. (p. 67)

The therapist identified the theme of Frank's story as that of excessive deprivation. The wife's money in the story represented the mother's love that Frank wanted so desperately but apparently could not have. The fact that the character killed his wife for her money is indicative of the rage Frank felt toward his mother, but interestingly enough, even by killing his wife, the story character achieved little satisfaction. The money he wanted so much was eventually lost. Frank seemed to realize that his anger toward his mother served little purpose and to believe that, just as his fictitious character lost the money because of his own personal shortcomings, he himself was unworthy of the love that he needed so much.

What follows is Gardner's retelling of Frank's story:

Once upon a time there was a guy [whose] mother was a very selfish person. She had a lot of money but she wouldn't part with a penny. . . . This poor guy felt starved for money and he felt very bad. He wanted to buy things. Other kids got allowances, other kids had a little extra bit of spending money to buy themselves things, and he was really sad. At times he would get so sad and mad that he would feel like killing her, but he realized that this would accomplish nothing.

So what he did was he decided to get a job. The first thing he did was to get a newspaper route and he was able to earn some money with that. As he got older, he was able to get bigger jobs. He went to school and he got trained in something so that he could earn a living. And then when he earned it on his own he met a wonderful girl whom he married. She had some earnings, and he earned, and they pooled their money together. They had a very good relationship, and they spent their life pleasurably.

The moral of that story is: if somebody is not giving you something that you want from them, don't kill them for it. Don't knock yourself out. Don't try to bug them when they can't give it. Try to find it elsewhere. Another way of saying the moral of that story is the old saying of W. C. Fields, If at first you don't succeed, try, try again. After that if you still don't succeed, forget about it. Don't make a damn fool of yourself. The end (p. 68).

Gardner began his story by acknowledging Frank's pain and deprivation. He also recognized Frank's underlying rage but indicated that anger alone would not solve the problem. Then he symbolically suggested to Frank that constructive approaches are more beneficial. The therapist let the boy know that instead of dwelling on what he was missing in life, he should realize that his mother might be unable to give him what he needed and truly deserved. He might be wise, therefore, to look for love elsewhere.

The point of this meaningful exchange between Frank and his therapist is that it probably would not have occurred without the safe, nonliteral element of make-believe. If he had to speak directly about his own life, Frank could never have been as eloquent in describing his problems. And to use the therapist's own phrase, if he had not replied to Frank in the boy's own language, he would have had a lesser chance of being heard.

Bibliocounseling

Many of us have had the experience of reading a story in which a character's life so closely resembled our own that we were comforted to discover that we are not so unusual after all. In fact, reading about the experiences of others often helps one gain insights into one's own lives. This phenomenon forms the rationale for **bibliocounseling,** in which troubled children are asked to read books about people whose life circumstances are similar to theirs or to listen while a book is read aloud to them by a counselor, and then encouraged to discuss with their counselors the characters' behaviors, thoughts, feelings, and problems (Thompson & Rudolph, 1988).

Reading about the experiences of other people can help children gain insights into their own lives.

The major goals of bibliocounseling, according to Watson (1980), are the following:

1. To encourage children to express their problems openly
2. To teach children to be able to analyze their own feelings and their behaviors
3. To stimulate children to consider a variety of possible alternatives in the solution of their problems
4. To allow children to realize that their problems are not unique to them, and thus to give them the comfort of knowing that they are not alone
5. To teach children to be constructive and positive in their thinking

An underlying assumption of bibliocounseling is that, if a character in a story has problems similar to those of a child in treatment, the child will identify with and gain insights from the character's experiences. To this end, story lines are specifically selected by the therapist to mirror the life experiences of the patient and often include themes like making friends, dealing with family changes caused by divorce or death, understanding the self, or finding love (Thompson, Davis, & Madden, 1986). Apparently it is easier for children to talk about a story character's problems than to talk about their own, and as they do so, they may learn to confront their own feelings and eventually to solve their own problems.

Does Play Really Help?

We have seen that play is a tool used by child psychotherapists of vastly different philosophical orientations. Now we close by asking whether there exists scientific proof of its therapeutic effectiveness. Before attempting to draw conclusions about the therapeutic effectiveness of play, we should remember that play, unlike psychoanalysis, behavioral therapy, or relationship therapy, is not in itself a particular philosophy of therapy. It is difficult, therefore, to determine precisely the effectiveness of play therapy, in the sense of offering statistical proof of its usefulness. Perhaps it is difficult to prove scientifically the effectiveness of any form of therapy, since techniques that work extremely well for one client may not work at all for another. Play is no exception to this general rule; exactly how and when play is incorporated into therapy seems to depend on the needs of the individual client. The proof of play's benefits in a therapeutic interaction must be obtained, therefore, from the testimonials of individual therapists who use it.

Numerous case studies described in the literature on child psychotherapy testify to the usefulness of play in a counseling setting. Successful results have been reported by therapists using puppet play (James & Myer, 1987), sand play (Allan & Berry, 1987; Vinturella & James, 1987; Weinrib, 1983), poetry and popular music (Mazza, 1986), and mutual storytelling (Kestenbaum, 1985). One of the more intriguing reports to appear recently concerned the effectiveness of computer art in helping a 10-year-old boy to discuss openly the painful feelings associated with his father's death, to gain self-confidence, and to relieve the anxiety he felt whenever his mother left the house (Johnson, 1987).

In summary, there appears to be little doubt that play has a number of curative powers. According to psychotherapist Charles E. Schaefer (1985), play releases tensions and pent-up emotions. It allows a child to compensate in fantasy for the hurtful experiences of reality. It encourages self-discovery. It provides the possibility for children to learn alternative, and more successful, methods for dealing with their problems. Finally, it is a child's natural medium for communication, and, because of this, play has been incorporated successfully into virtually every form of psychotherapy that is practiced on children today.

Summary

Because it allows children to communicate when no other forms of communication are possible, play has been found to be an extremely valuable asset in the process of child psychotherapy. Play provides a rare opportunity for adults to understand the world the from child's point of view, and since the activity is so enjoyable for them, play encourages children to relax, let down any defenses they might have, and express their feelings openly. It also helps them develop useful social skills and to try a variety of new problem-solving approaches.

Psychoanalytic therapists agree that play is an aid to therapy but disagree on the specific ways it should be used. Melanie Klein, for example, treated play as the equivalent of free association. She believed that children at play will divulge all of their innermost feelings, not directly but symbolically. In her work with children, Klein would observe their play and continuously translate into words what she perceived to be the underlying symbolic messages. She assumed that children have enough insight to recognize the meaning of their behaviors if the symbolism is pointed out to them, and that, as children come to understand their needs and feelings better, they gradually develop new and more effective ways of adapting to the world around them.

Anna Freud rejected the analogy of play as free association and was critical of what she saw as Klein's overreliance on interpretation. Such interpretations can often be incorrect, she argued. Instead, Freud used play primarily to diagnose a child's problems. She felt that the observation of children at play could allow adults to see in one stroke the whole of the child's psychological world in the limited space of the therapy room.

The relationship approach to psychotherapy emphasizes the importance for the therapist of creating an atmosphere of total acceptance of the child, of refraining from criticism, communicating instead a feeling of warmth, openness, and respect. A basic assumption of such therapy is that children have within themselves the motivation and the ability to change their lives for the better, but they can do so only after they have identified, expressed, and accepted their own feelings. The goal of therapy is self-awareness and self-direction on the part of the child.

A number of the basic principles of nondirective relationship therapy were articulated more than 40 years ago by psychotherapist Virginia Axline. Axline believed that the therapist must establish a friendly relationship with the child, accept the child completely, neither praising nor criticizing, communicate an attitude of permissiveness, recognize and reflect the child's feelings, respect the child's ability to solve his or her own problems, and be patient enough to allow the child to lead the way in therapy. The therapist must also keep the child anchored in reality even in the very permissive playroom by setting limits on time and on the possibility of damage to the materials or harm to the child or the therapist.

Modern psychotherapists are likely to use a variety of different approaches to the incorporation of play into their therapy. Guided less by a particular philosophical orientation and more by the practical constraints of reality, they tend to prefer a middle road between the extremes of directiveness represented by the early psychoanalytic therapists, on the one hand, and the relationship therapists, on the other. Thus, we have a variety of structured approaches, in which the client's problem is identified by the therapist, and play materials and/or activities are suggested that are most relevant in dealing with the problem. Among the most often used structured approaches to play in therapy are release therapy, which is based on the assumption that a child needs to release pent-up emotions in order to learn how to deal with them most effectively, costume drama, storytelling, and biblicounseling.

The effectiveness of play as an adjunct to therapy is difficult to assess through the use of statistical procedures, because the ways in which play is used differ considerably from therapist to therapist and even from client to client. However, numerous case studies can be found in the literature on child psychotherapy that describe individual successes based on a variety of play approaches. The curative powers of play have been widely documented.

Key Terms

Active Play Therapy
Bibliocounseling
Costume Play Therapy
Free Association
Mutual Storytelling

Passive Play Therapy
Play Analysis
Release Therapy
Transference

Glossary

Accommodation. In Jean Piaget's cognitive theory, the adjustment of the intellectual structures in response to the incorporation of new information from the outside world.

Active Play Therapy. A type of therapy in which the therapist decides in advance what the child's problem is and then tailors the therapy to the patient's specific needs, perhaps presenting specific toys and making suggestions for play activities.

Activity/Recreation Play Programs. Hospital play programs that emphasize doing things, such as arts-and-crafts projects, so that the child can gain the sense of accomplishment that comes from being busy and productive.

Adrenogenital Syndrome. A condition in which the adrenal glands produce excessively high levels of male sex hormones in a female fetus, which has a pronounced masculinizing effect on a genetically female child.

Arousal Modulation Theory. The theory of children's play that assumes some optimal level of central nervous system arousal that a human being tries to maintain, with play being a way of maintaining this level.

Assimilation. In Jean Piaget's cognitive theory, the taking of new material from the outside world and fitting it into one's already existing intellectual structures.

Associative Play. A form of play in which each child is engaged in a separate activity but there is a considerable amount of cooperation and communication.

Autocosmic Play. According to psychoanalytic theorist Erik Erikson, a type of play that occurs during the first year of life, centering on the exploration of the child's own body.

Behaviorism. The psychological theory developed by John B. Watson, who believed that the mind is a blank slate at birth, that people grow to be what they are made to be by the environment, and that the only legitimate area of inquiry for psychologists is the study of behavior.

Bibliocounseling. A form of therapy in which troubled children are asked to read books about people whose life circumstances are similar to their own or listen while such a book is read aloud to them by a counselor and are then encouraged to discuss with their counselors the characters' behaviors, thoughts, feelings, and problems.

Character Roles. Dramatic play roles based on characters that are either stereotyped or fictional.

Child Development Play Programs. Hospital play programs that include curricula ordinarily found in preschool or elementary school classrooms.

Collectivism. A societal philosophy that stresses the importance of group goals, group loyalty, and group identification, encourages communal labor and communal property, and discourages the formation of potentially divisive allegiances to subgroups like the family.

Comprehensive Child Life Play Programs. Hospital play programs that focus on all aspects of the hospitalized child's development, seen in both an individual and a social context.

Conative Hypothesis. The belief that, rather than suffering from a specific intellectual deficit, autistic children may simply not want to engage in symbolic play to the extent that normal children do.

Concrete Operations. In Jean Piaget's theory of cognitive development, the stage at which the child has a logical system to organize representational acts but is limited in the use of logic to reasoning about concrete situations or events.

Conservation. The ability to realize that even though the physical appearance changes, the amount of matter remains the same if nothing is added or taken away.

Convergent Problem Solving. The ability to bring a variety of isolated pieces of information together to come up with the one correct solution.

Cooperative Play. A form of play that occurs when two or more children are engaged in a play activity with a common goal.

Costume Play Therapy. A form of therapy in which clients dress in costume and act out imaginary conflicts, and, in doing so, unintentionally reveal much about their own problems.

Decentration. The underlying element of symbolic play that refers to the degree to which the child is able to shift the focus of its interest from self to external objects. More generally, the ability to attend simultaneously to two or more features of the environment.

Decontextualization. The underlying element of symbolic play that refers to the use of one object as a substitute for another.

Divergent Problem Solving. The ability to branch out from a starting point and consider a variety of possible solutions.

Diversionary Play Programs. Hospital play programs characterized by an implicit assumption that children are better off if they do not directly confront the stressful experience of hospitalization.

Enactive Representation. Motoric encoding of information about the world, illustrated by the way a person learns to ride a bicycle or tie a knot in a necktie.

Equivalency. The recognition that space can be divided into different-size units and that a certain number of units of one size correspond to a different number of units of another.

Euclidean Spatial Concept. A conception of space as an overall network, independent of the number or the arrangement of elements within it.

Family Roles. Dramatic play roles of family members, the most common roles assumed by preschool children.

Formal Operations. In Jean Piaget's theory of cognitive development the highest stage, occurring during adolescence and adulthood. Formal thinkers are able deal with abstract, hypothetical propositions.

Free Association. An essential characteristic of psychoanalysis, in which patients put into words, in the presence of their therapist, their innermost thoughts and feelings.

Functional Roles. Dramatic play roles that are defined by specific plans of action.

Games of Chance. Competitive games in which the outcome is determined by sheer blind luck.

Games of Construction. A type of play that Jean Piaget saw as representing an area of transition between symbolic play and "nonplayful activities, or serious adaptation."

Games of Physical Skill. Competitive games in which the outcome is determined solely by the physical skills of the players.

Games of Strategy. Competitive games in which the outcome is determined by the rational choices made by the players, and which require a degree of intellectual skill for success.

Games-with-Rules. The games of elementary school children that involve competition be-

tween two or more players and are governed by a set of regulations agreed to in advance by all the players.

Gender Constancy. The recognition that gender always remains the same, regardless of surface physical changes in appearance.

Gender Identity. The preschool child's realization that males and females are different on the basis of their physical characteristics.

Gender Stability. The realization that gender will always remain the same, and that boys and girls will grow up to become either men or women.

Graphic Collections. Pleasing or interesting arrangements of figures that are produced by preschool children when they are asked to sort objects into groups.

Hypothetico-Deductive Reasoning. A type of problem solving in which the formal thinker sets up a variety of hypotheses, or "if-then" statements, ranks them in order of probability, and then tests them out systematically in sequence.

Identity. The adolescent stage of personality development, according to Erikson, in which teenagers test themselves in a variety of ways as they seek deeper levels of self-awareness.

Imaginary Audience. Adolescents' egocentric belief that they are "on stage" and that other people are as interested in them as they are in themselves.

Individualism. A societal philosophy characterized by a belief that loyalty to self comes before group loyalty, that people should develop their own individual identities, rather than identifying with the group, that the purpose of work is more to benefit individual workers and their families than to benefit the state, and that individuals have a right to own property.

Induction. A technique of discipline in which parents stress the impact on other people of their child's undesirable behaviors.

Industry. In Erik Erikson's theory, the need that grade school children have to apply themselves to a variety of skills and tasks that are necessary for success in the larger world of adults.

Instinctual Anxiety. In psychoanalytic theory, a type of anxiety that occurs when children recognize in themselves instincts that would be disapproved of by society at large. These forbidden feelings, whether or not they are translated into behaviors, trigger an anxiety reaction.

Integration. The underlying element of symbolic play that refers to the child's ability to organize play into increasingly complex patterns during the second year of life.

Logical Classification. The ability, which first appears at the age of five or six, to sort objects according to their logically defining properties.

Macrosphere Play. According to psychoanalytic theorist Erik Erikson, a type of play that appears during the preschool years, as children at play begin to acquire mastery in social interactions.

Microsphere Play. According to psychoanalytic theorist Erik Erikson, a type of play that appears during the second year, in which the child begins to acquire mastery over objects.

Mutual Storytelling. Richard Gardner's therapeutic technique of asking children to make up a story, identifying the story's symbolic significance, and retelling the story in a revised version in which conflicts expressed in the original story are resolved constructively.

Naturalism. A philosophical theory expressed by Jean-Jacques Rousseau in the eighteenth century that stressed the natural goodness of human beings, suggested that nature equips children with a plan for their development, and questioned the need for firm direction in childrearing.

Objective Anxiety. Fear of the external world that results when a young child realizes the degree of his or her helplessness.

Onlooker Play. Play in which a child watches another child or children at play, is definitely involved as a spectator, even to the point of asking questions or offering suggestions, but does not become an active participant.

Parallel Play. A form of activity in which children play separately at the same activity at the same time and in the same place.

Passive Play Therapy. An approach in which the therapist does not specify which toys the child should play with or how, and the child at play is free to include or exclude the therapist. If included by the child, the therapist feels free to offer interpretations and encouragement.

Personal Fable. A form of adolescent egocentrism in which adolescents see themselves as both unique and immortal.

Personal Movement. A type of creative movement activity that allows children to express their inner moods, feelings, and perceptions of the world, using only their bodies.

Phonological Aspects of Language. Aspects of language that pertain to the production of sound.

Play Analysis. The directive and interpretive form of play therapy that was originally used by the psychoanalyst Melanie Klein.

Play Observation Scale. An instrument developed by psychologist Kenneth Rubin to study children's behaviors when they are at play to identify children who may be at risk in terms of their social development.

Pragmatic Aspects of Language. The aspect of language that deals with the rules that govern the behaviors for engaging in effective communication.

Primary Circular Reaction. One of the earliest forms of sensorimotor play, a behavior that occurs when a baby accidentally discovers an interesting sensory or motor experience related to its own body, apparently enjoys it, and later continues to repeat it.

Recapitulation Theory. G. Stanley Hall's early twentieth-century belief that each person's development reflects the evolutionary progression of the entire human species.

Release Therapy. A form of therapy developed by David Levy, based on the idea that if children are strong enough to tolerate significant emotional upheaval, they will benefit from releasing their pent-up emotions.

Reversibility. A characteristic of thinking that does not appear before the age of five or six, this is the ability mentally to reverse an action.

Rough-and-Tumble Play. A form of play that is characterized by play fighting, including hitting and wrestling, and chasing with the intent of fighting.

Schemes. The consistent action patterns found in infancy that Jean Piaget viewed as the sensorimotor equivalents of concepts.

Secondary Circular Reaction. A type of sensorimotor play that appears after the age of four months and involves infants' repetition of behaviors that bring about pleasing effects on their surrounding world.

Semantic Aspects of Language. Aspects of a language that deal with the selection of words that appropriately convey the intended meaning.

Sensorimotor Play. Also referred to as practice play (Piaget, 1962), the sensorimotor play of the infant involves the repetition of already assimilated sensory or motor activities for the sheer pleasure of doing so.

Shared Meanings. Themes that organize the social interactions of young toddlers, including social games like run-and-chase, peek-a-boo, stack-and-topple, and motor-copy (in which one child simply imitates the motor activity of another).

Sociodramatic Play. A form of pretend play that involves intense group interaction, with each group member taking a role that complements the roles played by all others in the group.

Solitary Play. A form of play in which the child is completely involved in an activity and physically and/or psychologically isolated from other children.

Strange Situation. An instrument developed by psychologist Mary Ainsworth to determine the degree of attachment between parent and child.

Surplus Energy Theory. The belief of philosopher Herbert Spencer (1873) that the function of play is to allow children to discharge pent-up energy.

Symbol Deficit Hypothesis. The belief that autistic children lack representational skills, which explains both the social impairment of autism and the failure to engage in symbolic play.

Symbolic Play. Make-believe, or pretend, play that first appears at the beginning of the infant's second year of life and continues as the dominant form of play throughout the pre-school years.

Syntactic Aspects of Language. The aspects of language concerning the rules by which words are put together into sentences.

Tabula Rasa. A blank slate, the term often used to refer to theories of human development that described human beings as empty organisms at birth who develop under the influence of the environment.

Tertiary Circular Reaction. A characteristic sensorimotor activity in the second year of life, the infant's repetition of behaviors that bring about pleasing effects on the surrounding world but now accompanied by an attempt to vary the activity instead of repeating it precisely.

Therapeutic Play Programs. Hospital play programs based on the assumption that children cope better with a hospital stay if they can release their feelings freely.

Transference. A necessary condition of psychoanalysis: A patient must be open to the possibility of thinking of the therapist as a substitute for someone of great significance in his or her life.

Vigorous Activity Play. A form of solitary or social play that is characterized by intense physical activity but does not contain elements of aggression.

Bibliography

Ainsworth, M. D. S. (1977). Attachment theory and its utility in cross-cultural research. In P. H. Leiderman, S. R. Tulkin, & R. Rosenfeld (Eds.), *Culture and infancy* (pp. 49–67). New York: Academic Press.

Ainsworth, M. D. S. (1979). Attachment as related to mother-infant interaction. In J. S. Rosenblatt, R. A. Hinde, C. Beer, & M. Busnell (Eds.), *Advances in the study of behavior* (Vol. 9). New York: Academic Press.

Ainsworth, M. D. S., Blehar, M. C., Waters, E., & Wall, S. (1978). *Patterns of attachment: A psychological study of the Strange Situation*. Hillsdale, NJ: Erlbaum.

Aldis, O. (1975). *Play fighting*. New York: Academic Press.

Allan, J., & Berry, P. (1987). Sandplay. *Elementary School Guidance and Counseling, 21,* 300–306.

American Psychiatric Association (1980). *Diagnosis and statistical manual of mental disorders (DSM-III: 3rd ed.)*. Washington, DC: Author.

Ames, L. B., Gillespie, C., Haines, J., & Ilg, F. M. (1979). *The Gesell Institute's child from one to six*. New York: Harper & Row.

Ammar, H. (1954). *Growing up in an Egyptian village*. London: Routledge & Kegan Paul.

Amster, F. (1943). Differential uses of play in treatment of young children. *American Journal of Orthopsychiatry, 13,* 62–68.

Anshel, M. H., Muller, D., & Owens, V. L. (1986). Effect of a sports camp experience on the multidimensional self-concepts of boys. *Perceptual and Motor Skills, 63,* 363–366.

Aries, P. (1962). *Centuries of childhood: A social history of family life*. New York: Knopf.

Asher, S. R., Hymel, S., & Renshaw, P. D. (1984). Loneliness in children. *Child Development, 55,* 1456–1464.

Athey, I. (1984). Contributions of play to development. In T. D. Yawkey & A. D. Pellegrini (Eds.), *Child's play: Developmental and applied* (pp. 9–28). Hillsdale, NJ: Erlbaum.

Atlas, J. A., & Lapidus, L. B. (1987). Patterns of symbolic expression in subgroups of the childhood psychoses. *Journal of Clinical Psychology, 43,* 177–188.

Attwood, A. J. (1984). *Gestures of autistic children*. Unpublished doctoral thesis, The University of London. Cited in Baron-Cohen, Leslie, & Frith. (1985).

Axline, V. (1950). Emotions and how they grow. *Childhood Education, 27,* 104–108.

Axline, V. (1969). *Play therapy* (rev. ed.). New York: Ballantine Books.

Bailey, D., & Wolery, M. (1984). *Teaching infants and preschoolers with handicaps*. Columbus, OH: Merrill.

Bakeman, R., & Brownlee, J. (1980). The strategic use of parallel play: A sequential analysis. *Child Development, 51,* 873–878.

Barnard, K. E., Bee, H. L., & Hammond, M. A. (1984). Home environment and cognitive development in a healthy, low-risk sample: The Seattle study. In A. W. Gottfried (Ed.), *Home environment and early cognitive development: Longitudinal research*. New York: Academic Press.

Baron-Cohen, S. (1987). Autism and symbolic play. *British Journal of Developmental Psychology, 5,* 139–148.

Baron-Cohen, S., Leslie, A. M., & Frith, U. (1985). Does the autistic child have a "theory of mind"? *Cognition, 21,* 37–46.

Barron, F., & Harrington, D. M. (1981). Creativity, intelligence, and personality. *Annual Review of Psychology, 32,* 439–476.

Bartak, L., Rutter, M., & Cox, A. (1975). A comparative study of infantile autism and specific developmental receptive language disorder: 1. The children. *British Journal of Psychiatry, 126,* 127–145.

Bayley, N. (1969). *The Bayley Scales of Infant Development*. New York: Psychological Corporation.

Bearison, D. J., & Cassel, T. Z. (1975). Cognitive decentration and social codes: Communicative effectiveness in young children from differing family contexts. *Developmental Psychology, 11,* 29–36.

Beckwith, L. (1986). Parent-infant interaction and infants' social-emotional development. In A. W. Gottfried & C. C. Brown (Eds.), *Play interactions: The contributions of play materials and parental involvement to children's development* (pp. 279–292). Lexington, MA: Heath.

Bednersh, F., & Peck, C. A. (1986). Assessing social

environments: Effects of peer characteristics on the social behavior of children with severe handicaps. *Child Study Journal, 16,* 315–329.

Bekoff, M. (1972). The development of social interaction, play, and metacommunication in mammals: An ethological perspective. *Quarterly Review of Biology, 47,* 412–434.

Belsky, J., Garduque, L., & Hrncir, E. (1984). Assessing performance, competence, and executive capacity in infant play: Relations to home environment and the security of attachment. *Developmental Psychology, 20,* 406–417.

Belsky, J., Gilstrap, B., & Rovine, M. (1984). The Pennsylvania Infant and Family Development Project: I. Stability and change in mother-infant and father-infant interaction in a family setting at one, three, and nine months. *Child Development, 55,* 692–705.

Belsky, J., & Most, R. K. (1981). From exploration to play: A cross-sectional study of infant free-play behavior. *Developmental Psychology, 17,* 630–639.

Belsky, J., & Steinberg, L. D. (1978). The effects of day care: A critical review. *Child Development, 49,* 929–949.

Belsky, J., & Volling, B. (1985). Mothering, fathering, and marital interaction in the family triad during infancy: Exploring family systems processes. In P. Berman & F. Pedersen (Eds.), *Men's transition to parenthood: Longitudinal studies of early family experience.* Hillsdale, NJ: Erlbaum.

Benbow, C. P. (1986). *Home environments and toy preferences of extremely precocious students.* Paper presented at the annual meeting of the American Educational Research Association, San Francisco.

Benish, J. (1978). *Blocks: Essential equipment for young children.* Charleston: West Virginia State Department of Education. (ERIC Document Reproduction Service No. 165–901).

Berk, L. E. (1989). *Child development.* Boston, MA: Allyn and Bacon.

Berlyne, D. E. (1969). Laughter, humor, and play. In G. Lindzey & E. Aronson (Eds.), *Handbook of social psychology (Vol. 3).* Reading, MA: Addison-Wesley.

Berndt, T. J. (1982). The features and effects of friendship in early adolescence. *Child Development, 53,* 1447–1460.

Bianchi, B. D. & Bakeman, R. (1978). Sex-typed affiliation preferences expressed in preschoolers: Traditional and open school differences. *Child Development, 49,* 910–912.

Bierman, K. L. (1986). Process of change during social skills training with preadolescents and its relation to treatment outcome. *Child Development, 57,* 230–240.

Bierman, K. L., & Furman, W. F. (1984). The effects of social skills training and peer involvement on the social adjustment of preadolescents. *Child Development, 55,* 151–162.

Bigelow, B. J. (1977). Children's friendship expectations: A cognitive-developmental study. *Child Development, 48,* 246–253.

Blehar, M. C., Lieberman, A. F., & Ainsworth, M. D. S. (1977). Early face-to-face interaction and its relation to later mother-infant attachment. *Child Development, 48,* 182–194.

Blurton-Jones, N. G. (1967). An ethological study of some aspects of social behavior of children in nursery school. In D. Morris (Ed.), *Primate ethology.* London: Weidenfeld and Nicholson.

Blurton-Jones, N. G., & Konner, M. J. (1973). Sex differences in behavior of London and Bushman children. In R. P. Michael & J. H. Crook (Eds.), *Comparative ethology and behavior of primates.* New York: Academic Press.

Boivin, M,, & Begin, G. (1989). Peer status and self-perception among early elementary school children: The case of the rejected children. *Child Development, 60,* 591–596.

Bolig, R. (1984). Play in hospital settings. In T. D. Yawkey & A. D. Pellegrini (Eds.), *Child's play: Developmental and applied* (pp. 323–346). Hillsdale, NJ: Erlbaum.

Borgh, K., & Dickson, W. P. (1986). Two preschoolers sharing one computer: Creating prosocial behavior with hardware and software. In P. F. Campbell & G. G. Fein (Eds.), *Young children and microcomputers* (pp. 37–44). Englewood Cliffs, NJ: Prentice-Hall.

Borstelmann, L. J. (1983). Children before psychology. In P. H. Mussen (Ed.), Handbook of child psychology. New York: Wiley.

Bradley, R. H. (1986). Play materials and intellectual development. In A. W. Gottfried & C. C. Brown (Eds.), *Play interactions: The contributions of play materials and parental involvement to children's development* (pp. 227–252). Lexington, MA: Heath.

Bradley, R. H., & Caldwell, B. M. (1984). 174 children: A study of the relationship between home environment and cognitive development during the first five years. In A. W. Gottfried (Ed.), *Home environment and early cognitive development: Longitudinal research.* New York: Academic Press.

Bredemeier, B. J., & Shields, D. L. (1985, October). Values and violence in sports today: The moral reasoning athletes use in their games and in their lives. *Psychology Today,* pp. 23–31.

Bredemeier, B., & Shields, D. (1986). Moral growth among athletes and non-athletes: A comparative analysis of males and females. *Journal of Genetic Psychology, 147,* 7–18.

Bredemeier, B. J., Shields, D. L., Weiss, M. R., & Cooper, B. A. B. (1986). The relationship of sport involvement with children' s moral reasoning and aggression tendencies. *Journal of Sport Psychology, 8,* 304–318.

Brenner, J., & Mueller, E. (1982). Shared meaning in boy toddlers' peer relations. *Child Development, 53,* 380–381.

Bretherton, I. (1984). Representing the social world in symbolic play: Reality and fantasy. In I. Bretherton (Ed.), *Symbolic play: The development of social understanding* (pp. 3–41). New York: Academic Press.

Bretherton, I. (1986). Representing the social play: Reality and fantasy. In I. Bretherton (Ed.), *Symbolic play: The development of social understanding* (pp. 3–41). New York: Academic Press.

Bretherton, I. (1986). Representing the social world in symbolic play: Reality and fantasy. In A. W. Gottfried & C.C. Brown (Eds.), *Play interactions: The contributions of play materials and parental involvement to children's development* (pp. 119–148). Lexington, MA: Heath.

Bretherton, I., & Waters, E. (Eds.) (1985). Growing points of attachment theory and research. *Monographs of the Society for Research in Child Development, 50* (1 & 2, Serial No. 209).

Brindley, C., Clarke, C., Hutt, P., Robinson, I., & Wehtli, E. (1973). Sex differences in the activities and social interactions of nursery school children. In R. P. Michael & J. H. Crook (Eds.), *Comparative ethology and behavior of primates.* New York: Academic Press.

Brody, G. H., Graziano, W. G., & Musser, L. M. (1983). Familiarity and children's behavior in same-age and mixed-age peer groups. *Developmental Psychology, 19,* 568–576.

Brody, G. H., & Stoneman, Z. (1981). Selective imitation of same-age, older, and younger peer models. *Child Development, 52,* 717–720.

Bronfenbrenner, U. (1972). *Two worlds of childhood: U.S. and U.S.S.R.* New York: Simon and Schuster.

Bronstein, P. (1988). Marital and parenting roles in transition: An overview. In P. Bronstein & C. P. Cowan (Eds.), *Fatherhood today: Men's changing role in the family.* New York: Wiley.

Brownell, C. A. (1982). *Effects of age and age-mix on toddler peer interaction.* Paper presented at the International Conference on Infant Studies, Austin, TX.

Brownell, C. A. (1986). Convergent developments: Cognitive-developmental correlates of growth in infant/toddler peer skills. *Child Development, 57,* 275–286.

Bruner, J. S. (1972). The nature and uses of immaturity. *American Psychologist, 27,* 687–708.

Bruner, J. S. (1973a). Going beyond the information given. In J. M. Anglin (Ed.), *Beyond the information given* (pp. 218–240). New York: Norton.

Bruner, J. S. (1974). The growth of representational processes in children. In J. M. Anglin (Ed.), *Beyond the information given* (pp. 313–324). New York: Norton.

Bruner, J. S. (1983). *Child's talk.* New York: Norton.

Burg, K. (1984, March). The microcomputer in the kindergarten. *Young Children,* pp. 28–33.

Burns, S. M., & Brainerd, C. J. (1979). Effects of constructive and dramatic play on perspective-taking in very young children. *Developmental Psychology, 15,* 512–521.

Caldera, Y. M., Huston, A. C., & O'Brien, M. (1989). Social interactions and play patterns of parents and toddlers with feminine, masculine, and neutral toys. *Child Development, 60,* 70–76.

Cameron, E., Eisenberg, N., & Tryon, K. (1985). The relations between sex-typed play and preschoolers' social behavior. *Sex Roles, 12,* 601–615.

Casby, M. W., & Ruder, K. F. (1983). Symbolic play and early language development in normal and mentally retarded children. *Journal of Speech and Hearing Research, 26,* 404–411.

Chalmers, N. (1984). Social play in monkeys: Theories and data. In P. K. Smith (Ed.), *Play in animals and humans* (pp. 119–146). Oxford: Basil Blackwell.

Chalmers, N., & Locke-Haydon, J. (1985). Correlations among measures of playfulness and skillfulness in captive common marmosets (*Callithrix jacchus jacchus*). *Developmental Psychobiology, 17,* 191–208.

Chance, P. (1979). *Learning through play.* Piscataway, NJ: Johnson & Johnson.

Children's Defense Fund (1990). *S.O.S. America! A children's defense budget.* Washington, DC: Author.

Churchill, D. W. (1978). *Language of autistic children.* Washington, DC: Winston.

Cialdini, R. B., Baumann, D. J., & Kendrick, D. T. (1981). Insights from sadness: A three-step model of the development of altruism as hedonism. *Developmental Review, 1,* 207–223.

Clarke-Stewart, A. (1973). Interactions between mothers and their young children: Characteristics and consequences. *Monographs of the Society for Research in Child Development, 38,* (6 & 7).

Clarke-Stewart, A. (1978). And daddy makes three: The father's impact on the mother and young child. *Child Development, 49,* 466–478.

Clarke-Stewart, A. (1984). Day care: A new context for research and development. In M. Perlmutter (Ed.), *The Minnesota Symposia on Child Psychology: Vol. 17* (pp. 61–100). Hillsdale, NJ: Erlbaum.

Coie, J. D. (1985). Fitting social skills intervention to the target group. In B. H. Schneider, K. H. Rubin, & J. D. Ledingham (Eds.), *Children's peer relations* (pp. 141–156). New York: Springer-Verlag.

Coie, J.D., & Krehbiel, G. (1984). Effects of academic tutoring on the social status of low-achieving, socially rejected children. *Child Development, 55,* 1465–1478.

Collins, W. A. (Ed.). (1984). *Development during middle childhood: The years from six to twelve.* Washington, DC: National Academy Press.

Comstock, G., Chaffee, S., Katzman, N., McCombs, M., & Roberts, D. (1978). *Television and human behavior.* New York: Columbia University Press.

Connolly, J. A. (1980). *The relationship between social pretend play and social competence in preschoolers: Correlational and experimental studies.* Unpublished doctoral dissertation, Concordia University.

Connolly, J., Doyle, A., & Ceschin, F. (1983). Forms and functions of social fantasy play in preschoolers. In M. B. Liss (Ed.), *Social and cognitive skills: Sex roles and children's play* (pp. 71–92). New York: Academic Press.

Connor, J. M., & Serbin, L. A. (1977). Behaviorally based masculine and feminine activity—reference scales for preschoolers: Correlates with other classroom behaviors and cognitive tests. *Child Development, 48,* 1411–1416.

Copple, C. E., Cocking, R. R., & Matthews, W. S. (1984). Objects, symbols, and substitutes: The nature of the cognitive activity during symbolic play. In T. D. Yawkey & A. D. Pellegrini (Eds.), Child's play: Developmental and applied (pp.

105–124). Hillsdale, NJ: Erlbaum.

Crawley, S. B., Rogers, P., Friedman, S., Iacobbo, M., Criticos, A., Richardson, L., & Thompson, M. (1978). Developmental changes in the structure of mother-infant play. *Developmental Psychology, 14,* 30–36.

Crawley, S. B., & Sherrod, K. B. (1984). Parent-infant play during the first year of life. *Infant Behavior and Development, 7,* 65–75.

Creasey, G. L., & Myers, B. J. (1986). Video games and children: Effects on leisure activities, schoolwork, and peer involvement. *Merrill-Palmer Quarterly, 32,* 251–262.

Cunningham, C. C., Glenn, S. M., Wilkinson, P., & Sloper, P. (1985). Mental ability, symbolic play, and receptive and expressive language of young children with Down's syndrome. *Journal of Child Psychology and Psychiatry, 26,* 255–265.

Damon, W. (1983). Social and personality development. New York: Norton.

Dansky, J. L. (1980). Make-believe: A mediator of the relationship between play and associative fluency. *Child Development, 51,* 576–579.

Dansky, J. L., & Silverman, I. W. (1973). Effects of play on associative fluency in preschool-aged children. *Developmental Psychology, 9,* 38–43.

Dansky, J. L., & Silverman, I. W. (1975). Play: A general facilitator of associative fluency. *Developmental Psychology, 11,* 104.

Darbyshire, J. O. (1977). Play patterns in young children with impaired hearing. *Volta Review, 79,* 19–26.

Davidson, L., McKernon, P., & Gardner, H. (1981). *The Acquisition of Song.* Documentary Report of the Application of Psychology to the Teaching of Music. Reston, VA: MENC.

Davis, G. (1976). *Childhood and history in America.* New York: Psychohistory Press.

Dawber, T. (1980). *The Framingham Study: Epidemiology of atherosclerotic disease.* Cambridge, MA: Harvard University Press.

Day, B. (1988). *Early childhood education: Creative learning activities* (3rd ed.). New York: Macmillan.

DeMyer, M. K., Mann, N. A., Tilton, J. R., & Loew, L. H. (1967). Toy play behavior and use of body by autistic and normal children as reported by mothers. *Psychological Reports, 21,* 975–981.

DePietro, J. A. (1981). Rough-and-tumble play: A function of gender. *Developmental Psychology, 17,* 50–58.

Diaz, R. M., & Berndt, T. J. (1982). Children's knowledge of a best friend: Fact or fancy?

Developmental Psychology, 18, 787–794.

Dodge, K. A. (1983). Behavioral antecedents of peer social status. *Child Development, 54,* 1386–1399.

Dodge, K. A., Coie, J. D., & Brakke, N. P. (1982). Behavior patterns of socially rejected and neglected preadolescents: The roles of social approach and aggression. *Journal of Abnormal Child Psychology, 10,* 389–410.

Dowell, L., Badgett, J., & Landis, C. (1976). A study of the relationship between selected physical attributes and self-concept. In G. Kenyon (Ed.), *Contemporary psychology of sport.* North Palm Beach, FL: Athletic Institute.

Doyle, A. B., Connolly, J., & Rivest, L. P. (1980). The effect of playmate familiarity on the social interactions of young children. *Child Development, 51,* 217–223.

Dunn, J. (1983). Sibling relationships in early childhood. *Child Development, 54,* 787–811.

Egeland, B., & Farber, E. A. (1984). Infant–mother attachment: Factors related to its development and changes over time. *Child Development, 55,* 753–771.

Ehrhardt, A. A., & Baker, S. W. (1974). Fetal androgens, human central nervous system differentiation, and behavioral sex differences. In R. C. Friedman, R. M. Richart, & R. L. Vande Wiele (Eds.), *Sex differences in behavior* (pp. 33–51). New York: Wiley.

Ehrhardt, A. A., & Meyer-Bahlburg, H. F. L. (1981). Effects of prenatal sex hormones on gender-related behavior. *Science, 211,* 1312–1318.

Eifermann, R. (1971). Social play in childhood. In R. Herron & B. Sutton-Smith (Eds.), *Child's play.* New York: Wiley.

Eisenberg, N. (1983). Sex-typed toy choices: What do they signify? In M. B. Liss (Ed.), *Social and cognitive skills: Sex roles and children's play* (pp. 45–70). New York: Academic Press.

Eisenberg, N., Boothby, R., & Matson, T. (1979). Correlates of preschool girls' feminine and masculine toy preferences. *Developmental Psychology, 15,* 354–355.

Eisenberg, N., Murray, E., & Hite, T. (1982). Children's reasoning regarding sex-typed toy choices. *Child Development, 53,* 81–86.

Eisenberg, N., Tryon, K., & Cameron, E. (1984). The relation of preschoolers' peer interaction to their sex-typed toy choices. *Child Development, 55,* 45–70.

Eisenberg, N., Wolchik, S. A., Hernandez, R., & Pasternack, J. F. (1985). Parental socialization

of young children's play. *Child Development, 56,* 1506–1513.

Elder, J. L., & Pederson, D. R. (1978). Preschool children's use of objects in symbolic play. *Child Development, 49,* 500–504.

Elkind, D. (1981). *The hurried child: Growing up too fast too soon.* Reading, MA: Addison-Wesley.

Elkind, D. (1987). *Miseducation: Preschoolers at risk.* New York: Knopf.

Ellis, M. J. (1973). *Why people play.* Englewood Cliffs, NJ: Prentice-Hall.

Erikson, E. (1963). *Childhood and society* (2nd ed.). New York: Norton

Escalona, S. (1968). *The roots of individuality.* Chicago: Aldine.

Esposito, B. G., & Koorland, M. A. (1989). Play behavior of hearing impaired children: Integrated and segregated settings. *Exceptional Children, 55,* 412–419.

Etaugh, C. (1983). Introduction: The influence of environmental factors on sex differences in children's play. In M. B. Liss (Ed.), *Social and cognitive skills: Sex roles and children's play.* New York: Academic Press.

Fagen, R. M. (1984). Play and behavioural flexibility. In P. K. Smith (Ed.), *Play in animals and humans.* (pp. 159–174) Oxford: Basil Blackwell.

Fagen, R. M., & George, T. K. (1977). Play behavior and exercise in young ponies. *Behavioral Ecology and Sociobiology, 2,* 267–269.

Fagot, B. I. (1978). The influences of sex of child on parental reactions to toddler children. *Child Development, 49,* 459–465.

Fagot, B. I. (1984). The child's expectations of differences in adult male and female interactions. *Sex Roles, 11,* 593–600.

Fagot, B. I., Hagan, R., Leinsbach, M. D., & Kronsberg, S. (1985). Differential reactions to assertive and communicative acts of toddler boys and girls. *Child Development, 56,* 1499–1505.

Fein, G. G. (1975). A transformational analysis of pretending. *Developmental Psychology, 11,* 291–296.

Fein, G. G. (1981). Pretend play: An integrative review. *Child Development, 52,* 195–1118.

Fein, G. G., & Apfel, N. (1979). Some preliminary observations on knowing and pretending. In M. Smith & M. B. Franklin (Eds.), *Symbolic functioning in childhood.* Hillsdale, NJ: Erlbaum.

Fein, G. G., Campbell, P. F., & Schwartz, S. S. (1987). Microcomputers in the preschool: Effects on social participation and cognitive play. *Journal of Applied Developmental Psychology, 8,* 197–208.

Fein, G. G., Johnson, D., Kosson, N., Stork, L., & Wasserman, L. (1975). Stereotypes and preferences in the toy choices of 20-month-old boys and girls. *Developmental Psychology, 11,* 527–528.

Fein, G. G., & Stork, L. (1981). Socio-dramatic play: Social class effects in an integrated classroom. *Journal of Applied Developmental Psychology, 2,* 267–279.

Feitelson, D. (1979). *Imaginative play and the educational process.* Paper presented at the International Year of the Child Conference. Yale University, New Haven, CT, June 21–28.

Feldstein, J. H., & Feldstein, S. (1986). Sex differences on televised toy commercials. *Sex Roles 8,* 581–587.

Fenson, L. (1986). The developmental progression of play. In A. W. Gottfried & C. C. Brown (Eds.), *Play interactions: The contribution of play materials and parental involvement to children's development* (pp. 53–66). Lexington, MA: Heath.

Fenson, L., Kagan, J., Kearsley, R. B., & Zelazo, P. R. (1976). The developmental progression of manipulative play in the first two years. *Child Development, 47,* 232–236.

Fenson, L., & Ramsay, D. S. (1980). Decentration and integration of play in the second year of life. *Child Development, 51,* 171–178.

Feshbach, N. D. (1979). Empathy training: A field study of affective education. In S. Feshbach & A. Fraazeh (Eds.), *Aggression and behavior change: Biological and social processes.* New York: Praeger.

Fields, W. (1979). *Imaginative play of four-year-old children as a function of toy realism.* Unpublished master's thesis, Merrill-Palmer Institute.

Fink, R. S. (1976). Role of dramatic play in cognitive development. *Psychological Reports, 39,* 895–906.

Flavell, J. H. (1985). *Cognitive development* (2nd ed.). Englewood Cliffs, NJ: Prentice-Hall.

Fogel, A. (1979). Peer vs. mother-directed behavior in 1- to 3-month-old infants. *Infant Behavior and Development, 2,* 215–216.

Fortes, M. (1970). Social and psychological aspects of education in Taleland. In J. Middleton (Ed.), *From child to adult.* New York: Natural History Press.

Fraiberg, S. (1978). *Insights from the blind.* London: Souvenir Press.

French, D. C. (1988). Heterogeneity of peer-rejected boys: Aggressive and non-aggressive subtypes. *Child Development, 59,* 976–985.

French, V. (1977). History of the child's influence: Ancient Mediterranean civilizations. In R. Q. Bell & L. V. Harper (Eds.), *Child effects on adults.* Hillsdale, NJ: Erlbaum.

Freud, A. (1968). *The psychoanalytical treatment of children.* New York: International Universities Press.

Freud, A. (1974). *The ego and the mechanisms of defense.* New York: International Universities Press.

Frith, U. (1984). A new perspective in research on autism. In Association pour la Recherche sur l'Autisme et les Psychoses Infantiles (ARAPI). (Ed.), *Contributions à la recherche scientifique sur l'autisme: Aspects cognitifs.* Paris: Author.

Froming, W. J., Allen, L., & Jensen, R. (1985). Altruism, role-taking, and self-awareness: The acquisition of norms governing altruistic behavior. *Child Development, 56,* 1223–1228.

Frost, J. L., & Klein, B. L. (1979). *Children's play and playgrounds.* Boston: Allyn and Bacon.

Gardner, R. (1972, March). "Once upon a time there was a doorknob . . ." *Psychology Today,* pp. 67–71.

Gardner, R. (1986). *Therapeutic communication with children: The mutual storytelling technique.* New York: Science House.

Garvey, C. (1977). *Play.* Cambridge, MA: Harvard University Press.

Garvey, C. (1983). Some properties of social play. In W. Damon (Ed.), *Social and personality development: Essays on the growth of the child.* New York: Norton.

Garvey, C. (1984). *Children's talk.* Cambridge, MA: Harvard University Press.

Garvey, C., & Berndt, R. (1977). *Organization of pretend play.* Paper presented at the meeting of the American Psychological Association, Chicago.

Geismar-Ryan, L. (1986). Infant social activity: The discovery of peer play. *Childhood Education* (October), 24–29.

Giddings, M., & Halverson, C. F. (1981). Young children's use of toys in home environments. *Family Relations, 30,* 69–74.

Gilligan, C. (1982). *In a different voice.* Cambridge, MA: Harvard University Press.

Glickman, C. D. (1984). Play in public school settings: A philosophical question. In T. D. Yawkey & A. D. Pellegrini (Eds.), *Child's play:*

Developmental and applied. (pp. 255–271). Hillsdale, NJ: Erlbaum.

Glomset, J. (1980). High-density lipoproteins in human health and disease. *Advances in Internal Medicine, 25,* 91.

Goldberg, S., & Lewis, M. (1969). Play behavior in the year-old-infant: Early sex differences. *Child Development, 40,* 21–32.

Golomb, C. (1979). Pretense play: A cognitive perspective. N. Smith & M. Franklin (Eds.), *Symbolic functioning in childhood.* New York: Wiley.

Golomb, C., & Cornelius, C. B. (1977). Symbolic play and its cognitive significance. *Developmental Psychology, 13,* 246–252.

Gottfried, A. W. (1986). The relationships of play materials and parental involvement to young children's cognitive development. In A. W. Gottfried & C. C. Brown (Eds.), *Play interactions: The contribution of play materials and parental involvement to children's development* (pp. 327–334). Lexington, MA: Heath.

Gottfried, A. W., & Gottfried, A. E. (1984). Home environment and cognitive development in young children of middle-socioeconomic-status. In A. W. Gottfried (Ed.), *Home environment and early cognitive development: Longitudinal research.* New York: Academic Press.

Gottman, J. M. (1977). Toward a definition of social isolation in children. *Child Development, 48,* 513–517.

Gould, J. (1986). The Lowe and Costello Symbolic Play Test in socially impaired children. *Journal of Autism and Developmental Disorders, 16,* 199–213.

Gouldner, H. (1978). *Teacher's pets, troublemakers, and nobodies.* Westport, CT: Greenwood Press.

Goy, R. W. (1975). Early hormonal influences on the development of sexual and sex-related behaviors. In R. K. Unger & F. L. Denmark (Eds.), *Woman: Dependent or independent variable* (pp. 447–472). New York: Psychological Dimensions.

Greif, E. B. (1976). Sex-role playing in preschool children. In J. S. Bruner, A. Jolly, & K. Sylva (Eds.), *Play: Its role in development and evolution* (pp. 385–393). Englewood Cliffs, NJ: Prentice-Hall.

Gresham, F. M., & Nagel, R. (1980). Social skills training with children: Responsiveness to modeling and coaching as a function of peer orientation. *Journal of Consulting and Clinical Psychology, 18,* 718–729.

Griffing, P. (1980). The relationship between socioeconomic status and sociodramatic play among black kindergarten children. *Genetic Psychology Monographs, 101,* 3–34.

Grinder, E. L., & Liben, L. S. (1989). *Quality of same- and cross-sex toy play in young children.* Paper presented at the biennial meeting of the Society for Research in Child Development, Kansas City, MO.

Groos, K. (1901). *The play of man.* New York: Appleton.

Guerney, L. F. (1984). Play therapy in counseling settings. In T. D. Yawkey & A. D. Pellegrini (Eds.), *Child's play: Developmental and applied* (pp. 291–322). Hillsdale, NJ: Erlbaum.

Guilford, J. P. (1967). *The nature of human intelligence.* New York: McGraw-Hill.

Gumauer, J. (1984). *Counseling and therapy for children.* New York: The Free Press.

Gustafson, G. E., Green, J. A., & West, M. J. (1979). The infant's changing role in mother–infant games: The growth of social skills. *Infant Behavior and Development, 2,* 301–308.

Guyot, G. W., Fairchild, L., & Hill, M. (1981). Physical fitness, sport participation, body build, and self-concept of elementary school children. *International Journal of Sport Psychology, 12,* 105–116.

Harkness, S., & Super, C. M. (1983). *The cultural structuring of children's play in a rural African community.* Paper presented at the annual meeting of the Association for the Anthropological Study of Play, Baton Rouge, LA.

Harlow, H. F., & Harlow, M. K. (1962). Social deprivation in monkeys. *Scientific American, 207,* 137–146.

Harlow, H. F., & Suomi, S. J. (1971). Social recovery by isolation-reared monkeys. *Proceedings of the National Academy of Science, 68,* 1534–1538.

Harter, S. (1983). Developmental perspectives on the self-system. In P. H. Mussen (Ed.), *Handbook of child psychology* (4th ed., Vol. 4, pp. 275–385). New York: Wiley.

Hartley, R. E. (1971). Play: The essential ingredient. *Childhood Education,* November, 80–84.

Hartley, R. E., Frank, L. K. & Goldenson, R. M. (1952). *Understanding children's play.* New York: Columbia University Press.

Hartley, R. E., & Goldenson, R. M. (1963). *The complete book of children's play* (rev. ed.). New York: Crowell.

Hartup, W. W. (1982). Peer relations. In C. B. Copp & J. B. Krakow (Eds.), *The child: Development* in a social context. Reading, MA: Addison-Wesley.

Hartup, W. W. (1983). Peer relations. In P. H. Mussen (Ed.), *Handbook of child psychology* (4th ed., Vol. 4, pp. 103–196). New York: Wiley.

Hartup, W. W. (1986). On relationships and development. In W. W. Hartup & Z. Rubin (Eds.), *Relationships and development*. Hillsdale, NJ: Erlbaum.

Hartup, W. W., Glazer, J. A., & Charlesworth, R. (1967). Peer reinforcement and sociometric status. *Child Development, 38,* 1017–1024.

Haslum, M. (1988). Length of preschool hospitalization, multiple admissions, and later educational attainment. *Child: Care, Health, and Development, 14,* 275–291.

Hawkins, J., Sheingold, K., Gearhart, M., & Berger, C. (1982). Microcomputers in schools: Impact on the social life of elementary school classrooms. *Journal of Applied Developmental Psychology, 3,* 361–373.

Hay, D. L., Pederson, J., & Nash, A. (1982). Dyadic interaction in the first year of life. In K. H. Rubin & H. S. Ross (Eds.), *Peer relationships and social skills in childhood.* New York: Springer-Verlag.

Hazen, N. L., & Black, B. (1989). Preschool peer communication skills: The role of social status and interaction context. *Child Development, 60,* 867–876.

Heaton, K. (1983). *A study of rough-and-tumble play and serious aggression in preschool children.* Unpublished bachelor's thesis, University of Sheffield, England.

Hetherington, E. M., Cox, M., & Cox, R. (1979). Play and social interaction in children following divorce. *Journal of Social Issues, 35,* 26–49.

Higginbotham, D. J., & Baker, B. M. (1981). Social participation and cognitive play differences in hearing-impaired and normally hearing preschoolers. *Volta Review, 83,* 135–149.

Hill, P., & McCune-Nicolich, L. M. (1981). Pretend play and patterns of cognition in Down's syndrome children. *Child Development, 52,* 611–617.

Hodapp, R. M., Goldfield, E. C., & Boyatzis, C. J. (1984). The use and effectiveness of maternal scaffolding in mother-infant games. *Child Development, 55,* 772–781.

Hoffman, L. W. (1979). Maternal employment. *American Psychologist, 34,* 859–865.

Horne, E. M., & Philleo, C. F. (1942). A comparative study of the spontaneous play activities of normal and mentally defective children. *Journal of Genetic Psychology, 61,* 32–36.

Howes, C. (1988). Peer interaction of young children. *Monographs of the Society for Research in Child Development, 53* (Serial No. 17).

Howes, C., & Olenick, M. (1986). Family and child care influences on toddlers' compliance. *Child Development, 57,* 202–216.

Howes, C., Unger, O., & Seidner, L. B. (1989). Social pretend play in toddlers: Parallels with social play and with solitary pretend. *Child Development, 60,* 77–84.

Hoyenga, K .B., & Hoyenga, K. T. (1979). *The question of sex differences.* Boston: Little, Brown.

Hudson, L. (1966). *Contrary imaginations.* London: Methuen.

Hughes, F. P., Noppe, L. D., & Noppe, I. C. (1988). *Child development.* St. Paul, MN: West.

Hughes, M. (1978). Sequential analysis of exploration and play. *International Journal of Behavioral Development, 1,* 83–97.

Hughes, M., & Hutt, C. (1979). Heartrate correlates of childhood activities: Play, exploration, problem-solving, and day-dreaming. *Biological Psychology, 8,* 253–263.

Hull, C. L. (1943). *Principles of behavior.* New York: Appleton-Century-Crofts.

Hulme, I., & Lunzer, E. A. (1966). Play, language and reasoning in subnormal children. *Journal of Child Psychology and Psychiatry, 7,* 107–123.

Humphreys, A. P. (1983). *The developmental significance of rough-and-tumble play in children.* Final report to Foundation for Child Development, New York.

Humphreys, A. P., & Smith, P. K. (1984). Rough-and-tumble in preschool and playground. In P.K. Smith (Ed.), *Play in animals and humans* (pp. 241–270). London: Basil Blackwell.

Hunter, F. T., McCarthy, M. E., MacTurk, R. H., & Vietze, P. M. (1987). Infants' social-constructive interactions with mothers and fathers. *Developmental Psychology, 23,* 249–254.

Huston, A. C. (1983). Sex typing. In P. H. Mussen (Ed.), *Handbook of child psychology* (4th ed., Vol. 4, pp. 387–467). New York: Wiley.

Hutt, C. (1979). Exploration and play. In B. Sutton-Smith (Ed.), *Play and learning.* New York: Gardner Press.

Hutt, C., & Bhavnani, R. (1976). Predictions from play. In J. S. Bruner, A. Jolly, & K. Sylva (Eds.), *Play: Its role in development and evolution* (pp. 216–221). Englewood Cliffs, NJ: Prentice-Hall.

Ianotti, R. J. (1978). Effect of role-taking experiences on role-taking, empathy, altruism, and aggression. *Developmental Psychology, 14,* 119-124.

Illick, J. E. (1974). Child-rearing in seventeenth-century England and America. In L. DeMause (Ed.), *The history of childhood.* New York: Psychohistory Press.

Inhelder, B., & Piaget, J. (1964). *The early growth of logic in the child.* New York: Norton.

Jackowitz, E. R., & Watson, M. W. (1980). The development of object transformations in early pretend play. *Developmental Psychology, 16,* 543-549.

James, R., & Myer, R. (1987). Puppets: The elementary school counselor's right or left arm. *Elementary School Guidance and Counseling, 21,* 292-299.

Jeffree, D. M., & McConkey, R. (1976). An observation scheme for recording children's imaginative doll play. *Journal of Child Psychology and Psychiatry, 17,* 189-197.

Joffe, L. S., & Vaughn, B. E. (1982). Infant-mother attachment: Theory, assessment, and implications for development. In B. B. Wolman (Ed.), *Handbook of developmental psychology* (pp. 190-207). Englewood Cliffs, NJ: Prentice-Hall.

Johnson, D. L., Breckenridge, J. N., & McGowan, R. J. (1984). Home environment and early cognitive development in Mexican-American children. In A. W. Gottfried (Ed.), *Home environment and early cognitive development: Longitudinal research.* New York: Academic Press.

Johnson, J. E. (1976). Relations of divergent thinking and intelligence test scores with social and non-social make-believe play of preschool children. *Child Development, 47,* 1200- 1203.

Johnson, J. E., & Ershler, J. (1981). Developmental trends in preschool play as a function of classroom program and child gender. *Child Development, 52,* 995-1004.

Johnson, J. E., & Roopnarine, J. L. (1983). The preschool classroom and sex differences in children's play. In M. B. Liss (Ed.), *Social and cognitive skills: Sex roles and children's play* (pp. 193-218). New York: Academic Press.

Johnson, R. (1987). Using computer art in counseling children. *Elementary School Guidance and Counseling, 21,* 276-283.

Kagan, S., & Madsen, M. C. (1972). Experimental analyses of cooperation and competition of Anglo-American and Mexican children. *Developmental Psychology, 6,* 49-59.

Kanner, L. (1971). Follow-up study of eleven autistic children originally reported in 1943. *Journal of Autism and Childhood Schizophrenia, 1,* 217-250.

Kestenbaum, C. J. (1985). The creative process in child psychotherapy. *American Journal of Psychotherapy, 39,* 479-489.

King, N. R. (1979). Play: The kindergartner's perspective. *Elementary School Journal, 80,* 81-87.

Kinsman, C. A., & Berk, L. E. (1979). Joining the block and housekeeping areas: Changes in play and social behavior. *Young Children, 35,* 66-75.

Klein, M. (1955). The psychoanalytic play technique. *American Journal of Orthopsychiatry, 55,* 223-227.

Knight, G. P., & Kagan, S. (1977). Acculturation of prosocial and competitive behaviors among second- and third-generation Mexican-American children. *Journal of Cross-Cultural Psychology, 8,* 273-284.

Kogan, N. (1983). Stylistic variation in childhood and adolescence: Creativity, metaphor, and cognitive styles. In P. H. Mussen (Ed.), *Handbook of child psychology* (4th ed., Vol. 3, pp. 630-706). New York: Academic Press.

Kohl, F. L., & Beckman, P. J. (1984). A comparison of handicapped and non-handicapped preschoolers' interactions across classroom activities. *Journal of the Division for Early Childhood, 8,* 49-56.

Kohlberg, L. (1966). A cognitive-developmental analysis of children's sex-role concepts and attitudes. In E. Maccoby (Ed.), *The development of sex differences* (pp. 82-173). Stanford, CA: Stanford University Press.

Kuczaj, S. A. (1982). Language play and language acquisition. In R. H. Reese (Ed.), *Advances in child development and behavior.* New York: Academic Press.

Kuczaj, S. A. (1985). Language play. *Early Child Development and Care, 19,* 53-67.

Kurdek, L. A., & Krile, D. (1982). A developmental analysis of the relation between peer acceptance and both interpersonal understanding and perceived social self-competence. *Child Development, 53,* 1485-1491.

La Freniere, P., Strayer, F. F., & Gauthier, R. (1984). The emergence of same-sex affiliative preferences among preschool peers: A developmental/ethological perspective. *Child Development, 55,* 1958-1965.

Labov, W. (1972). *Language in the inner city: Studies in the black English vernacular.* Philadelphia: University of Pennsylvania Press.

Ladd, G. W. (1981). Effectiveness of a social learning method for enhancing children's social interaction and peer acceptance. *Child Development, 52,* 171–178.

Ladd, G. W., & Price, J. M. (1987). Predicting children's social and school adjustment following the transition from preschool to kindergarten. *Child Development, 58,* 171–178.

Ladd, G. W., Price, J. M., & Hart, C. H. (1988). Predicting preschoolers' peer status from their playground behaviors. *Child Development, 59,* 986–992.

Lamb, M. (1977). The development of parental preferences in the first years of life. *Sex Roles, 3,* 495–497.

Lamb, M. (1978). Interactions between eighteen-month-olds and their preschool-age siblings. *Child Development, 49,* 51–59.

Lamb, M. (1981). The development of father-infant relationships. In M. Lamb (Ed.), *The role of the father in child development* (2nd ed., pp. 1–70). New York: Wiley.

Lamb, M. E., Frodi, A. M., Hwang, C. P., Frodi, M., & Steinberg, J. (1982). Effects of gender and caretaking role on parent-infant interaction. In M. E. Lamb (Ed.), *Nontraditional families.* Hillsdale, NJ: Erlbaum.

Landreth, G. (1987). Play therapy: Facilitative use of child's play in elementary school counseling. *Elementary School Guidance and Counseling, 21,* 253–261.

Langer, J. L. (1969). *Theories of development.* New York: Holt, Rinehart, & Winston.

Langlois, J. H., & Downs, A. C. (1980). Mothers, fathers, and peers as socialization agents of sex-typed play behaviors in young children. *Child Development, 51,* 1217–1247.

Lederberg, A. R., Chapin, S. L., Rosenblatt, V., & Vandell, V. L. (1986). Ethnic, gender, and age preferences among deaf and hearing peers. *Child Development, 57,* 375–386.

Leslie, A. M. (1984). Pretend play and representation in infancy: A cognitive approach. In Association pour la Recherche sur l'Autisme et les Psychoses Infantiles (ARAPI) (Ed.), *Contributions à la recherche scientifique sur l'autisme: Aspects cognitifs.* Paris: Author.

Leslie, A. M., & Frith, U. (1988). Autistic children's understanding of seeing, knowing, and believing. *British Journal of Developmental Psychology, 6,* 315–324.

Lever, J. (1976). Sex differences in the games children play. *Social Problems, 23,* 478–487.

LeVine, R., & LeVine, B. (1963). Nyansongo: A Gusii community in Kenya. In B. Whiting (Ed.), *Six cultures: Studies of childrearing.* New York: Wiley.

Levy, D. M. (1939). Release therapy. *American Journal of Orthopsychiatry, 9,* 713–736.

Lewis, V., & Boucher, L. (1988). Spontaneous, instructed, and elicited play in relatively able autistic children. *British Journal of Developmental Psychology, 6,* 325–339.

Li, A. K. F. (1985). Toward more elaborate pretend play. *Mental Retardation, 23,* 131–136.

Lieberman, A. F. (1977). Preschoolers' competence with a peer: Relations with attachment and peer experience. *Child Development, 48,* 1277–1287.

Lloyd, B., & Smith, C. (1985). The social representation of gender and young children's play. *British Journal of Developmental Psychology, 3,* 65–73.

Locke, J. (1964). *Some thoughts concerning education.* (Abridged and edited by F. W. Garforth). Woodbury, NY: Barron's Educational Series.

Lockheed, M. E. (1986). Reshaping the social order: The case of gender segregation. *Sex Roles, 14,* 617–628.

Logan, R. D. (1977). Sociocultural change and the emergence of children as burdens. *Child and Family, 16,* 295–304.

Lombardino, L., & Sproul, C. (1984). Patterns of correspondence and non-correspondence between play and language in developmentally-delayed preschoolers. *Education and Training of the Mentally Retarded, 19,* 5–14.

Lombardino, L. L., Stein, J. E., Kricos, P. B., & Wolf, M. A. (1986). Play diversity and structural relationships in the play and language of language-impaired and language-normal preschoolers: Preliminary data. *Journal of Communication Disorders, 19,* 475–489.

Lord, C. (1984). The development of peer relations in children with autism. In F. J. Morrison, C. Lord, & D. P. Keating (Eds.), *Advances in applied developmental psychology* (pp. 165–229). New York: Academic Press.

Lovell, K., Hoyle, H. W., & Siddall, N. Q. (1968). A study of some aspects of the play and language of young children with delayed speech. *Journal of Child Psychology and Psychiatry, 9,* 41–50.

Lowe, M., & Costello, A. J. (1976). *Manual for the Symbolic Play Test* (experimental ed.). Windsor: NFER.

Lynch-Fraser, D. (1982). *Dance play: Creative movement for very young children.* New York: Walker.

Maccoby, E. E., & Jacklin, C. N. (1974). *The psychology of sex differences.* Stanford, CA: Stanford University Press.

MacDonald, K., & Parke, R. D. (1986). Parent-child physical play: The effects of sex and age on children and parents. *Sex Roles, 15,* 367–378.

Madsen, M. C. (1967). Cooperative and competitive motivation of children in three Mexican sub-cultures. *Psychological Reports, 20,* 1307–1320.

Madsen, M. C. (1971). Developmental and cross-cultural differences in the cooperative and competitive behaviors of young children. *Journal of Cross-Cultural Psychology, 2,* 365–371.

Madsen, M. C., & Shapira, A. (1970). Cooperative and competitive behavior of urban Afro-American, Anglo-American, Mexican-American, and Mexican village children. *Developmental Psychology, 3,* 16–20.

Magill, R. A., & Ash, M. J. (1979). Academic, psycho-social, and motor characteristics of participants and non-participants in children's sports. *Research Quarterly, 50,* 240.

Main, M. (1981). Avoidance in the service of attachment: A working paper. In K. Immelmann, G. Barlow, L. Petrinoviich, & M. Main (Eds.), *Behavioral development: The Bielefeld Interdisciplinary Project* (pp. 651–693). New York: Cambridge University Press.

Mann, B. L. (1984). Effects of realistic and unrealistic props on symbolic play. In T. D. Yawkey & A. D. Pellegrini (Eds.), *Child's play: Developmental and applied* (pp. 359–376). Hillsdale, NJ: Erlbaum.

Mann, L. F. (1984). Play behaviors of deaf and hearing children. In D. S. Martin (Ed.), *International Symposium on Cognition, Education, and Deafness.* Washington, DC: Gallaudet College Press.

Marcus, I. (1966). Costume play therapy. *American Academy of Child Psychiatry Journal, 5,* 441–451.

Markus, H. J., & Nurius, P. S. (1984). Self-understanding and self-regulation in middle childhood. In W. A. Collins (Ed.), *Development during middle childhood: The years from six to twelve* (pp. 147–183). Washington, DC: National Academy Press.

Marvick, E. W. (1974). Nature versus nurture: Patterns and trends in seventeenth-century French childrearing. In L. DeMause (Ed.), *The history of childhood.* New York: Psychohistory Press.

Matthews, W. S. (1977). Modes of transformation in the initiation of fantasy play. *Developmental Psychology, 13,* 212–216.

Mazza, N. (1986). Poetry and popular music in social work education: The liberal arts perspective. *The Arts in Psychotherapy, 13,* 293–299.

McConkey, R. (1985). Changing beliefs about play and handicapped children. *Early Child Development and Care, 19,* 79–94.

McCune, L. (1986). Play-language relationships: Implications for a theory of symbolic development. In A. W. Gottfried & C. C. Brown (Eds.), *Play interactions: The contribution of play materials and parental involvement to children's development* (pp. 67–80). Lexington, MA: Heath.

McCune-Nicolich, L., & Fenson, L. (1984). Methodological issues in studying early pretend play. In T. D. Yawkey & A. D. Pellegrini (Eds.), *Child's play: Developmental and applied* (pp. 81–104). Hillsdale, NJ: Erlbaum.

McCutcheon, B., & Calhoun, K. (1976). Social and emotional adjustment of infants and toddlers to a day care setting. *American Journal of Orthopsychiatry, 46,* 104–108.

McGrew, W. C. (1972). *An ethological study of children's behavior.* London: Academic Press.

McGuire, K. D., & Weisz, J. R. (1982). Social cognition and behavior correlates of preadolescent chumship. *Child Development, 53,* 1478–1484.

McLoyd, V. (1980). Verbally expressed modes of transformation in the fantasy play of black preschool children. *Child Development, 51,* 1133–1139.

McLoyd, V. C. (1983). The effects of the structure of play objects on the pretend play of low-income preschool children. *Child Development, 54,* 626–635.

McLoyd, V. C. (1986). Social class and pretend play. In A. W. Gottfried & C. C. Brown (Eds.), *Play interactions: The contribution of play materials and parental involvement to children's development* (pp. 175–196). Lexington, MA: Heath.

Mead, M. (1937). *Cooperation and competition among primitive people.* New York: McGraw-Hill.

Mead, M. (1975). *Growing up in New Guinea.* New York: Morrow.

Meador, B. D., & Rogers, C. R. (1984). Person-centered therapy. R. D. Corsini & D. Wedding (Eds.), *Current psychotherapies* (3rd ed.) Itasca, IL: Peacock.

Meaney, M. J. (1988). The sexual differentiation of social play. *Trends in Neuroscience, 7,* 54–58.

Menyuk, P. (1982). Language development. In C. B. Kopp & J. B. Krakow (Eds.), *The child: Devel-*

opment in a social context. Reading, MA: Addison-Wesley.

Minuchin, P. P. (1977). *The middle years of childhood.* Monterey, CA: Brooks/Cole.

Money, J., & Ehrhardt, A. A. (1972). *Man and woman: Boy and girl.* Baltimore: Johns Hopkins University Press.

Montague, S. P., & Morais, R. (1976). Football games and rock concerts: The natural enactment. In W. Arens & S. P. Montague (Eds.), *The American dimension: Cultural myths and social realities.* Port Washington, NY: Alfred.

Moustakas, C. (1959). *Psychotherapy with children: The living relationship.* New York: Ballantine Books.

Muller-Schwarze, D. (1984). Analysis of play behavior: What do we measure and when? In P. K. Smith (Ed.). *Play in animals and humans.* Oxford: Basil Blackwell.

Mundy, P., Sigman, M., Ungerer, J., & Sherman, T. (1987). Non-verbal communication and play correlates of language development in autistic children. *Journal of Autism and Developmental Disorders, 17,* 349–364.

Nickerson, E. (1973). The application of play therapy to a school setting. *Psychology in the Schools, 10,* 362–365.

Nicolich, L. (1977). Beyond sensorimotor intelligence: Assessment of symbolic maturity through analysis of pretend play. *Merrill-Palmer Quarterly, 23,* 89–99.

Novak, M. A., & Harlow, H. F. (1975). Social recovery of monkeys isolated for the first year of life: 1. Rehabilitation and therapy. *Developmental Psychology, 11,* 453–465.

O'Brien, M, & Huston, A. C. (1985). Development of sex-typed play behavior in toddlers. *Developmental Psychology, 21,* 866–871.

Oden, S, & Asher, S. R. (1977). Coaching children in social skills for friendship making. *Child Development, 48,* 495–506.

Ogilvie, B. C., & Tutko, T. A. (1971). If you want to built character, try something else. *Psychology Today, 5,* 60–63.

Opie, I., & Opie, P. (1957). Nursery rhymes. In W. Targ (Ed.), *Bibliophile in the nursery.* Cleveland: World.

Parke, R. D., & Tinsley, B. J. (1987). Family interaction in infancy. In J. D. Osofsky (Ed.), *Handbook of infant development* (2nd ed.). New York: Wiley.

Parker, S. T. (1984). Playing for keeps: An evolutionary perspective on human games. In P. K. Smith (Ed.), *Play in animals and humans* (pp. 271–294). Oxford: Basil Blackwell.

Parten, M. (1933). Social play among preschool children. *Journal of Abnormal and Social Psychology, 28,* 136–147.

Patrick, G. T. W. (1916). *The psychology of relaxation.* Boston: Houghton Mifflin.

Peck, J., & Goldman, R. (1978, March). *The behaviors of kindergarten children under selected conditions of the physical and social environment.* Paper presented at the meeting of the American Educational Research Association, Toronto, Canada.

Pedersen, F. A. (Ed.), (1980). *The father-infant relationship: Observational studies in the family setting.* New York: Praeger.

Pederson, D. R., Rook-Green, A., & Elder, J. L. (1981). The role of action in the development of pretend play in young children. *Developmental Psychology, 17,* 756–759.

Pellegrini, A. D. (1985). Social-cognitive aspects of children's play: The effects of age, gender, and activity centers. *Journal of Applied Developmental Psychology, 6,* 129–140.

Pellegrini, A. D., & Galda, L. (1982). The effects of thematic fantasy play training on the development of children's story comprehension. *Child Development, 52,* 1202–1210.

Pepler, D. J. (1979). *Effects of convergent and divergent play experience on preschoolers' problem-solving behaviors.* Unpublished doctoral dissertation, University of Waterloo, Ontario.

Pepler, D. J., & Ross, H. S. (1981). The effects of play on convergent and divergent problem-solving. *Child Development, 52,* 1202–1210.

Perner, J., Frith, U., Leslie, A. M., & Leekam, S. R. (1989). Exploration of the autistic child's theory of mind: Knowledge, belief, and communication. *Child Development, 60,* 689–700.

Perry, D. G., White, A. J., & Perry, L. C. (1984). Does early sex-typing result from children's attempts to match their behavior to sex-role stereotypes? *Child Development, 55,* 2114–2121.

Phillips, D., McCartney, K., & Scarr, S. (1987). Child-care quality and children's social development. *Developmental Psychology, 23,* 537–543.

Piaget, J. (1962). *Play, dreams, and imitation in childhood.* New York: Norton.

Piaget, J. (1963). *The origins of intelligence in children.* New York: Norton.

Piaget, J. (1965). *The moral judgment of the child.* New York: Free Press.

Piaget, J. (1983). Piaget's theory. In P. H. Mussen

(ed.), *Handbook of child psychology.* New York: Wiley.

Piaget, J., & Inhelder, B. (1956). *The child's conception of space.* London: Routledge & Kegan Paul.

Piaget, J., & Inhelder, B. (1969). *The psychology of the child.* New York: Basic Books.

Piazza, C. L., & Riggs, S. (1984). Writing with a computer: An invitation to play. *Early Child Development and Care, 17,* 63–76.

Pinchbeck, I., & Hewitt, M. (1969). *Children in English society.* London: Routledge & Kegan Paul.

Plato (1961). The laws. In E. Hamilton & H. Cairns (Eds.), *The collected dialogues.* New York: Pantheon Press.

Plattner, S., & Minturn, L. (1975). A comparative and longitudinal study of the behavior of communally-raised children. *Ethos, 3,* 469–480.

Power, T. G. (1985). Mother– and father–infant play: A developmental analysis. *Child Development, 56,* 1514–1524.

Power, T. G., & Parke, R. D. (1980). Play as a context for early learning: Lab and home analyses. In I. E. Sigel & L. J. Laosa (Eds.), *The family as a learning environment* (pp. 147–178). New York: Plenum.

Power, T. G., & Parke, R. D. (1983). Patterns of mother and father play with their 8-month-old infants: A multiple analyses approach. *Infant Behavior and Development, 6,* 453–459.

Power, T. G., & Parke, R. D. (1986). Patterns of early socialization: An analysis of mother– and father–infant interaction in the home. *International Journal of Behavioral Development, 9,* 331–341.

Premack, D., & Woodruff, G. (1978). Does the chimpanzee have a "theory of mind"? *Behavioral and Brain Sciences, 4,* 515–526.

Pulaski, M. A. (1973). Toys and imaginative play. In J. L. Singer (Ed.), *The child's world of make-believe.* New York: Academic Press.

Putallaz, M., & Gottman, J. M. (1981). Social skills and group acceptance. In S. R. Asher & J. M. Gottman (Eds.), *The development of children's friendships* (pp. 116–149). New York: Cambridge University Press.

Quay, L. C., & Jarrett, O. S. (1986). Social reciprocity in handicapped and non-handicapped children in a dyadic play situation. *Journal of Applied Developmental Psychology, 7,* 383–390.

Quinn, J., & Rubin, K. (1984). The play of handicapped children. In T. D. Yawkey & A. Pellegrini (Eds.), *Child's play: Developmental and applied* (63–80). Hillsdale, NJ: Erlbaum.

Rabinowitz, F. M., Moely, B. E., Finkel, N., & McClinton, S. (1975). The effects of toy novelty and social interaction on the exploratory behavior of preschool children. *Child Development, 46,* 286–289.

Rappaport, J., Bernstein, D. A., Hogan, M., Kane, J., Plunk, M., & Sholder, M. (1972). Fraternal and communal living: Values and behavior on the campus. *Journal of Counseling Psychology, 19,* 296–300.

Ratner, N., & Bruner, J. (1978). Games, social exchange, and the acquisition of language. *Journal of Child Language, 5,* 391–401.

Repetti, R. L. (1984). Determinants of children's sex-typing: Parental sex-role traits and television viewing. *Personality and Social Psychology Bulletin, 10,* 457–468.

Reynolds, P. C. (1976). Play, language, and human evolution. In J. Bruner, A. Jolly, & K. Sylva (Eds.), *Play: Its role in development and evolution.* New York: Basic Books.

Reynolds, P. C. (1981). *On the evolution of human behavior: The argument from animals to man.* Berkeley, CA: University of California Press.

Rheingold, H. L., & Cook, K. V. (1975). The contents of boys' and girls' rooms as an index of parents' behavior. *Child Development, 46,* 459–463.

Robinson, C. C., & Morris, J. J. (1986). The gender-stereotyped nature of Christmas toys by 36-, 48-, and 60-month-old children: A comparison between non-requested vs. requested toys. *Sex Roles, 15,* 21–32.

Rogers, D. L. (1985). Relationships between block play and the social development of children. *Early Child Development and Care, 20,* 245–261.

Rogers-Warren, A., Warren, S. F., & Baer, D. M. (1977). A component analysis-modeling, self-reporting, and reinforcement of self-reporting in the development of sharing. *Behavior Modification, 1,* 307–322.

Romance, T. (1984). *A program to promote moral development through elementary school physical education.* Unpublished doctoral dissertation, University of Oregon.

Roopnarine, J. L. (1986). Mothers' and fathers' behaviors toward the toy play of their infant sons and daughters. *Sex Roles, 14,* 59–68.

Roopnarine, J. L., & Johnson, J. E. (1984). Socialization in a mixed-age experimental program. *Developmental Psychology, 20,* 828–832.

Rosen, C. E. (1974). The effects of sociodramatic play on problem-solving behavior among culturally-disadvantaged preschool children. *Child Development, 45,* 920–927.

Rosenblatt, D. (1977). Developmental trends in infant play. In B. Tizard & D. Harvey (Eds.), *The biology of play.* Philadelphia: Lippincott.

Ross, H. S., & Kay, D. A. (1980). The origins of social games. In K. H. Rubin (Ed.), *Children's play* (pp. 17–31). San Francisco: Jossey-Bass.

Ross, H. S., & Lollis, S. P. (1987). Communication within infant social games. *Developmental Psychology, 23,* 241–248.

Rosseau, J. J. (1911). *Emile, or On Education.* (Translated by B. Foxley). London: Dent. (Original work published 1762).

Rubenstein, J. L. (1976). Concordance of visual and manipulative responsiveness to novel and familiar stimuli: A function of test procedures or of prior experience? *Child Development, 47,* 1197–1199.

Rubenstein, J. L., & Howes, C. (1976). The effect of peers on toddler interaction with mother and toys. *Child Development, 47,* 597–605.

Rubenstein, J. L., & Howes, C. (1979). Caregiving and infant behavior in day care and in homes. *Developmental Psychology, 15,* 1–24.

Rubin, K. H. (1980). Fantasy play: Its role in the development of social skills and social cognition. In K. H. Rubin (Ed.), *Children's play.* San Francisco: Jossey-Bass.

Rubin, K. H. (1982). Non-social play in preschoolers: Necessary evil? *Child Development, 53,* 651–657.

Rubin, K. H. (1986). Play, peer interaction, and social development. In A. W. Gottfried & C. C. Brown (Eds.), *Play interactions: The contribution of play materials and parental involvement to children's development* (pp. 163–174). Lexington, MA: Heath.

Rubin, K. H., & Clark, L. (1983). Preschool teachers' ratings of behavioral problems. *Journal of Abnormal Child Psychology, 11,* 273–285.

Rubin, K. H., Fein, G. C., & Vandenberg, B. (1983). Play. In P. H. Mussen (Ed.), *Handbook of child psychology* (4th ed., 693–774). New York: Wiley.

Rubin, K. H., & Maioni, T. (1975). Play preference and its relationship to egocentrism, popularity, and classification skills in preschoolers. *Merrill-Palmer Quarterly, 21,* 171–179.

Rubin, K. H., Maioni, T. L., & Hornung, M. (1976). Free play behaviors in middle- and lower-class preschoolers: Parten and Piaget revisited. *Child Development, 47,* 414–419.

Rubin, K. H., & Pepler, D. J. (1982). Children's play: Piaget's views reconsidered. *Contemporary Educational Psychology, 7,* 289–299.

Ruff, H. A. (1984). Infants' manipulative exploration of objects: Effects of age and object characteristics. *Developmental Psychology, 20,* 9–20.

Rutter, M. (1975). *Helping troubled children.* New York: Plenum.

Rutter, M. (1978) Diagnosis and definition. In M. Rutter & E. Schopler (Eds.) *Autism: A reappraisal of concepts of treatment.* New York: Plenum.

Rutter, M. (1983). Cognitive deficits in the pathogenesis of autism. *Journal of Child Psychology and Psychiatry, 24,* 513–531.

Ryan, J., & Smollar, J. (1978). *A developmental analysis of obligation in parent–child and friend relations.* Unpublished manuscript, Catholic University of America, Washington, DC

Sachs, J., Goldman, J., & Chaille, E. (1982). *Planning in pretend play: Using language to coordinate narrative development.* Paper presented at the annual conference of the American Educational Research Association, New York.

Sagi, A., Lamb, M. E., Shoham, R., Dvir, R., & Lewkowicz, K. S. (1985). Parent-infant interaction in families on Israeli kibbutzim. *International Journal of Behavioral Development, 8,* 273–284.

Salomon, G. (1977). *The language of media and the cultivation of mental skills.* Report of the Spencer Foundation, Chicago.

Saltz, E., Dixon, D., & Johnson, J. (1977). Training disadvantaged preschoolers on various fantasy activities: Effects on cognitive functioning and impulse control. *Child Development, 48,* 367–380.

Saltz, E., & Johnson, J. (1974). Training for thematic-fantasy play in culturally disadvantaged children: Preliminary results. *Journal of Educational Psychology, 66,* 623–630.

Schaefer, C. E. (1985). Play therapy. *Early Child Development and Care, 19,* 95–108.

Schaffer, H. R. & Crook, C. K. (1979). Maternal control techniques in a directed play situation. *Child Development, 50,* 989–996.

Schiller, F. (1954). *On the aesthetic education of man.* New Haven, CT: Yale University Press.

Schindler, P. J., Moely, B. E., & Frank, A. L. (1987). Time in day care and social participation of young children. *Developmental Psychology, 23,* 255–261.

Schwartz, L. A., & Markham, W. T. (1985). Sex

stereotyping in children's toy advertisements. *Sex Roles, 12,* 157–170.

Schwartzman, H. B. (1984). Imaginative play: Deficit or difference? In T. D. Yawkey & A. D. Pellegrini (Eds.), *Child's play: Developmental and applied* (pp. 49–62). Hillsdale, NJ: Erlbaum.

Schwartzman, H. B. (1986). A cross-cultural perspective on child-structured play activities and materials. In A. W. Gottfried & C. C. Brown (Eds.), *Play interactions: The contribution of play materials and parental involvement to children's development* (pp. 13–30). Lexington, MA: Heath.

Selman, R. L. (1980). *The growth of interpersonal understanding.* New York: Academic Press.

Selman, R. L., & Byrne, D. F. (1974). A structural-developmental analysis of levels of role-taking in middle childhood. *Child Development, 45,* 803–806.

Selman, R. L., & Jacquette, D. (1978). Stability and oscillation in interpersonal awareness: A clinical-developmental analysis. In C. B. Keasey (Ed.), *The XXV Nebraska Symposium on Motivation.* Lincoln: University of Nebraska Press.

Serbin, L. A., & Conner, J. A. (1979). Sex-typing, children's play preferences, and patterns of cognitive performance. *Journal of Genetic Psychology, 134,* 315–316.

Serbin, L. A., Conner, J. A., Burchardt, C. J., & Citron, C. C. (1979). Effects of peer presence on sex-typing of children's play behavior. *Journal of Experimental Child Psychology, 27,* 303–309.

Serbin, L. A., Tonick, I. J., & Sternglanz, S. H. (1977). Shaping cooperative cross-sex play. *Child Development, 48,* 924–929.

Seymour, S. (1981). Cooperation and competition: Some issues and problems in cross-cultural analysis. In R. H. Munroe, R. L. Munroe, & B. B. Whiting (Eds.), *Handbook of cross-cultural development* (pp. 717–738). New York: Garland.

Shantz, C. U. (1983). Social cognition. In P. H. Mussen (Ed.), *Handbook of child psychology* (4th ed., Vol. 3, 495–555). New York: Wiley.

Shapira, A. (1976). Developmental differences in competitive behavior in kibbutz and city children in Israel. *Journal of Social Psychology, 98,* 19–26.

Shapira, A., & Madsen, M. C. (1974). Between and within group cooperation and competition among kibbutz and non-kibbutz children. *Developmental Psychology, 10,* 1–12.

Shatz, M. (1983). Communication. In J. Flavell & E. Markman (Eds.), *Handbook of child psychol-*

ogy. Vol 3: Cognitive development. New York: Wiley.

Shimada, S., Sano, R., & Peng, F. C. C. (1979). A longitudinal study of symbolic play in the second year of life. *The Research Institute for the Education of Exceptional Children, Research Bulletin.* Tokyo: Gakugei University.

Shonkoff, J. P. (1984). The biological substrate and physical health in middle childhood. In W. A. Collins (Ed.), *Development during middle childhood: The years from six to twelve* (pp. 24–69). Washington, DC: National Academy Press.

Sidorowicz, L. S., & Lunney, G. S. (1980). Baby X revisited. *Sex Roles, 6,* 67–73.

Siegel, L. S (1984). Home environmental influences on cognitive development in pre-term and full-term children during the first five years. In A. W. Gottfried (Ed.), *Home environment and early cognitive development: Longitudinal research.* New York: Academic Press.

Silvern, S. B., Williamson, P. A., Taylor, J. B., Surbeck, E., & Kelly, M. F. (1982, March). *The effects of self-directed dramatization on story recall.* Paper presented at the annual meeting of the American Educational Research Association, New York.

Silvern, S. B., Williamson, P. A., & Waters, B. (1982). Play as a mediator of comprehension: An alternative to play training. *Educational Research Quarterly, 7,* 16–21.

Simon, T. (1985). Play and learning with computers. *Early Child Development and Care, 19,* 69–78.

Singer, D. G., & Singer, J. L. (1976). Family television viewing habits and the spontaneous play of preschool children. *American Journal of Orthopsychiatry, 46,* 496–502.

Singer, J. L. (Ed.) (1973). *The child's world of make-believe: Experimental studies of imaginative play.* New York: Academic Press.

Singer, J. L., & Streiner, B. F. (1966). Imaginative content in the dreams and fantasy play of blind and sighted children. *Perceptual and Motor Skills, 22,* 475–482.

Skipper, J. K., & Leonard, R. C. (1968). Children, stress, and hospitalization: A field experiment. *Journal of Health and Social Behavior, 9,* 275–287.

Slade, A. (1987). Quality of attachment and early symbolic play. *Developmental Psychology, 23,* 78–85.

Smilansky, S. (1968). *The effects of sociodramatic play on disadvantaged preschool children.* New York: Wiley.

Smiley, S. S., & Brown, A. L. (1979). Conceptual preference for thematic or taxonomic relations: A non-monotonic trend from preschool to old age. *Journal of Experimental Child Psychology, 28,* 249–257.

Smith, A. B., & Bain, H. (1978). Dependency in day care and play centre children. *New Zealand Journal of Educational Studies, 13,* 163–173.

Smith, C., & Lloyd, B. (1978). Maternal behavior and perceived sex of infant: Revisited. *Child Development, 49,* 1263–1266.

Smith, P. K. (1983). Differences or deficits? The significance of pretend and sociodramatic play. *Developmental Review, 3,* 6–10.

Smith, P. K. (1989, April). *Rough-and-tumble play and its relationship to serious fighting.* Paper presented at the biennial meeting of the Society for Research in Child Development, Kansas City, MO.

Smith, P. K., & Connolly, K. J. (1972). Patterns of play and social interaction in preschool children. In N. Blurton-Jones (Ed.), *Ethological studies of child behavior.* Cambridge: Cambridge University Press.

Smith, P. K., & Connolly, K. J. (1976). Social and aggressive behavior in preschool children as a function of crowding. *Social Science Information, 16,* 601–620.

Smith, P. K., & Connolly, K. J. (1980). *The ecology of preschool behavior.* Cambridge: Cambridge University Press.
77). Sex differences in parent and infant behavior in the home. *Child Development, 48,* 1250–1254.

Smith, P. K., Dalgleish, M., & Herzmark, G. (1981). A comparison of the effects of fantasy play tutoring and skills tutoring in nursery classes. *International Journal of Behavioral Development, 4,* 421–441.

Smith, P. K., & Dodsworth, C. (1976). Social class differences in the fantasy play of preschool children. *Journal of Genetic Psychology, 133,* 183–190.

Smith, P. K., & Dutton, S. (1979). Play and training in direct and innovative problem-solving. *Child Development, 50,* 830–836.

Smith, P. K., & Sydall, S. (1978). Play and non-play tutoring in preschool children: Is it play or tutoring which matters? *British Journal of Educational Psychology, 48,* 315–325.

Smith, T. L. (1986). Self-concepts of youth sports participants and nonparticipants in grades 3 and 6. *Perceptual and Motor Skills, 62,* 863–866.

Smollar, J., & Youniss, J. (1982). Social development through friendship. In K. H. Rubin & H. S. Ross (Eds.), *Peer relationships and social skills in childhood.* New York: Springer-Verlag.

Snow, M., Jacklin, C., & Maccoby, E. (1983). Sex-of-child differences in father–child interaction at one year of age. *Child Development, 54,* 227–232.

Somerville, J. (1982). *The rise and fall of childhood.* Beverly Hills, CA: Sage.

Spencer, H, (1973). *Principles of psychology.* New York: Appleton-Century-Crofts.

Stern, V., Bragdon, N., & Gordon, A. (1976). *Cognitive aspects of young children's symbolic play.* Unpublished paper. Cited by McLoyd (1986).

Stevenson, M. B., Leavitt, L.A., Thompson, R. H., & Roach, M. A. (1988). A social relations model analysis of parent and child play. *Developmental Psychology, 24,* 101–108.

Strein, W., & Kachman, W. (1984). Effects of computer games on young children's cooperative behavior: An exploratory study. *Journal of Research and Development in Education, 18,* 40–43.

Sugarman-Bell, S. (1978). Some organizational aspects of pre-verbal communication. In I. Markova (Ed.), *The social context of language* (pp. 49–66). Chichester, England: Wiley.

Sutton-Smith, B. (1967). The role of play in cognitive development. *Young Children, 22,* 361–370.

Sutton-Smith, B. (1979). The play of girls. In C. B. Kopp & M. Kirkpatrick (Eds.), *Becoming female: Perspectives on development.* New York: Plenum.

Sutton-Smith, B. (1980). Children's play: Some sources of play theorizing. In K. H. Rubin (Ed.), *Children's play.* San Francisco: Jossey-Bass.

Sutton-Smith, B. (1985). The child at play. *Psychology Today, 19,* 64–65.

Sutton-Smith, B., & Kelly-Byrne, D. (1984). The idealization of play. In P. K. Smith (Ed.), *Play in animals and humans.* Oxford, England: Basil Blackwell.

Sutton-Smith, B., & Roberts, J. M. (1970). The cross-cultural and psychological study of games. In G. Luschen (Ed.), *The cross-cultural analysis of games.* Champaign, IL: Stipes.

Sutton-Smith, B., & Roberts, J. M. (1981). Play, games, and sports. In H. C. Triandis & A. Heron (Eds.), *Handbook of cross-cultural psychology. 4. Delopmental psychology.* Boston: Allyn and Bacon.

Sylva, K. (1977). Play and learning. In B. Tizard & D. Harvey (Eds.), *Biology of play.* London: Heinemann.

Sylva, K., Bruner, J. S., & Genova, P. (1976). The role of play in the problem-solving of children

3–5 years old. In J. S. Bruner, A. Jolly, & K. Sylva (Eds.), *Play: Its role in development and evolution.* New York: Basic Books.

Symons, D. (1978). *Play and aggression: A study of rhesus monkeys.* New York: Columbia University Press.

Tait, P. (1973). Behavior of young blind children in a controlled play setting. *Perception and Motor Skills, 34,* 963–969.

Tan, L. E. (1985). Computers in preschool education. *Early Child Development and Care, 19,* 319–336.

Terrell, B., Schwartz, R., Prelock, P., & Messick, C. (1984). Symbolic play in normal and language-impaired children. *Journal of Speech and Hearing Research, 27,* 424–429.

Thompson, C. L., Davis, J. M., & Madden, L. (1986). Children as consultants and bibliocounseling. *Elementary School Guidance and Counseling, 21,* 89–95.

Thompson, C. L., & Rudolph, L. B. (1988). *Counseling children* (2nd ed.). Pacific Grove, CA: Brooks/Cole.

Tilton, J. R., & Ottinger, D. R. (1964). Comparisons of the toy play of and behavior of autistic, retarded, and normal children. *Psychological Reports, 15,* 967–975.

Toqueville, A. de. (1946) *Democracy in America.* (H. Reeves, Trans.). New York: Knopf. (Original work published in 1835).

Tower, R. B., Singer, D. G., Singer, J. L., & Biggs, A. (1979). Differential effects of television programming on preschoolers' cognition, imagination, and social play. *American Journal of Orthopsychiatry, 49,* 265–280.

Tracy, D. M. (1987). Toys, spatial ability, and science and mathematics achievement: Are they related? *Sex Roles, 17,* 115–138.

Travers, J., Goodson, B. D., Singer, J. D., & Connell, D. B. (1980). *Research results of the National Day Care Study.* Cambridge, MA: Abt Books.

Troll, L. E. (1972). *The salience of members of three-generation families for one another.* Paper presented at the annual meeting of the American Psychological Association, Honolulu.

Tronick, E. Z. (1982). Affectivity and sharing. In E. Z. Tronick (Ed.), *Social interchange in infancy. Affect, cognition, and communication.* Baltimore: University Park Press.

Tucker, M. J. (1974). The child as beginning and end: Fifteenth and sixteenth century English childhood. In L. DeMause (Ed.), *The history of childhood.* New York: Psychohistory Press.

Ungerer, J. A., Zelazo, P. R., Kearsley, R. B., &

O'Leary, K. (1981). Developmental changes in the representation of objects in symbolic play from 18 to 34 months of age. *Child Development, 52,* 186–195.

U.S. Bureau of the Census (1987). Who's minding the kids? *Current population report.* (Series P-70). Washington, DC: U.S. Government Printing Office.

Vandell, D. L., & Wilson, K. S. (1983). *The relationship between infants' interactions with mother, sibling, and peer.* Paper presented at the biennial meeting of the Society for Research in Child Development, Detroit.

Vandenberg, B. (1978). Play and development from an ethological perspective. *American Psychologist, 33,* 724–738.

Vinturella, L., & James, R. (1987). Sand play: A therapeutic medium with children. *Elementary School Guidance and Counseling, 21,* 229–238.

Volpe, J. (1976). *The development of children's conceptions of friendship.* Unpublished master's thesis, Catholic University of America, Washington, DC.

Vygotsky, L. S. (1976). Play and its role in the mental development of the child. In J. Bruner, A. Jolly, & K. Sylva (Eds.), *Play: Its role in development and evolution.* New York: Basic Books. (Original work published 1933, *Soviet Psychology, 5,* 6–18.

Wachs, T. D. (1979). Proximal experience and early cognitive intellectual development. *Merrill-Palmer Quarterly, 25,* 3–41.

Wachs, T. D. (1986). Models of physical environmental action: Implications for the study of play materials and parent-child interaction. In A. W. Gottfried & C. C. Brown (Eds.), *Play interactions: The contribution of play materials and parental involvement to children's development* (pp. 253–278). Lexington, MA: Heath.

Waldrop, M. L., & Halverson, C. F. (1975). Intensive and extensive peer behavior: Longitudinal and cross-sectional analyses. *Child Development, 46,* 19–26.

Wallach, M. A. (1985). Creativity testing and giftedness. In F. D. Horowitz & M. O'Brien (Eds.), *The gifted and talented: Developmental perspectives.* Washington, DC: American Psychological Association.

Walzer, J. F. (1974). A period of ambivalence: Eighteenth century American childhood. In L. deMause (Ed.)., *The history of childhood.* New York: Psychohistory Press.

Watson, J. B. (1925). *Behaviorism.* New York: Norton.

Watson, J. (1980). Bibliotherapy for abused children. *School Counselor, 27,* 204–208.

Watson, J. S., & Ramey, C. T. (1972). Reactions to response contingent stimulation in early infancy. *Merrill-Palmer Quarterly, 18,* 219–227.

Watson, M. M., & Jackowitz, E. R. (1984). Agents and recipient objects in the development of early symbolic play. *Child Development, 55,* 1091–1097.

Weiner, E. A. & Weiner, E. J. (1974). Differentiation of retarded and normal children through toy-play analysis. *Multivariate Behavior Research, 9,* 245–252.

Weinrib, E. (1983). *The sandplay therapy process: Images of the self.* Boston: Sigo Press.

Weir, R. H. (1962). *Language in the crib.* The Hague: Mouton.

Werner, H., & Kaplan, B. (1963). *Symbol formation.* New York: Wiley.

Werner, P. H., & Burton, E. C. (1979). *Learning through movement: Teaching cognitive content through physical activities.* St. Louis: Mosby.

Whiting, B., & Edwards, C. P. (1973). A cross-cultural analysis of sex differences in the behavior of children aged three through eleven. *Journal of Social Psychology, 91,* 171–188.

Whiting, J. W., & Whiting, H. W. (1968). *Proverbs, sentences, and proverbial phrases from English writings mainly before 1500.* Cambridge, MA: Harvard University Press.

Will, J. A., Self, P. A., & Datan, N. (1976). Maternal behavior and perceived sex of infant. *American Journal of Orthopsychiatry, 46,* 135–139.

Williams, J. W., & Stith, M. (1980). *Middle childhood: Behavior and development* (2nd ed.). New York: Macmillan.

Williams, R. (1980, February). *Symbolic play in young language handicapped and normal speaking children.* Paper presented at the International Conference on Piaget and the Helping Professions, Los Angeles.

Williamson, P. A., & Silvern, S. B. (1984). Creative dramatic play and language comprehension. In T. D. Yawkey & A. D. Pellegrini (Eds.), *Child's play: Developmental and applied* (pp. 347–358). Hillsdale, NJ: Erlbaum.

Wills, D. M. (1972). Problems of play and mastery in the blind child. In E. P. Trapp & P. Himelstein (Eds.), *Readings on the exceptional child.* New York: Appleton-Century-Crofts.

Wilson, J. M. (1986). Parent–child play interaction in hospital settings. In A. W. Gottfried & C. C. Brown (Eds.), *Play interactions: The contribution of play materials and parental involvement to children's development* (pp. 213–224). Lexington, MA: Heath.

Wing, L., Gould, J., Yeates, S. R., & Brierly, L. M. (1977). Symbolic play in severely mentally retarded and in autistic children. *Journal of Child Psychology and Psychiatry, 18,* 167–178.

Winner, E. (1982). *Invented worlds: The psychology of the arts.* Cambridge MA: Harvard University Press.

Wohlwill, J. F. (1984). Relationships between exploration and play. In T. D. Yawkey & A. D. Pellegrini (Eds.), *Child's play: Developmental and applied* (pp. 143–170). Hillsdale, NJ: Erlbaum.

Wolfgang, C. H., & Stakenas, R. G. (1985). An exploration of toy content of preschool children's home environments as a predictor of cognitive development. *Early Child Development and Care, 19,* 291–307.

Wright, J., & Samaras, A. (1986). Play and mastery. In G. G. Fein & P. F. Campbell (Eds.), *Young children and microcomputers* (pp. 73–86). Englewood Cliffs, NJ: Prentice-Hall.

Wulff, S. B. (1985). The symbolic and object play of children with autism: A review. *Journal of Autism and Developmental Disorders, 15,* 139–148.

Zaijka, A. (1983). Microcomputers in early childhood education? A first look. *Young Children, 38,* 61–67.

Zelazo, P. R., & Kearsley, R. B. (1980). The emergence of functional play in infants: Evidence for a major cognitive transition. *Journal of Applied Psychology, 1,* 95–117.

Subject Index

Author Index

Shatz, M., 63
Sheingold, K., 82
Sherman, T., 151
Sherrod, K. B., 61
Shields, D. L., 114
Shimada, S., 146
Sholder, M., 40
Shonkoff, J. P., 112
Siddall, N. Q., 146
Sidorowicz, L. S., 123
Siegel, L. S., 163
Sigman, M., 151
Silverman, I. W., 177, 178
Silvern, S. B., 175, 176
Simon, T., 82
Singer, D. G., 93, 145
Singer, J. D., 91
Singer, J. L., 86, 93
Skipper, J. K., 158
Slade, A., 88
Sloper, P., 149
Smilansky, S., 40, 41
Smiley, S. S., 168
Smith, A. B., 91
Smith, P. K., 41, 87, 113, 123, 129, 132–34, 177, 193
Smollar, J., 88, 105
Snow, M., 123
Somerville, J., 5, 9
Spencer, H., 14, 15
Sproul, C., 146
Stakenas, R. G., 164
Stein, J. E., 146
Steinberg, J., 61, 91
Stern, V., 41, 60
Sternglanz, S. H., 89
Stevenson, M. B., 60–62, 134
Stith, M., 100, 101, 109
Stoneman, Z., 90
Stork, L., 41, 130
Strayer, F. F., 89
Strein, W., 82
Streiner, B. F., 145
Sugarman-Bell, S., 62
Suomi, S. J., 29

Super, C. M., 31
Surbeck, E., 175
Sutton-Smith, B., 3, 15, 18, 19, 32, 34, 35, 38, 87, 130
Sydall, S., 87, 193
Sylva, K., 176, 177
Symons, D., 134

T

Tait, P., 145
Tan, L. E., 82
Taylor, J. B., 175
Terrell, B., 147
Thompson, C. L., 203, 213, 215, 217, 218
Thompson, R. H., 60–62, 134
Tilton, J. R., 148, 151
Tinsley, B. J., 61, 62, 134
Tonick, I. J., 89
Toqueville, A. de, 11
Tower, R. B., 93
Tracy, D. M., 127–29
Travers, J., 91
Troll, L. E., 184
Tronick, E. Z., 185
Tryon, K., 128, 129
Tucker, M. J., 4, 5
Tutko, T. A., 115

U

Unger, O., 65
Ungerer, J., 151, 164

V

Vandell, V. L., 62, 89, 90
Vandenberg, B., 2, 19, 28, 29, 47, 53, 56, 82, 86, 88, 93, 98, 111, 133, 142, 147, 164, 169, 170, 176, 178, 196
Vaughn, B. E., 21, 88
Vietze, P. M., 61

This page constitutes a continuation of the copyright page.

Text Credits

Excerpts reprinted on pp. 49–50 from *The Origins of Intelligence in Children* by Jean Piaget, © copyright 1952 by International Universities Press, Inc.

Excerpts reprinted on pp. 189–191 from *Understanding Children's Play* by R. E. Hartley, L. K. Frank, and R. M. Goldenson, © copyright 1952 Columbia University Press. Used by permission.

Excerpts on pp. 202–203 from *Psychotherapy with Children* by Clark E. Moustakas, © copyright by Clark E. Moustakas. Reprinted by permission of Harper & Row, Publishers, Inc.

Excerpts on pp. 204–205 from *Psychoanalytic Treatment of Children* by Anna Freud, © 1968 by International Universities Press, Inc.

Excerpts on pp. 215–16 from *Therapeutic Communication with Children: The Mutual Storytelling Technique* by Richard A. Gardner, © copyright 1986, 1971 Richard A. Gardner, M.D. Reprinted with permission of the publisher, Jason Aronson Inc.